D1557177

AMERICAN HISTORY BY ERA

Antebellum
America: 1784–1850

VOLUME 4

Other titles in the American History by Era series:

AMERICAN HISTORY BY ERA

Antebellum America: 1784–1850

—| VOLUME 4 |—

William Dudley, *Book Editor*

Daniel Leone, *President*
Bonnie Szumski, *Publisher*
Scott Barbour, *Managing Editor*

GREENHAVEN
PRESS®

THOMSON
——✦——™
GALE

San Diego • Detroit • New York • San Francisco • Cleveland
New Haven, Conn. • Waterville, Maine • London • Munich

THOMSON

GALE

© 2003 by Greenhaven Press. Greenhaven Press is an imprint of The Gale Group, Inc., a division of Thomson Learning, Inc.

Greenhaven® and Thomson Learning™ are trademarks used herein under license.

For more information, contact
Greenhaven Press
27500 Drake Rd.
Farmington Hills, MI 48331-3535
Or you can visit our Internet site at http://www.gale.com

ALL RIGHTS RESERVED.
No part of this work covered by the copyright hereon may be reproduced or used in any form or by any means—graphic, electronic, or mechanical, including photocopying, recording, taping, Web distribution or information storage retrieval systems—without the written permission of the publisher.

Every effort has been made to trace the owners of copyrighted material.

Cover credit: © Hulton/Archive by Getty Images

Dover Publications, 233
Library of Congress, 41, 54, 151, 252
National Archives, 90
North Wind Picture Archives, 206

Cover inset photo credits (from left): Planet Art; Corel; Digital Stock; Corel; Library of Congress; Library of Congress; Digital Stock; Painet/Garry Rissman

LIBRARY OF CONGRESS CATALOGING-IN-PUBLICATION DATA

Antebellum America : 1784–1850 / William Dudley, book editor.
p. cm. — (American history by era; v. 4)
Includes bibliographical references and index.
ISBN 0-7377-0718-6 (alk. paper) — ISBN 0-7377-0717-8 (pbk. : alk. paper)
1. United States—History—1783–1815. 2. United States—History—1815–1861.
I. Dudley, William, 1964– . II. Series.
E301 .A58 2003
973—dc21
2002070259

Printed in the United States of America

CONTENTS

Chapter 1: Building a New Government for a New Nation, 1784–1800

1. The Triumphs and Troubles of Independence

Following the successful conclusion of the eight-year war for independence, the United States of America faced new challenges in peacetime, including economic troubles and social unrest. The thirteen former colonies, now states, found it difficult to unite, leading some figures to call for a convention to reform America's national government.

2. The Constitutional Convention of 1787

The Constitutional Convention (also called the Philadelphia Convention) was a landmark in U.S. and world history. Its delegates, which included many of America's leading political figures, discarded the Articles of Confederation and created a new blueprint for a national government.

3. The Debate over Ratifying the Constitution

The U.S. Constitution was ratified by the states following a vigorous political campaign during which it came under severe criticism by its opponents. The willingness of these detractors to participate in the political process and not resort to violence, as well as the willingness of the Constitution's supporters to compromise and agree to amend the document, helped ensure both its ratification and its long-term success.

Chapter 2: Expansion, War, and Nationalism, 1800–1824

Chapter 3: The Jacksonian Age, 1824–1840

neurs, Transcendentalist philosophers, religious revivalists, or social reformers—believed that they could improve and perfect themselves and American society.

Chapter 4: Manifest Destiny, 1840–1850

D uring the sixteenth century, events occurred in North America that would change the course of American history. In 1512, Spanish explorer Juan Ponce de León led the first European expedition to Florida. French navigator Jean Ribault established the first French colony in America at Fort Caroline in 1564. Over a decade later, in 1579, English pirate Francis Drake landed near San Francisco and claimed the country for England.

These three seemingly random events happened in different decades, occurred in various regions of America, and involved three different European nations. However, each discrete occurrence was part of a larger movement for European dominance over the New World. During the sixteenth century, Spain, France, and England vied for control of what was later to become the United States. Each nation was to leave behind a legacy that would shape the political structure, language, culture, and customs of the American people.

Examining such seemingly disparate events in tandem can help to emphasize the connections between them and generate an appreciation for the larger global forces of which they were a part. Greenhaven Press's American History by Era series provides students with a unique tool for examining American history in a way that allows them to see such connections. This series divides American history—from the time that the first people arrived in the New World from Asia to the September 11, 2001, terrorist attacks—into nine discrete periods. Each volume then presents a collection of both primary and secondary documents that describe the major events of the period in chronological order. This structure provides students with a snapshot of events occurring simultaneously in all parts of America. The reader can then gain an appreciation for the political, social, and cultural movements and trends that shaped the nation. Students reading about the adventures of individual European explorers, for instance, are invited to consider how such expeditions compared in purpose and consequence to earlier and later expeditions. Rather than simply learning that Ponce de León was the first Spaniard to try to colonize Florida, for example, students can begin to understand his expedition in a larger context. Indeed, Ponce's voyage was an extension of Spain's desire to conquer the Caribbean and Mexico, and his expedition was to inspire other Spanish explorers to head north from Hispaniola and New Spain in search of rich empires to conquer.

Another benefit of studying eras is that students can view a "snapshot" of America at any given moment of time and see the various social, cultural, and political events that occurred simultaneously. For example, during the period between 1920 and 1945, Charles Lindbergh became the first to make a solo transatlantic flight, Babe Ruth broke the record for the most home runs in one season, and the United States dropped the atomic bomb on Hiroshima. Random events occurring in post–Cold War America included the torching of the Branch Davidian compound in Waco, Texas, the emergence of the World Wide Web, and the 2000 presidential election debacle in which ballot miscounts in Florida held up election results for weeks.

Each volume in this series offers features to enhance students' understanding of the era of American history under discussion. An introductory essay provides an overview of the period, supplying essential context for the readings that follow. An annotated table of contents highlights the main point of each selection. A more in-depth introduction precedes each document, placing it in its particular historical context and offering biographical information about the author. A thorough chronology and index allow students to quickly reference specific events and dates. Finally, a bibliography opens up additional avenues of research. These features help to make the American History by Era series an extremely valuable tool for students researching the political upheavals, wars, cultural movements, scientific and technological advancements, and other events that mark the unfolding of American history.

INTRODUCTION

In Washington Irving's famous story about Rip van Winkle, the title character falls asleep for twenty years, during which time the American Revolution is fought and won and the United States of America is born. Upon his return to his home village in the Catskill Mountains in New York state, Rip van Winkle does not recognize the people he runs into, and gets into trouble with them when he affirms his loyalty to King George III of Great Britain. However, the town itself and life's daily routines had not changed so much as to become totally alien to him. Eventually he is recognized and welcomed, settles down with his grown daughter, and happily lives out his days in the local tavern.

It is interesting to speculate whether, had van Winkle decided instead to take another long nap and awaken in 1850, he could so readily adapt to his new home or even recognize where he was. For few countries in world history have experienced as much change in so many ways as the United States did from 1783—the year it formally gained independence from Great Britain—to 1850, less than one human lifespan later. (This period, interestingly, corresponds closely with Irving's own lifespan; the diplomat and writer was born in 1783 and died in 1859.) The United States grew from a collection of thirteen former colonies hugging the Atlantic Coast to a nation of thirty-one states whose lands reached both the Pacific Ocean and the Gulf of Mexico. Its population grew from 4 million in 1790 to 23 million in 1850. One of three Americans in 1850 resided in areas that were not part of America in 1790. One out of ten were foreign-born, a result of a large influx of immigrants from Ireland, Germany, and other European nations (370,000 immigrants came to the United States in 1850 alone). The United States evolved from a small nation wary of antagonizing European powers to a self-confident continental power (and emerging world power) that faced few external enemies.

A reawakened van Winkle would also find out that ways of living in America had changed immensely. While many Americans still lived on farms and small villages, a growing proportion lived in larger towns and cities. The harnessing of steam and water power revolutionized how things were made and how people traveled. A reawakened Rip van Winkle in 1850 would have been confronted by new factories, new churches, new schools, and new ideas of social reform.

The challenge of historical study of antebellum America is not only to catalog the enormous technological, social, and political changes of this time. Historians also strive to analyze what caused these changes and to try to identify continuities in American life and thought as the revolutionary generation passed. The following essay provides a brief overview of America's change during this turbulent era, focusing on five key areas of growth: America's territorial expansion as its people moved westward (and the displacement of Native Americans such expansion caused), the burgeoning of America's industrialized economy and the accompanying social changes, America's rise as a diplomatic power, the evolution and democratization of America's government, and the growth of slavery as an institution and source of national division. Each of these developments affected both the nation as a whole, and everyday life in places such as van Winkle's New York town.

WESTWARD EXPANSION

In 1783, Rip van Winkle's small town in upstate New York was at or close to the edge of America's western frontier. The United States of America consisted of thirteen states—the former thirteen colonies—that ran on a North-South axis along the Atlantic Ocean coastline. In addition, America had possession of former British territory that extended westward across the Appalachian mountain chain to the Mississippi River (the fact that some of the original thirteen states had official claims to western territories and others did not was a serious source of discord in the early republic—one resolved when states ceded their western claims to the national government). The first U.S. census, conducted in 1790, counted 891,364 square miles of American territory—although much of that land was also claimed by Native American groups and various European powers. The bulk of America's population lived on or close by the Atlantic, however.

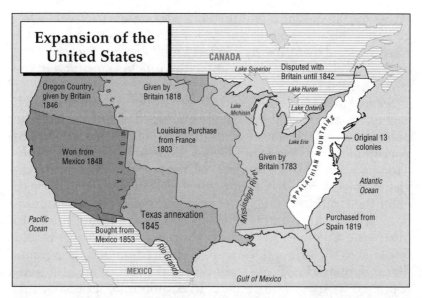

Expansion of the United States

CANADA
Lake Superior
Disputed with Britain until 1842
Oregon Country, given by Britain 1846
Given by Britain 1818
Lake Huron
Lake Michigan
Lake Ontario
Louisiana Purchase from France 1803
Lake Erie
Original 13 colonies
Won from Mexico 1848
Given by Britain 1783
Atlantic Ocean
Pacific Ocean
Texas annexation 1845
Mississippi River
Purchased from Spain 1819
Bought from Mexico 1853
Rio Grande
MEXICO
Gulf of Mexico
ROCKY MOUNTAINS
APPALACHIAN MOUNTAINS

Travel and commerce flowed both across the Atlantic Ocean to Europe and up and down the coast much more freely than between the coastal and interior regions.

Over the next few decades, the United States would expand from less than 900,000 square miles to almost 3 million. The United States acquired territory by means both military and diplomatic, or in some cases combinations of the two. It purchased the Louisiana Territory from France in 1803. Spain ceded Florida to the United States in an 1819 treaty (after American military incursions into the territory). America annexed the independent nation of Texas in 1845, nine years after Texas settlers (most of whom were of U.S. origin) had declared independence from Mexico. An 1846 treaty with Great Britain settled boundaries of the Oregon Territory and added almost 300,000 square miles to America. Finally, the United States took a large portion of Mexico, including what is now the state of California, in the 1846–1848 Mexican War.

The addition of territory both preceded and followed waves of settlement, as American explorers, fur traders, farmers, and miners attempted to make new lives for themselves on the frontier. American individuals and families streamed westward at the rate of sixty thousand per year. By the 1830s, the American frontier line had been pushed across the Mississippi River and into what is now Iowa, Missouri, Arkansas, and eastern Texas. In the 1840s many pioneers made the difficult trek beyond, across the Great Plains and the Rocky Mountains, to reach Oregon and California along the Pacific coast. Woods and prairies were replaced by farms; by 1850, 114 million acres of forest were cleared or improved. Towns and cities quickly sprouted in the newly settled lands.

Some American founders harbored doubts on whether such vast territory could be effectively governed as one nation. The political fate of these new communities was charted by an important piece of early federal legislation—the Northwest Ordinance. Passed by Congress in 1787, the law provided for the division of western territory into territories that could petition to enter the Union as states once they reached a certain population. By 1850, the number of states had grown from thirteen to thirty-one. By establishing the principle that new states would be equal to the original thirteen, it ensured potential migrants that they would not lose their political liberties and thus encouraged westward movement. In addition, Congress encouraged westward expansion by federal laws providing for the sale of public lands in family-farm-size lots.

As a result, the demographic center of America's population steadily moved west; by 1840 it was west of the Appalachian mountains. A reawakened Rip van Winkle in 1850 might have found the young people of his town looking westward for their future. His town was no longer on the far reaches of the frontier, but instead part of the established East. "Europe stretches to the Alleghenies [part of the Appalachian chain]; America lies beyond," wrote American philosopher Ralph Waldo Emerson in 1844.

NATIVE AMERICAN DISPLACEMENT

The flip side of settler expansion was Native American displacement. Even before Rip van Winkle's original nap, few of the aboriginal inhabitants of the thirteen former British colonies remained in their original homelands. (In Washington Irving's story, Indians were, like ghosts and witches, fodder for van Winkle's tales he told children.) Many remained, however, in the territory beyond. Their existence was seen by some as a barrier to America's destiny as a growing nation. James Monroe, America's fifth president, spoke for many whites when he declared in 1817 that "the hunter or savage state requires a greater extent of territory to sustain it than is compatible with . . . civilized life, and must yield to it." Between 1783 and 1850, Native

Americans were under continuous pressure to withdraw from their traditional homelands, adapt European models of "civilized life," or both.

Indians who sought to resist white settlement with force were unable to achieve sustained success. Little Turtle led a confederacy of tribes to defeat American armies in a series of battles in the 1790s, but met defeat in the 1794 Battle of Fallen Timbers, destroying Indian power in what is now Ohio. The Shawnee leader Tecumseh sought a pan-tribal alliance of resistance in the early 1800s, but was killed in 1813 during the War of 1812. Andrew Jackson led American forces in defeating the Creek tribe of Georgia in 1814 during the same war (which proved to be a crucial turning point after which Native Americans could no longer depend on Spain or Great Britain to be allies).

Some Indian tribes eschewed military resistance and sought instead to adapt their culture and political structures to European models. They were helped in their efforts by both private Christian missionaries and by the federal government, which appropriated funds to agricultural and vocational instruction for Indians. The Cherokee in Georgia, for example, had constructed a state with private property, a written language and legal code, and a written constitution. (Some Cherokee even owned black slaves.) In 1830, Jackson, who had parlayed his fame as an Indian fighter into a successful run for the presidency, signed the Indian Removal Act, which led to the forced uprooting of more than 100,000 Cherokee and other Native Americans to territory beyond the Mississippi River. By 1850, most Native Americans had been "removed" to territory west of the Mississippi River.

The growth in America's territory and population was matched by what some historians have called the "economic miracle"—the stunning economic growth and industrial development of the United States in the first half of the nineteenth century. Historians have identified three interrelated social and economic revolutions behind America's economic transformation: the transportation revolution, the market revolution, and the industrial revolution.

THE MARKET AND TRANSPORTATION REVOLUTIONS

In 1800, 94 percent of Americans lived on farms, in villages, or in towns of less than twenty-five hundred people (and many townspeople remained engaged in raising livestock, gardening, or other agricultural pursuits). People in Rip van Winkle's village in the Catskill Mountains, like most small rural communities, lived an insular existence. Communities not on major rivers or the seacoast could be reached only by horseback or by foot; roads were generally poor. The farms and communities most Americans lived in were economically self-sufficient. Family members—husbands, wives, children, and in some cases servants or slaves—raised their own food, created their own clothing and household goods, and bartered with neighbors for what they could not make on their own. While some American cities on the coast developed a flourishing trade exporting American lumber and agricultural products and importing European manufactured goods and other luxuries, this trade had relatively little impact on life in America's interior. This was the pattern of Rip van Winkle and his neighbors lived in both before, and to a lesser extent after, his twenty-year nap. (Washington Irving gives a sense of this isolation by describing a favorite pastime of van Winkle and his cronies—debating the contents of the occasional months-old newspaper that would reach them from the outside.)

By 1850 the isolation of many Americans had been greatly reduced by improvements in America's transportation and communication network. These included better roads, the development of the steamboat (which enabled goods and people to be transported upriver), the invention of the telegraph, and the creation and development of railroads. By 1840, the United States had more than three thousand miles of canals. By 1850 the country had nine thousand miles of railroad lines in operation. The transportation revolution greatly diminished western isolation and led to greater trade, as western farmers sold their goods to eastern markets and eastern manufacturers sold their goods to farmers. In Rip van Winkle's time, the Hudson River was an important water highway connecting New York City with the rest of the state. But the completion of the Erie Canal in 1825 connected the Hudson River to the Great Lakes in the Midwest, and thus made it possible for goods, farm produce, and people to be transported by boat and barge to and from New York City to much of the United States. The Erie Canal was just one of many projects that created national markets for farmers and reduced the isolation of America's towns.

INDUSTRIALIZATION

The rise of the market economy in America was accompanied by industrial development. The industrial revolution began in Great Britain around 1750, when a group of inventors perfected machines for the mass production of textiles. The first factory on American soil was made in 1791 by Samuel Slater, a British mechanic who memorized plans for a textile factory before emigrating to the United States. However, industrialization was slow to take root in America. Its progress was slowed by a lack of capital, labor, and consumers. American financiers with capital to invest preferred to place their money in trade or land. Factory work was seen as degrading by many potential workers who would rather pursue their fortune in the frontier. The few American consumers wealthy enough to buy manufactured goods preferred English products. While some American leaders such as Alexander Hamilton called for federal government promotion of manufacturing, others such as Thomas Jefferson envisioned a future expanding America populated by self-sufficient farmers.

Beginning around 1810, these obstacles to industrialization began to be overcome. Capital was raised by New England merchants and bankers, and aided by the development of the corporation—a legal device through which money was raised through the selling of shares of stock—and by laws that limited liability of shareholders to the amounts of their investments. Capital was also raised by banks, which rose in number in the United States from about thirty to eight hundred between 1800 and 1850. The demand for labor was met by recruiting children, young women, and immigrants. The growing canal and railroad network created a large national market for manufactured goods. The American government took steps to encourage industrialization by enacting protective tariffs. By 1850 fifty thousand factories in America produced items ranging from fabric to firearms.

The economic transformation affected different regions of the country in different ways. Historian Raymond H. Robinson in his book *The Growing of America* argues that four identifiable regions in the United States existed in the middle of the nineteenth century that were able to benefit from each other economically.

> The Northeast was the urban and industrial center, the
> Old Northwest [now the upper Midwest] raised food;

the South was the domain of King Cotton; and the New West was significant for mining and ranching. . . . The Northeast sold manufactured goods—textiles, shoes, iron products, and the like—to the other sections and bought food, cotton, and hides from other parts of the country. The Old Northwest provided foodstuffs and bought manufactured items from the Northeast. . . . The South sold its fiber to the Northeast. And the New West sent its gold and hides to eastern markets for manufactured goods.

The rise of an industrial market economy had profound social effects. In 1790, most Americans lived on farms or villages; only two cities (Philadelphia and New York) had a population of over 20,000. By 1860 forty-three cities had at least 20,000 residents. New York, with 800,000, had overtaken Philadelphia as the nation's largest city (and the third largest in the western world, behind London and Paris). As late as 1820, more than three-quarters of American workers labored on farms. By 1850 roughly half were so employed. Many households abandoned self-sufficiency and had yoked themselves to the burgeoning (and national) market economy. They worked for wages at factories, or planted cash crops they sold for money to pay for their own food and household goods. The revolution especially affected women's work as the household ceased to become a center of economic production and instead became a refuge from economic life and the special "domestic sphere" of women.

GROWTH IN DIPLOMATIC STATURE

The growth of America—in territory, population, and gross domestic product—was also reflected in the growth of America's international stature. In 1783, the United States, despite its victorious war of independence with Great Britain, was viewed by Britain and other European powers as a weak and divided country. Great Britain refused to send a minister to the United States for eight years, refused to make a commercial treaty, and continued to station soldiers and agents on trading posts on America's northern boundary with Canada, where they maintained relations with hostile Native American tribes. Relations with Spain, whose colonial possessions formed America's southern boundary (and whose territorial claims reached into American territory), were not much better. Spain claimed territory the British had granted the United States, worked with Native American tribes to resist American expansion, and in 1784 dealt a blow to American farmers by closing the port of New Orleans to American commerce. France, America's wartime ally, demanded repayment of war loans while restricting West Indies trade.

American foreign relations became further complicated by the fact that, from 1793 to 1815, the major European powers were embroiled in war. While some Americans called for the United States to take sides with either Great Britain or France, others feared that another war so soon after the American Revolution would be devastating for the new nation. President George Washington instead issued in 1793 a proclamation of neutrality regarding the war between Great Britain and France. The efforts of Washington and his successors, John Adams and Thomas Jefferson, to maintain neutrality and keep out of war were sorely tried by the actions of both nations. Great Britain sold firearms to Native Americans on America's western frontier, seized hundreds of American ships in the West Indies, and arrested and impressed thousands of American sailors. France in turn seized American ships and, in an act widely seen as insulting, demanded monetary concessions from American diplomats. America's hostilities with France peaked in an undeclared naval war that lasted from 1798 to 1800—a conflict that then-president Adams narrowly prevented from turning into an official war. Hostilities with Great Britain culminated in the War of 1812, which lasted from 1812 to 1815.

In that conflict, Americans had some naval success, but were unable to dislodge Britian's supremacy on the oceans. American expeditions seeking to invade and conquer Canada were hampered by the reluctance of some state militia troops to participate and were ultimately repelled. By the summer of 1814, British troops had burned the public buildings in Washington, D.C., and had gathered a strong force to invade New York state. British negotiators made sweeping demands as the price for ending hostilities, including the creation of an Indian buffer state in the Great Lakes region and British military control of the Great Lakes themselves. But American victories in Baltimore and New York caused Britain to drop these demands. The 1814 Treaty of Ghent was essentially an agreement to stop fighting and restore conquered territory.

The conclusion of the War of 1812 ended an era in which the

United States was continually affected by constant European wars. The final defeat of French dictator Napoleon in the Battle of Waterloo in 1815 began a long period of peace on the European continent. America was able instead to concentrate its energies on domestic expansion and development and to bask in a wave of patriotic nationalism following the War of 1812. While relations with Great Britain steadily improved (there would be no more wars between America and Britain), the threat posed by the Spanish empire to American interests declined as its Latin American colonies fought for their own independence; Spain ceded Florida to the United States in 1819. By the early 1820s treaties with Spain, Russia, and Great Britain had resolved American boundary questions all the way to the Pacific Ocean and freed the United States from serious diplomatic entanglements for the next thirty years. The United States took advantage of this situation to concentrate on domestic affairs. In 1823 President James Monroe issued the Monroe Doctrine, in which he pronounced that all of the Western Hemisphere would be off-limits to European colonization (such a stance was largely made possible by Great Britain, a naval power that had decided that supporting the United States in this particular area was in its own interests).

THE DEVELOPMENT OF DEMOCRACY AND AMERICA'S NATIONAL GOVERNMENT

The growth in the United States in land, people, economic wealth, and diplomatic stature coincided with (and some would say was created by) the growth of a national government. In 1783, America was a loose confederation of states without a strong national government. By 1850 a remarkably stable national government had been created. Historians identify several key steps in the development of America's national government in the years between 1783 and 1850.

The first was the creation of a written constitution. Many prominent Americans believed the national government under the Articles of Confederation, created in 1781 during the Revolutionary War, was inadequate to the challenges the new nation faced. The government could not collect money, regulate trade, or issue money. In the summer of 1787 delegates meeting in Philadelphia created a new blueprint for a national government—the United States Constitution.

The Constitution was a product of debate and compromise

between large and small-state representatives, and between proponents and opponents of a strong central government. It created a two-house legislature—a House of Representatives based on population, and a Senate where all states had equal representation—an executive branch headed by the president, and a federal judiciary including the Supreme Court. Completed in September 1787, the Constitution was ratified by special conventions called in the separate states. It was ratified in 1789. It was amended several times at first (most notably adding the Bill of Rights), but then remained unchanged between 1804 and the Civil War. Its proper interpretation became the frame of reference for many if not most of America's political debates.

Two other elements important in the development of America's national government was the rise in suffrage and the development of political parties. Both elements can be found in Washington Irving's story, in which the reawakened Rip van Winkle finds himself in the middle of election day (the first question asked of him is whether he voted, the second was what political party he supported). Ironically, these two elements—the popular vote and political parties—now seen as central to American politics, were not necessarily considered as important or desirable by many of the Constitution's creators.

America's Declaration of Independence had declared that "all men are created equal" and the revolutionary era resulted in the democratization of many state and local governments. However, many leaders of that time continued to doubt the ability of the "common man" to govern himself and considered direct democracy a dangerously reckless way of governing a nation. One result of this belief was a Constitution filled with checks and layers through which the voice of the people would be filtered and interpreted by a social and political elite. Thus the president would be elected by "electors" chosen by the state legislators (state legislatures also elected U.S. senators). Members of the House of Representatives would be elected by popular vote every two years, but voting was generally limited to substantial men of property.

By 1824, however, state constitutions had been rewritten to eliminate the property requirement for voting (in newer western states, voting was permitted from the start to all adult white males). In addition, in many states the selection of the presidential electors (the electoral college) passed from the state legislature to the direct popular vote of the people, thus giving people increased say in electing their president and presidential candidates greater motive in appealing directly to the people. By 1850 political campaigns had become a source of entertainment for many as well as a means of having a voice in government (without resorting to violent revolution).

It is important to remember that "universal" suffrage in antebellum America was still limited to white males. Many of the voter reform laws in the early 1800s that provided for white voters placed restrictions on free blacks voting (black slaves were of course never allowed to vote). By 1837 only the New England states north of Connecticut retained black suffrage. Suffrage was also denied to women—something that activists who gathered in Seneca Falls, New York, in 1848, found cause to complain.

The individual who symbolized the changing face of politics was Andrew Jackson, the nation's seventh president, who was elected in 1828. Jackson's six predecessors had all been well-schooled and well-heeled planters or lawyers from the influential states of Virginia or Massachusetts. Jackson was a self-made man and political outsider from the frontier. He was elected president in 1828 (after winning a popular vote plurality in 1824), in a contest that many believe marked the tilting of America's political balance of power westward. As president, Jackson cast himself as a battler for majoritarian democratic rule against special interests and social elites.

POLITICAL PARTIES

Jackson's presidency also marked the comeback of the two-party system. Although George Washington, among other early leaders, deplored political parties as malevolent "factions" that smacked of conspiracy and did not help create a virtuous republic, divisions within his own administration evolved into separate political parties—Federalists and Jeffersonian Republicans. The Federalist Party faded into obscurity following the War of 1812 in the so-called Era of Good Feelings, but during Jackson's two terms as president (1828–1836) the Democratic Party (the organization of Jackson and his backers) and the Whig Party (which evolved out of Jackson's political opponents) both grew into strong national institutions that mediated between the people and government. Rip van Winkle's New York village may well have had local Democratic and Whig party organizations, each publishing their own newspaper and working for their own candidates.

SLAVERY AND SECTIONAL DIVISION

Most of the above described developments affected different regions in different ways. One region that followed a different path from the rest of America was the South, which included the older southern colonies (Virginia, the Carolinas, and Georgia) and the southern frontier states (Mississippi, Alabama, and Tennessee). The South had fewer cities, factories, canals, railroads, and foreign immigrants than the rest of the nation. Its economy became dependent on one cash crop—cotton. The trend toward universal white male suffrage was slower to affect southern states, where a small planter elite generally remained in control of state and local government. In examining what and why the American South was different, historians have mostly focused on one social institution that for many people defines antebellum America—slavery.

Prior to America's independence, slavery was legal in all thirteen colonies. Southern planters were enriched by the growing of tobacco and indigo and other cash crops on plantations cultivated by slave labor, while traders based in Massachusetts and Rhode Island prospered through the African slave trade. During and immediately after the Revolutionary War, however, slavery was abolished in the northern states (New York, Rip van Winkle's state, abolished slavery in 1799). The Constitution protected the international slave trade, but only until 1808; many American leaders predicted the institution's eventual demise. In 1793, however, the invention of the cotton gin, coupled with demand for cotton from textile factories in England and the United States, gave new economic life to slavery. A "Cotton Kingdom" emerged that relied on virgin soils of southern frontier states and on slave labor. By 1840 cotton accounted for half the value of America's exports. However, the profits to be gained from selling cotton discouraged diversification in agriculture and manufacturing in the region.

Three million African Americans lived in slavery in 1850—all in the South. However, a reawakened Rip van Winkle in 1850 might well have found that the issue of slavery to have a greater impact on his life than it would have in 1783. Back then he may have seen the occasional black slave, but slaves were not as common where he lived than they were elsewhere in America (there is no mention of slaves in Washington Irving's story). However, by 1850 the institution of slavery may well have had a significant impact on life in his small New York community.

It may have been home to chapters of abolitionist societies. Such groups, who promoted their cause with newspapers or lectures, often found their offices and meetings to be the targets of mob violence. Van Winkle, had he reawakened in 1850, might also have seen the disturbing spectacle of an escaped slave (or a free black) being dragged through the street in chains after being captured and sent South, pursuant to the Fugitive Slave Act, passed at the South's insistence in 1850.

Another topic of frequent discussion would be whether slavery should be extended into new territories as the nation grew. In 1819 the nation became divided over whether to admit Missouri as a slave state. In 1820 Congress passed the Missouri Compromise, which seemed to settle the issue by establishing a dividing line between slave and free regions. But the victory over Mexico and the territory the United States gained raised the issue anew, and set America to a course that would eventually take it to civil war.

THE SPIRIT OF THE AGE

Perhaps the element that Rip van Winkle might find most different in America in 1850 goes beyond changes in America's size, power, economy, and government. The character of van Winkle, as created by Washington Irving, was a lazy, indolent person with "an insuperable aversion to all kinds of profitable labor." This would place him at odds with many Americans of the antebellum era. A consistent observation found in both contemporaneous and historical accounts is an appreciation of the drive and energy and hard work of Americans, whether it be for the purpose of clearing forest for a new farm, starting a new business enterprise, forming a new church or religion, or embarking on a new social reform. "The whole continent presents a scene of *scrambling* and roars with greedy hurry," commented one foreign visitor. "Go ahead! is the order of the day." The essays in this volume present and analyze the major developments of American society during this significant and transformative time when millions of Americans worked energetically to grow and transform the United States.

Building a New Government for a New Nation, 1784–1800

CHAPTER 1

THE TRIUMPHS AND TROUBLES OF INDEPENDENCE

THOMAS FLEMING

Historian and novelist Thomas Fleming writes that the years following America's victory in the Revolutionary War were marked by an increase in liberty for many. Many slaves were emancipated, laws were passed protecting religious freedom, and arts and education flourished. However, the thirteen former colonies were not able to unite effectively as one nation. In Shays' Rebellion and similar incidents, disgruntled Americans staged violent protests against state taxes. Many Americans shared George Washington's fears that the new nation would not prove viable.

A merican liberty had survived the challenges of war. But could it meet the demands of peace? The eight-year see-saw conflict had convinced many people that a strong union was essential to the survival of American liberty. Far and away the most important and most influential of these federal-minded Americans was ex-General George Washington. As one of his last official acts, he sent a circular letter to the governors of the thirteen states, urging them to give the Congress the power it needed to create a genuine union. He warned them that a failure to solve this fundamental problem would make Americans "the sport of European politics, which may play one state against another." Grimly, he reminded them that it was not

Thomas Fleming, *Liberty: The American Revolution*, New York: Viking Penguin, 1997. Copyright © 1997 by Viking Penguin. Reproduced by permission.

yet decided "whether the Revolution must ultimately be considered as a blessing or a curse."

No one paid much attention to Washington's admonition. The steep decline in the Congress's power, so evident in the closing years of the war, accelerated without the threat of a British army and navy to inspire even a feeble unity. After wandering from Princeton to Annapolis to Trenton in search of hospitality, the Congress settled in New York. More often than not, the national legislature could not muster a quorum. Delegates often sat around for weeks waiting for missing members to appear.

With no hope of acquiring the power to tax, the Congress tried to persuade the states to authorize them to collect a duty on imports. After years of negotiation, twelve states agreed. But New York, prospering as a port of entry for New Jersey and Connecticut as well as for her own merchants, said no. Under the Articles of Confederation, all thirteen states had to agree to any amendment to the federal government's powers. The campaign for an "impost" collapsed and with it Congress's last hope of solvency. As a result, the United States had no army to repel an invader or suppress internal insurrections. England displayed its contempt for the weakling federal government by refusing to withdraw its troops from six forts on American soil in the West. Spain prohibited Western settlers from shipping farm produce and other exports from New Orleans. Lacking a navy, the United States could do nothing about Arab pirates who made a specialty of capturing American ships and soon destroyed the country's Mediterranean trade. There was also no way to repay the millions the nation had borrowed from France and Holland to finance the war for independence.

Washington found this failure to maintain America's public credit particularly painful. "To be more exposed in the eyes of the world and more contemptible than we already are, is hardly possible," he wrote to a friend. . . .

LIBERTY'S FERMENT

In the United States one of the things that held the Congress together during the postwar years was the vast swath of Western wilderness between the Alleghenies and the Mississippi. By persuading Virginia and other states with often overlapping claims to cede everything to the federal government, the Congress hoped to be able to sell huge tracts to land speculators who were organizing companies in several states. Fortunately, some members of the Congress had more meaningful visions of the future of this enormous territory. One was a returning delegate from Virginia, Thomas Jefferson.

The author of the Declaration of Independence was the driving force behind an ordinance that the Congress passed in 1784, dividing the territory into ten rectangular sections, each of which would become a future state when its population reached 20,000. This vision of an expanding union evolved into the Ordinance of 1787, which provided different population figures and shapes for the emerging states. But it had at its heart a stipulation that Jefferson warmly approved: "There shall be neither slavery nor involuntary servitude in the said territory." This simple statement, which barred slavery from the future states of Ohio, Indiana, Illinois, Michigan and Wisconsin, was the most significant achievement of the postwar Congress. It was encouraging evidence that liberty would remain a dynamic force in American life.

There were many other signs of liberty's impact on slavery. In 1781 a slave named Quok Walker sued for his freedom, pointing out that the Massachusetts state constitution said: "All men are born free and equal." He won his case, and slavery ended in Massachusetts. In the other New England states and in Pennsylvania, where Quakers had been agitating against slavery for decades, a policy of gradual manumission began. All children born of slave parents were declared free. On September 22, 1783, Lemuel Haynes became the first African-American to be ordained as a Congregational minister. Later in the year, James Durham became the first member of his race to begin practicing as a licensed physician. In Boston, Phillis Wheatley, a young African-American who had been educated and freed, celebrated the end of the war with a poem, "Liberty and Peace."

In Virginia the Methodist Church urged the legislature to begin a gradual emancipation program, basing its petition on the Christian religion and the state's Declaration of Rights. The lawmakers rejected the proposal unanimously. Because of the huge numbers of blacks in the South, most Southerners did not believe slavery could be ended without exposing the region to a race war. But Virginia freed all slaves who had fought in the Revolution and joined Delaware and the Northern States in banning the slave trade. Between 1775 and 1800 the number of free African-Americans rose from 14,000 to 100,000. "There is not a man living," George Washington wrote to Robert Morris in 1786, "who wishes more sincerely than I do to see a plan adopted for the gradual abolition of [slavery]."

Another example of liberty's ferment was the enthusiasm for educating women. While their husbands were fighting the war or sitting in state legislatures or the Congress, many women were forced to raise children, run farms and sell crops and cattle, relying on their own judgment. This experience led to large leaps in feminine self-confidence. Abigail Adams had long criticized "the trifling narrow contracted Education of the females" in America, as she put it in one of her letters to John. In the 1780s, with the war over, women—and some men—began doing something about it.

In 1786 Timothy Dwight announced that he had opened his Connecticut school to girls as well as boys, promising to teach both sexes "belles lettres, Geography, Philosophy and Astronomy." Soon, in the words of Yale's Ezra Stiles, a "spirit of academy making" spread through the country. Many of these schools were open to young women or created specifically to educate them. Before the war, parents expected a girl to acquire only good work habits. Now many began to see it as their "republican duty" to educate their daughters. When John Jay's wife, Sarah, sent their daughter to the Moravian Seminary for Young Ladies in Bethlehem, Pennsylvania, considered the best girls' school in the nation, she told the young woman that training her mind would give her "the satisfaction of rearing a family agreeable to your wishes." A New Hampshire woman who sent her daughter to a local academy exclaimed: "What an advantage the youth of the present have, compared with former times."

All the arts profited from liberty's growth, especially the theater, which Sam Adams and his fellow Puritans in the Congress had banned during the war. When some people tried to continue the ban, supporters of the theater argued that no government should have the authority to intrude on the freedom of citizens to enjoy themselves. "The same authority which proscribes our amusements may . . . dictate the shape and texture of our dress or the modes and ceremonies of worship," warned one Philadelphian.

In 1787 Royall Tyler excited audiences with *The Contrast*, the first successful American play. Tyler invented a character who would reappear in a thousand other dramas: Brother Jonathan, the comic stage Yankee. The playwright used him to mock the Puritans: "Ain't the playhouse the shop where the devil hangs out the vanities of the world upon the tenterhooks of temptation?" Jonathan asked, looking down his long disapproving nose.

Perhaps the greatest example of liberty's expanding power was the Virginia legislature's approval of Thomas Jefferson's Statute for Religious Freedom. This landmark legislation guaranteed every citizen the freedom to worship in the church of his or her choice—and ended state support for the Anglican (Episcopal) church in Virginia. Jefferson had first proposed the idea in 1776, but fierce opposition forced him to set it aside. He was in Paris serving as American ambassador when the statute passed, thanks to the unremitting efforts of his fellow Virginian James Madison.

TROUBLED TIMES

While liberty was expanding private lives, it was creating serious problems in the shaky American confederacy. The sovereign states began to act like thirteen independent countries. Rhode Island churned out millions of dollars of worthless paper money that her citizens forced local merchants to accept for debts—and tried to palm off on creditors in neighboring states. Other states, such as Maryland, edged toward similar schemes. New York laid import duties on every farmer's rowboat that crossed the Hudson River with produce from New Jersey. Pennsylvania played the same game on the state's western border until someone described New Jersey as "a barrel tapped at both ends." Massachusetts was levying duties on imports from England and other European countries and selling the goods at inflated prices in Connecticut and New Hampshire. One infuriated New Jersey politician predicted the victimized states would soon go to war against their oppressors.

After a brief burst of postwar prosperity, the United States experienced its first economic depression. The British, playing the states off against each other as Washington had feared, persuaded some to charge no import duties and then dumped huge amounts of goods into their stores, driving prices down and throwing shoemakers, dressmakers and other artisans out of work. New England was especially hard hit by the British decision to bar American ships from the West Indies. Farm produce glutted the market. The shipbuilding industry, which had once launched dozens of vessels a year for English buyers, collapsed. Compounding the problem in Massachusetts was the high-tax financial policy of the state legislature, which was controlled by eastern merchants determined to pay off the state's war debt.

ENTER DANIEL SHAYS

As 1786 began former Continental army Captain Daniel Shays was an unhappy man. He had fought at Bunker Hill, Saratoga and Stony Point. Now he was living from day to day, constantly fearful of losing his small Massachusetts farm. At one point he was unable to raise $12 to pay a debt. All around him men were losing their farms because they could not pay their taxes or their bills to local storekeepers. In two years, more than 4,000 men had been prosecuted for debt in Worcester County. No less than 80 percent of the inhabitants of the county jail were debtors. Was this the liberty for which they had fought? Shays asked himself.

Shays and a group of like-minded men, such as former Continental Major Luke Day, decided to solve their problem the way they had defeated taxation from another distant body, the British Parliament. They began organizing companies of men and drilling them with guns on their shoulders. When judges showed up to open the county courts, they were met by an angry mob and hastily left town. The protest movement swiftly spread to other Massachusetts counties and found vocal supporters in New Hampshire, Connecticut and Rhode Island.

The governor of Massachusetts, James Bowdoin, banned unlawful assemblies and called on the militia to disperse the protesters. He was backed by Samuel Adams, who took a dim view of this adaptation of his revolutionary techniques. The protesters responded by threatening to overthrow the Boston government. The alarmed governor called on the Congress for help.

Bankrupt as usual, the Congress voted to ask the states to raise $530,000 for an army. Twelve of the thirteen supposedly united states ignored the request. Only Virginia sent money. Without cash, Massachusetts could not enlist a man. In desperation, one Virginia delegate urged George Washington to rush to Massachusetts and use his influence to calm the rebels. Washington's reply was a growl: "Influence is no government."

Massachusetts was forced to ask wealthy private citizens to donate enough money to raise an army of 4,400 men. With former Major General Benjamin Lincoln in command, they slogged west on snowy roads. The insurgents decided to attack the federal arsenal at Springfield, which held 15,000 muskets and numerous cannon—more than enough weaponry to start another revolution.

Fortunately, the man in command of the arsenal was unintimidated by the radical rhetoric Daniel Shays and Luke Day showered on him. Backed by 400 loyal militia, he beat off their attack with several salvos of cannon fire. Benjamin Lincoln's force arrived in time to cut off Luke Day's retreat and accepted his surrender. Shays fell back thirty miles, determined to carry on the war. Lincoln took a leaf from Washington's Trenton book and marched all night through bitter cold to surprise the rebels' camp. Most of them surrendered; Shays fled to a neighboring state. Bands of Shaysites continued a guerrilla war through the spring of 1787, burning stores and factories and kidnapping merchants and judges. A pitched battle with loyal militia near Sheffield, Massachusetts, left 100 men dead or wounded.

Shays' Rebellion was not an isolated phenomenon. From New Jersey to South Carolina, other groups of disgruntled Americans staged similar protests. In York, Pennsylvania, a mob prevented the sheriff from selling cattle seized for taxes. Maryland's Charles County courthouse was closed down by another mob for similar reasons. In South Carolina judges fled the Camden courthouse under a rain of threats and insults. In Virginia a mob burned down the King William County courthouse, destroying all the records on which taxes were based.

Hearing reports of these disturbances and watching the feckless Congress trying to cope with them, George Washington became more and more dismayed. "I am mortified beyond expression," he told one correspondent, "when I view the clouds that have spread over the brightest morn that ever dawned upon any country." To another friend he exclaimed, "Good God! Who besides a Tory could have foreseen or a Briton predicted such a situation?"

"There are combustibles in every state," a worried Washington wrote to James Madison, the young Virginian whose abilities as a politician and political thinker had already impressed him. He urged Madison to persuade the Virginia legislature to issue a call for reform of the federal government. "Let us look to our national character and to things beyond the present moment," Washington wrote.

Virginia's summons inspired a meeting at Annapolis in the fall of 1786 to discuss the mounting chaos. Only twelve delegates from five states showed up, but James Madison prodded them into issuing a call for another convention of all the states to meet in Philadelphia in May 1787. Congress, understandably jealous of its dwindling powers, was not enthusiastic—until Shays' Rebellion escalated to the brink of civil war. The Congressmen seconded the motion but primly stipulated that the "sole and express purpose" of the meeting would be to revise the Articles of Confederation.

THE GRAND CONVENTION

Soon James Madison informed George Washington that he was one of seven delegates chosen to represent Virginia at this yet-unnamed convention. Should he go? Washington feared he could risk his prestige in such a venture only once. What if the states ignored the Congress and failed to send delegates? What if the delegates who showed up failed to agree? It would make a bad situation far worse if people decided not even George Washington could rescue the foundering ship of state.

Some of the ex-general's most trusted advisers, such as his former artillery commander, Henry Knox, urged him to stay home. For two months Washington brooded and pondered. Finally something deep within him said yes. "To see this country happy is so much the wish of my soul," he told Knox, "nothing on this side of Elysium can be placed in competition with it." On May 9, 1787, he stepped into his coach and began the journey to Philadelphia.

Before he left Mount Vernon, Washington hurled a final challenge at James Madison. "My wish," he wrote, "is that the convention may adopt no temporizing expedients, but probe [our] defects . . . to the bottom and provide radical cures." It would take three and one half exhausting, harrowing months, but Washington would get his wish—and then some.

THE CONSTITUTIONAL CONVENTION OF 1787

RICHARD B. BERNSTEIN

In 1787, some leading political figures, dissatisfied with the Articles of Confederation, gathered in Philadelphia to discuss ways of reforming America's fledgling national government. What they came up with is the Constitution that remains in use in the United States today. Historian Richard B. Bernstein provides a brief general overview of this historic gathering, including its background, who the delegates were, and the summer-long process by which they fashioned a new national government. Bernstein, an adjunct associate professor of law at New York Law School, has written and edited several books on American constitutional history.

T he Philadelphia Convention of 1787 (also known as the Federal Convention or the Constitutional Convention) was a landmark in American and world history. Both its handiwork, the Constitution of the United States, and its example of a people's representatives using reason and experience to decide how to govern themselves had profound influence on subsequent experiments in government.

The convention met in the State House (now called Independence Hall) in Philadelphia from May 25 to September 17, 1787. Fifty-five delegates from twelve of the thirteen states (Rhode Island did not send delegates) took part in its deliberations.

A CAMPAIGN FOR REFORM

The convention was the result of a campaign to reform the first charter of government of the United States, the Articles of Con-

Richard B. Bernstein, "Philadelphia Convention," *The Reader's Companion to American History*, edited by Eric Foner and John A. Garraty, Boston: Houghton Mifflin, 1991. Copyright © 1991 by Houghton Mifflin Company. Reproduced by permission.

federation. Throughout the 1780s, politicians who thought in national terms worried that the Confederation faced problems its government was too weak to solve. Former allies, such as France and Spain, and its former adversary, Great Britain, restricted trade with the new nation and hampered America's development of its western territories. The Confederation Congress lacked the power to resolve boundary disputes between the states, to prevent states from imposing tariffs and other restrictions on interstate commerce, or to compel the states to meet requisitions issued to finance the Confederation. The Confederation even lacked an independent source of revenue, and plans in 1781 and 1783 to grant Congress authority to levy a 5 percent tax on imports had failed. Because all thirteen states had to ratify amendments, one state's refusal could block any attempt to amend the Articles.

Advocates of reform exchanged correspondence to muster support for a convention to revise the Articles, laying the foundation for interstate conferences and conventions seeking similar goals. In 1785, delegates from Maryland and Virginia, meeting in the Mount Vernon Conference, set a precedent for interstate conferences on reform. In 1786, hoping to extend this success, some proposed that the states meet in a convention on commercial matters at Annapolis, Maryland. Twelve delegates from five states gathered there in September; their report, written by Alexander Hamilton of New York, urging a general convention spurred the calling of the Federal Convention.

On February 21, 1787, the Confederation Congress adopted a resolution authorizing the convention but limited its mandate to revision of the Articles. Several states already had named their delegates and, citing the Annapolis Convention's report, authorized them to take any measures "to render the constitution of government adequate to the exigencies of the Union." The convention thus began with an inconsistent mandate.

MEMBERS OF THE CONVENTION

The convention consisted of states' governors, chief justices, attorneys general, and many delegates to the Confederation Congress, as well as several distinguished Americans who had agreed to come out of retirement to participate one last time in American politics. Although they followed a wide range of callings—lawyers, physicians, soldiers, clergymen, merchants, and farmers—most of the delegates were well-to-do members of their states' elite; one historian called them the well-bred, well-fed, well-wed, and well-read. They fell into several groups:

1. *National political figures:* Benjamin Franklin of Pennsylvania and George Washington of Virginia composed this group. Their willingness to place their prestige at risk by attending the convention testified to its legitimacy and to the severity of the problems facing the United States.

2. *Senior statesmen of American politics:* John Dickinson of Delaware, William Livingston of New Jersey, George Mason of Virginia, John Rutledge of South Carolina, and Roger Sherman of Connecticut were among these men. Veterans of colonial politics, they had helped lead the struggle against Great Britain. They brought with them an ability to compromise and a sensitivity to the clashing interests of the several states.

3. *Advocates of state and local interests:* These included John Lansing, Jr., of New York, Luther Martin of Maryland, William Paterson of New Jersey, Charles C. Pinckney of South Carolina, and Robert Yates, Jr., of New York. Because they spoke for particular interests, they made it necessary at least to consider localist views and interests in framing the new charter of government.

4. *Architects of national government:* Alexander Hamilton of New York, James Madison of Virginia, Charles C. Pinckney of South Carolina, and James Wilson of Pennsylvania formed this group. Each of these men hoped to make his ideas the basis of the convention's deliberations.

5. *Quiet men:* Among these were John Blair of Virginia, Jacob Broome of Delaware, Jared Ingersoll of Pennsylvania, and James McHenry of Maryland. They provided the votes needed to build consensus and to establish grounds for compromise.

Some leading figures were not present: John Adams and Thomas Jefferson were the American ministers to London and Paris, John Jay was the Confederation's secretary for foreign affairs in New York City, and Patrick Henry was too interested in Virginia politics.

DEBATES AND DECISIONS

The convention elected Washington as its president and appointed a committee to prepare rules. Two of these were vital to the convention's success. First, as was customary among legislatures in the Anglo-American world, the convention met in secret, which would permit full and free discussion. Second, the

In 1787 political figures met in Philadelphia to discuss government reform. The result was the drafting of the U.S. Constitution.

delegates were free to change their minds and reopen any matters for further debate.

The delegates rotated between sessions in full convention and meetings of the Committee of the Whole House, the latter a useful parliamentary procedure permitting informal debate, freedom in stating views, and flexibility in reaching and reconsidering decisions. Select committees worked out compromises, prepared drafts, or formulated a range of solutions to a given problem. The delegates attacked questions piecemeal, debating and deciding on individual aspects. Often a decision on one issue would require them to reconsider other decisions they had reached. They traced a tortuous, crisscrossing route, at times pausing in dismay as they realized that a vote they had just taken had undone the accomplishments of hours or even days of grueling debate.

The convention discarded the Articles and framed an entirely new constitution. They based their work on a set of resolutions known as the Virginia Plan, largely the work of James Madison. These resolutions proposed the creation of a supreme national government with separate legislative, executive, and judicial branches.

The convention's principal task was the design of the national legislature. The delegates agreed on the powers they wished to lodge in the new Congress, but disagreed about how the states and the American people would be represented in it. Under the Virginia Plan, population or some other proportional measure would determine representation in both houses of Congress. To protect the principle of state equality, small-state delegates rallied behind William Paterson's New Jersey Plan, which would have preserved each state's equal vote in a one-house Congress with augmented powers. Although the delegates rejected the New Jersey Plan on June 19, it took them nearly a month of further argument before they adopted on July 16 what has been called the Great Compromise, under which the House of Representatives would be apportioned based on population and each state would have two votes in the Senate.

Other difficulties facing them included the method of electing the chief executive, or president—solved by the invention of the electoral college; the counting of slaves in the ratio for apportioning representation and taxation among the states—resolved with the "three-fifths" ratio, under which three-fifths of the slave population would be added to the free population; and the dispute over the need for a bill of rights, a proposal rejected by the convention in its last week. But the delegates devoted little attention to the powers of the president and almost none to the structure of the judiciary or the executive branch, leaving these matters to the new Congress.

THE FINAL PRODUCT

The document approved on September 17, the Constitution of the United States, was a terse outline of government—seven articles of four thousand words. In framing it, the delegates drew on their accumulated experience and memories of colonial, state, and national politics, their familiarity with English constitutional history and classical civilization, and the political ideas of the Age of Enlightenment. Thirty-nine delegates signed the Constitution; the convention sent it to the Confederation Congress for submission to the states, which were to refer it in turn to ratifying conventions chosen by the people.

James Madison took detailed notes of the convention's debates to educate future generations about the difficulties and challenges of constitution making. Together with convention documents, the notes kept by Madison, John Lansing, Jr., Robert Yates, James McHenry, and other delegates form the basis for the modern understanding of the convention's work. Although these documents had little influence on the workings of the Constitution in its first decades, modern constitutional lawyers use them in preparing arguments about the "original intent" of the Framers.

THE DEBATE OVER RATIFYING THE CONSTITUTION

JOHN P. KAMINSKI AND RICHARD LEFFLER

After delegates to the 1787 Constitutional Convention finished their plan for a new national government, at least nine states had to ratify the Constitution. What followed, historians John P. Kaminski and Richard Leffler write, was a hard-fought political campaign. Opponents of the Constitution, called Antifederalists, severely criticized the Constitution, arguing that it gave the federal government too much power, jeopardized people's hard-won freedoms, and favored the elite at the expense of the common people. Proponents (Federalists) sought to reassure the country that such fears were unfounded and that the Constitution was the best solution that could be devised that accommodated all the states. The Constitution was ratified, but Congress in 1789 proposed amendments to address the concerns of leading Antifederalists. These amendments, adopted in 1791, became known as the Bill of Rights.

Kaminski is professor of history at the University of Wisconsin, Madison, and director of that university's Center for the Study of the American Constitution. Leffler is deputy director of the center and senior associate editor of its *Documentary History of the Constitution* project.

John P. Kaminski and Richard Leffler, *Creating the Constitution: A History in Documents*, Madison, WI: The Center for the Study of the American Constitution, 1991. Copyright © 1991 by The Center for the Study of the American Constitution. Reproduced by permission.

W hen Supreme Court Justice Thurgood Marshall said, some time ago, that the Constitution was flawed and that he saw little wisdom or foresight in the Framers, it shocked a lot of people.

His remarks made news because most people today revere the Constitution. They would agree with Thomas Jefferson, who called the members of the Constitutional Convention "demi-gods." The great British statesman William Gladstone would probably get widespread agreement with his statement that the Constitution "is the most wonderful work ever struck off at a given time by the brain and purpose of man."

But Justice Marshall's criticism is mild compared to some of the things said about the Framers and their product in the debate that raged over the ratification of the Constitution in 1787–88. For instance, a pamphleteer in New York wrote of the Convention: "Some of the characters which compose it I revere; others I consider as of small consequence, and a number are suspected of being great public defaulters, and to have been guilty of notorious peculation and fraud, with regard to our public property in the hour of our distress."

The Convention, of course, had met behind closed doors. Little was known of its proceedings. This became the subject of severe criticism during the debate over the adoption of the Constitution. Samuel Bryan of Pennsylvania, one of the most prolific and virulent critics of the Constitution, writing as "Centinel," charged that "the evil genius of darkness presided at its birth, it came forth under the veil of mystery, its true features being carefully concealed, and every deceptive art has been and is practising to have this spurious brat received as the genuine offspring of heaven-born liberty."

WHAT ANTIFEDERALISTS BELIEVED

The opponents of the Constitution, called Antifederalists, believed that the current government under the Articles of Confederation needed fixing. The Confederation government had no power to tax. Its major source of money was to request the states to supply a yearly "requisition." Many of the states were badly in arrears. As a result, the Confederation government did not have enough money even to finance the interest on the debts owed to the foreign nations that had helped pay for the Revolution. The government was also unable to pay the interest on the money Americans had loaned to it during the Revolution. And there was no national currency. The "Continental" had long since become worthless.

The Confederation was also unable to regulate commerce, either between the states or with foreign nations. Some of the states adopted import duties that discriminated against other states. Great Britain, the major trading partner with America before the Revolution, was unwilling to enter into a commercial treaty with the United States. In fact, the British adopted trade regulations that discriminated against American shipping, which had a devastating effect on American merchants and shipping. Many people believed that if the government had the power to regulate trade, the British would be more willing to enter into a commercial treaty. In the mid-1780s, the United States suffered from a major economic depression; it was commonly believed that the cause of this depression was the inability of the government to regulate trade among the states and with foreign nations. Antifederalists agreed that the Confederation government should have such power.

But they were shocked that the Constitution went so far beyond simply giving the Confederation Congress these additional powers. The Constitution was not a revision of the Articles of Confederation but a totally new government with vastly more power, so much power that they feared for the liberty of the country and the future viability of the states.

Antifederalists believed that the Constitution would give the federal government enough power to destroy the states, which were then considered the bulwarks of liberty. They feared that the House of Representatives, the only branch of government directly elected by the people, was too small (only 65 members sat in the first House) to represent all the people and too weak to resist the power of the Senate and the President.

Antifederalists worried that the Senate would become a tool of the rich and the well-educated few (their shorthand way of referring to this elite was to call them the aristocracy) and that the President would, alternately, become either a king or be controlled by the aristocratic Senate. They were afraid that the Supreme Court and the inferior federal courts would defend the interests of the federal government at the expense of the states, would make justice available only to the wealthy, and would overwhelm the state courts, which Antifederalists believed were better able to defend the interests of the ordinary people.

CALLS FOR A BILL OF RIGHTS

Of all the shortcomings that Antifederalists saw in the Constitution, probably the most stunning was that the Constitution did not contain a bill of rights. Seven of the state constitutions contained a bill of rights; in the other states, protections for civil liberty were written into the body of their constitutions or enacted as legislation. Antifederalists asked why there was no protection in the proposed Constitution for freedom of the press and religion, the right to petition for redress of grievances, or critical procedural rights in criminal cases, such as the right against self-incrimination, the right to legal counsel, and the right to cross-examine witnesses and confront one's accusers. Some saw the absence of a bill of rights as a proof that the Framers intended to establish a despotism.

Antifederalists demanded that changes be made in the Constitution and especially that a bill of rights be added that would secure liberty. They warned against adopting this new government without amendments because, as Richard Henry Lee of Virginia wrote, it had "been found from Universal experience that the most express declarations and reservations are necessary to protect the just rights and liberty of mankind from the silent, powerful, and ever active conspiracy of those who govern."

FEDERALIST ARGUMENTS

Federalists, those who supported the Constitution, responded that none of these fears was justified and that no changes could be made in the Constitution until it was ratified and put into effect. They argued that the choice was: either accept this Constitution as it was, with the possibility of amendments after it goes into effect, or reject it and risk anarchy or civil war.

Federalists sought to assure the country that the concerns raised about the Constitution were unjustified. They argued that the federal government would not destroy the states because most power still remained with the states; the powers of the federal government were limited to those that were delegated to it by the Constitution. They argued that the checks and balances among the House of Representatives, the Senate, the President, and the courts guaranteed that no one person or small group could ever control the government. Federalists claimed that of the three branches, the judiciary would be the "least dangerous." They denied that a bill of rights was needed because of the strict limits placed on federal power. In fact, they argued that a bill of rights might be dangerous in two ways. First, a listing of rights could never be complete, and if a right were not mentioned the implication might be that it was left unprotected. Second, if the bill of rights mentioned freedom of the press, for instance, someone might argue that this implied that there was a power in the Constitution for the federal government to legislate in some way concerning the press—Congress might not prohibit freedom of the press, but it might pass "proper" regulations concerning the press.

RATIFYING THE CONSTITUTION

The Constitution specified that ratification had to be accomplished by conventions elected by the people in each state. Once nine states ratified, the Constitution was to go into effect among the ratifying states.

On December 7, 1787, Delaware's Convention became the first to ratify the Constitution, by a vote of 30–0. This was quickly followed by Pennsylvania on December 12 (46–23), New Jersey on December 18 (38–0), Georgia on December 31 (26–0), and Connecticut on January 9, 1788 (128–40). None of these state conventions proposed amendments. The minority in the Pennsylvania Convention presented amendments, but Federalists refused even to allow them to be entered on the journal.

Federalists in the Massachusetts Convention, however, ran into trouble. They could not ratify the Constitution without a compromise: the Convention would adopt the Constitution, but it would also instruct the state's representatives and senators in the first Congress under the Constitution to advocate a list of amendments. Similar demands for amendments were then made by the conventions of New Hampshire, South Carolina, Virginia, New York, and North Carolina. Antifederalists in Maryland's Convention would have proposed amendments, but the Federalist majority refused to allow amendments to come to the floor.

Finally, on June 21, 1788, New Hampshire became the ninth state to ratify the Constitution. Virginia and New York followed on June 25 and July 26, respectively. In addition to calling for amendments, New York's Convention called for a second constitutional convention to propose amendments. On August 2, North Carolina refused to ratify the Constitution until amendments were adopted. North Carolina did not ratify until November 1789 and Rhode Island delayed its ratification until May 1790.

But if Antifederalists were unable to prevent the ratification of the Constitution, they were successful in another important way. It was their insistent demand, throughout the long debate over ratification, that a bill of rights be added to the Constitution that would secure the rights of the people from the tyranny of a too-powerful federal government. Federalists denied that the government was too powerful and that tyranny was a real danger, but, finally, they were forced by necessity to agree that after the Constitution was operative amendments to it would be considered. Without this promise, it is unlikely that the Constitution could have been ratified in Massachusetts, Virginia, or New York.

Ultimately, the Antifederalist demand for a bill of rights was fulfilled. On June 8, 1789, James Madison proposed a bill of rights to an unreceptive House of Representatives. Many representatives—both Federalists and Antifederalists—felt that the consideration of amendments was premature; other issues needed the immediate attention of Congress, such as the establishment of the executive departments, the creation of the federal judiciary, and the enactment of tariffs to provide the new government with revenue. Madison, however, remained steadfast, arguing that amendments were necessary to satisfy the fears of Antifederalists. As the basis for his proposal, Madison used the amendments that had been proposed by the several state conventions. After considerable debate and alteration, on September 25 Congress adopted a proposal for amendments to the Constitution, including the ten amendments now known as the Bill of Rights. These amendments were adopted by the required number of states when Virginia ratified them on December 15, 1791. In March 1792 Secretary of State Thomas Jefferson declared the amendments to be in effect.

A WILLINGNESS TO COMPROMISE

What is extraordinary about the ratification of the Constitution is not that the Constitution was perfect and the people were unanimous in support of it. In fact, the people were badly divided over the wisdom of adopting the Constitution and Federalists and Antifederalists alike realized that the Constitution was imperfect. Many people were shocked and frightened because the Constitution did not have a bill of rights and feared that the liberty that had been fought for in the Revolution, at tremendous cost in blood and money, might be lost. Others objected to the compromises embodied in the document, particularly those in which concessions were made to the South concerning slavery. Federalists readily admitted that the Constitution had flaws, but they also maintained that, as the product of accommodation among thirteen different states, it was the best constitution that could be obtained at that time, and that amendments could be obtained when deficiencies became apparent.

Despite the grave reservations raised by Antifederalists, the states ratified the Constitution. Antifederalists, concerned though they were that freedom might be endangered, acceded to the will of the majority. They did not resist or resort to violence. They participated in the system created by the Constitution and the new government, and many of their fears were eliminated when Congress proposed the Bill of Rights.

The Constitution has served us well for 200 years. Part of the reason for its success goes back to the beginning: Americans have been willing to trust each other's devotion to liberty, to compromise when necessary, and to abide by the rule of law.

ERVIN TRASK MEM. LIBRARY
PLAINVILLE HIGH SCHOOL

HOW GEORGE WASHINGTON SAVED AMERICA

Seymour Martin Lipset

George Washington, who served as America's first president from 1789 to 1797, is arguably the most important single figure in American history, according to sociologist and political scientist Seymour Martin Lipset. He used his status as hero of the American Revolution to create respect for the new nation and to bolster the legitimacy of its government. In addition, by rejecting any suggestions of becoming president-for-life, Washington helped establish a tradition of peaceful and republican transitions of leadership. Lipset is a professor of public policy at George Mason University. His numerous books include *The First New Nation*.

George Washington is an underestimated figure. Abraham Lincoln, Thomas Jefferson, and Benjamin Franklin are seen as real people with lives and emotions; Washington is a painting on the wall. Yet I believe that he is the most important single figure in American history. Without him, the Revolution might have failed. This is not because of his military ability; he lost many of the battles he fought, and only French intervention brought victory. His first enormous achievement was to build and maintain the morale of the Continental Army's troops and the loyalty of its officers under depressing conditions. . . .

Little need be said here about Washington the general, or of

Seymour Martin Lipset, "George Washington and the Founding of Democracy," *Journal of Democracy*, vol. 9, October 1998, pp. 24–38. Copyright © 1998 by *Journal of Democracy*. Reproduced by permission.

what he did prior to the closing years of the Revolution, as important as such aspects of his career undoubtedly are. Instead, I will discuss Washington as a founder, the man who helped the United States to formulate an identity and to institutionalize a competitive electoral democracy—or, to put it in terms that Washington himself would have found more familiar, to establish a republic.

The relevance of individual greatness to history has been much debated. . . .

One cannot say . . . : No Washington, no American democratic republic. The United States would in all probability have eventually become a democracy, even had Washington not been on the scene. Elections predated independence in the British colonies, and as historian William Chambers noted, the new nation possessed many of the other "prerequisites for full democratic participation and practice." Yet Washington played a necessary role because of the charisma that flowed from his personality and his military leadership (which was something different from his generalship in a narrower sense). He inspired incredible trust and facilitated—as no one else alive at the time probably could have—the formation of the culture and institutions needed for a stable, legitimate, and effective democratic system. Washington, in short, was one of those "great men" without whom history would be very different.

THE PROBLEM OF WEAK LEGITIMACY

The postindependence experience of the entire non-British-ruled ex-colonial world, and much of the former British Empire as well, is a story of secessions, military coups, and dictatorships. The history of postcoup, postrevolutionary regimes is largely one of democratic failure. It is rare for all the major players, including the military, economic, and political elites, to accept the need to conform to the rules of the new system. New political regimes inherently have weak or low legitimacy.

[German sociologist] Max Weber suggested there are basically three ways in which authority may possess legitimacy. The first is *traditional,* as in a monarchy where kings have seemingly "always" ruled. *Rational-legal* authority exists in polities in which those in power are obeyed because of an acceptance of the system of rules under which they have won and hold office. It takes root as a result of prolonged periods of effectiveness, particularly in the economy. *Charismatic* authority rests upon faith in a leader who is believed to be endowed with great personal worth: This may come from God, as in the case of a religious prophet, or may arise from the display of extraordinary talents.

Old states possess traditional legitimacy, but where legitimacy is absent, it can be developed quickly only through charisma. Almost by definition, newly independent nations or revolutionary regimes begin with low legitimacy. Democratic norms require a willingness to accept political defeat: to leave office upon losing an election, to follow rules even when they work against one's interests. New democracies' weak legitimacy makes them unstable and potentially short-lived. For illustrations, one can turn to the history of Latin America, of much of Europe before 1945, and of most of Africa and Asia since that date.

The postrevolutionary United States, also marked by weak legitimacy, faced recurrent crises of authority as important "players" rejected the "rules of the game." The years from 1800 to the Civil War saw a number of attempts at secession, some in the North, some in the South, one in the West. Washington was privately pessimistic about the fledgling Union's prospects for survival, expecting a rupture between free and slave states during his lifetime. Even before the end of the War of Independence, he had to overcome a projected military coup. Soon after he left the presidency in 1797, the declining Federalist majority in Congress passed the Alien and Sedition Acts, curtailing free speech in hopes of suppressing their opponents.

Three years later, shortly after Washington's own death in December 1799, the leaders of the defeated Federalists tried to overturn the results of the 1800 presidential election, which had brought their enemy Thomas Jefferson to power. The intended victims of the Federalists, Jefferson and his own party, the Democratic-Republicans, behaved in a similar manner after they took office. Aaron Burr, Jefferson's rival and first vice-president, upon leaving office hatched a conspiracy to split the trans-Appalachian West from the rest of the country. Clearly, the conditions conducive to the breakdown of postrevolutionary regimes and new states were present in the early United States. But unlike almost all of Latin America and many latter-day "new nations," the United States was able to survive its first three-quarters of a century with its competitive electoral democracy intact. During this time, political parties became institutionalized, the suffrage was expanded to include all white male citizens, and the republic enlarged rapidly in population, productive wealth, and geographical extent, settling and adding new states as it grew. How was it able to do so? The answer in part is a form of charismatic legitimacy.

To understand why this happened we must examine the role of Washington, who consciously employed his status as military leader and hero of the Revolution to create respect for national authority and to bolster the legitimacy of the new nation. Unlike most leaders of new postcolonial regimes, Washington was committed to a free polity and understood the problem posed by weak legitimacy. The record suggests that he was the only person who could have created or sustained allegiance, building new respect for the new nation.

The mandate to obey newly created legal structures is necessarily a weak source of authority in societies in which law and government have been identified with the interests of an imperial power or a previous autocratic regime. Charismatic authority, by contrast, is well-suited to the needs of such polities. A charismatic leader plays several roles. He is first of all the symbol of the new nation or political system, a hero who embodies its values and aspirations. But more than merely symbolizing the polity, he, like the monarch in a traditional system, legitimizes the government by endowing it with his "gift of grace." Charismatic authority can be seen as a transitional phenomenon inducing citizens to observe the requirements for national stability out of trust in the leader until they learn to do so out of a more impersonal sense of loyalty to or satisfaction with the regime.

CHARISMA WITH MODERATION

Because it is so personalized, charismatic leadership is inherently unstable. Unlike traditional authority, new charismatic authority admits of little or no distinction between itself and its agents. (In a monarchy, by contrast, "the king can do no wrong"—fault is never imputed to the crown, but only to its ministers.) Under charismatic authority, dissatisfaction with particular policies or officials can easily produce generalized disaffection with the system and with the source of authority, who is also seen as the responsible agent. A charismatic leader, therefore, must either make public opposition or criticism impermissible, or he must transcend partisan conflict by playing

As America's first president, Washington (shown taking the oath of office) unified the nation and worked to stabilize the government.

the role of a constitutional monarch, who symbolizes the system but remains above the ordinary political fray. Even where opposition to specific policies on an individual or informal factional basis may be tolerated, there must not be organized opposition to the charismatic leader.

The difference between these options is fateful. Authoritarian regimes often break down because the charismatic head, inherently a policy actor, is blamed for adverse outcomes. Conversely, it may be argued that revolutionary dictatorships require efforts at charismatic legitimation, since the only alternative is the costly and difficult one of absolute repression. . . .

The republic that emerged from the American Revolution was legitimized by charisma. To a degree that we today often do not appreciate, Washington was idolized; his name, image, and person were held in almost sacred regard. He understood this role and, his biographers have stressed, cultivated a profound concern with acting properly, doing what was right, and setting a good example in matters large and small. His "great gifts to the presidency and to the Republic," as [historian] Clinton Rossiter put it, "were dignity, authority and constitutionalism." His self-consciousness about being a model began with the way he performed his role as commander of the Continental Army. To secure respect as head of a rebel force (as later, of a new government), he had to be aloof, to discourage familiarity, to demand deference. Although privately he enjoyed humor and conviviality (including dancing), publicly he practiced a studied reserve. . . .

As commander of an army whose men were not accustomed to military hierarchy, which had limited resources, and which won few battles, Washington's greatest contribution was to keep it viable, to command respect, and to maintain morale. He showed no personal weakness and never gave his soldiers any reason to lose faith in him. He lived with his troops, drew no pay, and rejected opportunities to take even the briefest leave to visit Mount Vernon. . . .

Always deferential to civilian authorities, Washington let them be the first to return to New York City after the British evacuated it. He then gave a series of farewell addresses, in most of which he stated his intention to withdraw from public life. His returning to his farm revived the legend of Cincinnatus, the Roman hero whose plowing had been interrupted by a call to save the republic from invaders, and who had gone back to his lands when the job was done. (Washington's behavior inspired the founding of the Order of Cincinnatus by former officers of the Revolutionary army; its name symbolizes that their greatest action was to return to being ordinary citizens again.) In retiring, Washington exhibited a disdain for office and power that only enhanced his charisma and increased his influence. He made it clear that he had no interest in any public position, certainly not as king, which many wanted him to become, but equally not as head of the republic. A disdain for office did not mean a lack of interest in the shape of the new nation. Washington understood that to have one nation, it would be necessary to have a central government with an executive—something not provided for in the Articles of Confederation. His resignation address to the Continental Congress had included a strong argument for such a government.

Washington feared that the opponents of the experiment in democratic government, who had predicted that the new polity would dissolve, might turn out to be right. The Congress-dominated government under the Articles of Confederation had revealed itself all too clearly as unequal to the challenges of handling either domestic or foreign affairs. Distressed by repeated crises, he wrote frequently to friends in different states urging that the Articles be revised.

LEGITIMIZING THE NEW SYSTEM

Changes of the type that he advocated were adopted at the Constitutional Convention, held in Philadelphia during the

summer of 1787. The meeting was called to propose revisions
to the Articles, but soon took up the work of drafting a new fundamental law. Washington had been reluctant to attend it, wor-
rying that he might be appearing to renege on his pledge to stay
out of public life. But Shays' Rebellion, an armed uprising by
western Massachusetts farmers in the fall of 1786, shocked him
and convinced him to take part. Critics' predictions that the new
nation would not be able to govern itself seemed to be coming
true. Washington went to the Philadelphia Convention, and as
everyone expected, was chosen as its presiding officer.

As chairman, he never spoke or voted. In typical Washing-
tonian fashion, he set an example for the delegates by never
missing a session or arriving late. His greatest influence, however, was exerted off the convention floor. Everyone knew that
he favored what became the Convention's basic outcome: a more
powerful central government led by a president, albeit one subject to elaborate checks and balances. It has been agreed, both
then and since, that the expectation that Washington would be
the first incumbent played a large role in the creation of this office, and in securing approval for the Constitution generally. No
one feared that he would misuse power. As noted earlier, his
genuine hesitancy, his reluctance to assume the position only
served to reinforce the almost universal desire that he do so.

In any case, it was agreed before, during, and after the
Philadelphia Convention that Washington's presence at the sessions, and his subsequent public approval of the Constitution,
were necessary to secure its passage. The opponents of the Constitution, who feared a more powerful executive, were quite numerous in many states, including New York and Virginia, without whose approval the new Constitution would have been
inoperative. Writing of the subsequent deliberations to secure
Virginia's ratification, James Monroe wrote privately to Jefferson, "Be assured, his influence carried the government."

Washington assumed the presidency in 1789 knowing that
his task was to create respect for the office so that the new polity
might survive. In ways large and small, therefore, Washington
sought to have his position recognized as supreme, as a symbol
of national unity. When he visited Massachusetts, for instance,
he insisted that the state's governor, John Hancock, recognize
the precedence of the federal government by calling on him,
holding that adherence to such "rules of proceeding" would be
"prudent for a young state."

If ever there was an example of charismatic legitimization of a polity, it was the way in which respect and veneration for Washington sanctified the new Republic. The man who would not be king, who was genuinely reluctant to take part in politics, who resisted and feared becoming president, was able to legitimate the new system.

IMPORTING VIRTUE

Washington knew what he was doing. He never used the phrase "charismatic legitimacy"—a modern coinage—but he understood that a stable and free polity required a set of values, a national character that subsumed the rule of law, respect for authority, and a willingness to subordinate private interest and factional conflict for the sake of the larger good. His task was to set an example, to be a model of "public virtue," to awe the politicians and the public into doing right. But he understood, as he noted in his Farewell Address, that "[t]ime and habit are at least as necessary to fix the true character of government as of other human institutions."

Washington's concern for inculcating virtue in the citizens and leaders of the young republic was evident in his effort to create a national university in the nation's capital. For Washington, "the guarantee that the American government would never degenerate into despotism lay in the ultimate virtue of the American people," and first-rate higher education contributed to that end. He believed that a "national university would help form the characters of future leaders by breaking down local attachments and state prejudices" and teaching them to understand "the principles of the Constitution [and] the laws." His first and last messages to Congress recommended its establishment, and in his last will and testament, which included a bequest for the university, he described the proposal as a "matter of infinite importance in my judgment."

Washington was capable of mistakes—for instance, in his belief that parties are intrinsically bad for democracy. He was distressed by factional strife, and by public pursuit of individual or group self-interest. Though he obviously knew he could not prevent interest-driven conflict, he was able during the first years of the Republic to keep it within bounds, to coax opponents to cooperate, to sustain among strong partisans allegiance to the nation and obedience to policies they opposed. But he was never reconciled to partisan struggles, and the outbreak of a maritime quasi-war with Revolutionary France seemingly pushed him to drop his initial opposition to the repressive Alien and Sedition Acts.

Alexander Hamilton and Thomas Jefferson, the leaders of the factions that would become the first parties, served in Washington's cabinet for most of his presidency and never let their antagonism break completely into the open. Privately, Washington sided with Treasury Secretary Hamilton and the Federalists, who favored a strong central government and the use of public resources to build up the economy, against Secretary of State Jefferson and his Democratic-Republicans, who tended to favor localism and agrarianism. In public, as we have seen, Washington was careful to stand above the fray and appear nonpartisan. Throughout the often bitter controversies of the 1790s, nearly all Americans continued to revere him.

RELIGION AND RACE

Washington tried to demonstrate by word and deed how to deal with religion in a pluralistic society. He clearly believed in God and formally belonged to the Episcopal Church for most of his life, but was not strongly committed to any particular creed. The evidence seems clear that he was a deist. But he set a model that all future presidents have followed by adding "so help me God" to the inaugural oath.

More important were his efforts to integrate minority religions and to command respect for them. His famous 1791 letter to the Touro Synagogue in Rhode Island stated his pleasure that Judaism was among the American creeds. He went on to criticize the idea of tolerance as invidious, saying, "It is now no more that toleration is spoken of, as if it was by the indulgence of one class of people, that another enjoyed the exercise of their inherent natural rights." Jews were not merely to be tolerated; they were Americans. During the Revolution, he forbade a New England festivity called "Pope's Day" as offensive to his Catholic soldiers. After the war, he opposed the continued "establishment" of the Episcopal Church in Virginia, urging that members of all religious groups should instead pay legally required assessments to their respective religious bodies, while nonbelievers paid levies to charity.

Barry Schwartz notes how Washington reached out to the various religious minorities:

The Baptists, for example, were delighted when the nation's hero urged them to be persuaded that "no one would be more zealous than myself to establish effectual barriers against the horrors of spiritual tyranny, and every species of religious persecution." The Quakers rejoiced to know that the new President considered them "exemplary and useful citizens," despite their refusal to aid him in war. Catholics, who were in many respects the most despised of the religious minorities, saw an end to persecution when the chief magistrate assured them that all citizens "are equally entitled to the protection of civil government. . . . And I presume that your fellow-citizens will not forget the patriotic part which you took in the accomplishment of the revolution, and the establishment of their government." Jews found in Washington's policy an unprecedented expression of friendship from a head of state. . . . The Universalists, disdained by the pious for their liberal religious views, were congratulated by Washington for their "political professions and practices," which were "almost universally friendly to the order and happiness of our civil institutions." Acknowledging in each instance that respect for diversity was a fair price for commitment to the nation and its regime, Washington abolished deep-rooted fears that would have otherwise alienated a large part of the population from the nation-building process. For this large minority, he embodied not the ideal of union, nor even that of liberty, but rather the reconciliation of union and liberty.

SLAVERY

Discussion of Washington's liberality as regards religious minorities leads inevitably to the subject of Washington as a slave owner. Virginia in his time contained about two-fifths of all the slaves in the original 13 states, and Washington himself owned more than a hundred slaves to maintain the several farms, numerous outbuildings, and gracious riverfront mansion that made up Mount Vernon. As Washington matured, he faced up to the immorality of slavery, with opinions that put him squarely on the liberal side of the Southern spectrum regarding "the peculiar institution" and its future. He appears to have begun thinking about the problem with great seriousness during the War of Independence. Foreign and domestic friends raised the obvious question of how slavery could be reconciled with a war for freedom.

Washington considered ways of freeing the slaves, but expressed concern over the prospects awaiting largely unskilled and uneducated people who also would face discrimination. After the war, he tried to enhance the skills of his slaves and to collect enough money to support them after manumission. His personal situation was difficult because the many slaves that his wife Martha had brought into their marriage had belonged to a previous husband who had died without a will. Under the laws of Virginia, these so-called "dower" slaves belonged neither to Washington nor his wife, but to the estate of her first husband. Washington could have freed his own slaves during his lifetime, but neither Martha nor he could have freed hers.

Washington saved enough money to free his own and his wife's slaves after he died, and to provide a fund for their support. Their children were to be educated. Washington's estate made payments to former Mount Vernon slaves until 1833, a third of a century after his death. A hint as to the depth of his feelings shows through in conversations he had early in his presidency, when he privately expressed fears that the new nation would break up along North-South lines. At that time, this proud Virginian told friends, including fellow Virginian Edmund Randolph, that such an event would force him to move to the North. Washington exceeded Jefferson and almost all his fellow southern Founders in the generosity with which he dealt with his slaves.

INSTITUTIONALIZING DEMOCRACY

Washington wished to retire after one term in office, but the conflict between Hamilton and Jefferson would not permit it. At the urging of these two principal lieutenants and of many others, he agreed to serve another term. As much as he regretted the emergence of embryonic parties, he was thereby unwittingly permitting the further peaceful extension of factional conflict under his administration. Yet the decision to stay on turned out to be a crucial one. His second term saw the country badly torn by conflicting attitudes toward the French Revolution, and also faced with a Western antitax uprising, the so-called Whiskey Rebellion, that required the dispatch of federal troops to the Allegheny Mountains of Pennsylvania.

In sum, it is clear that Washington was an indispensable

charismatic leader. Yet there can be no doubt that he pushed the United States toward a legal-rational system of authority by his firm refusal to take advantage of his status. He rejected all suggestions that he assume autocratic powers or become president-for-life. He retired while still in good health, identifying himself to the end with the laws and spirit of the nation. His brand of charismatic leadership had a critical stabilizing effect on the society's evolution. The first succession contest, between Jefferson and Vice-President John Adams, took place while Washington still held office, enabling him to set a precedent as the first head of a modern state to hand over the reins to a duly elected successor (Adams). Had Washington continued in office until his death, it is quite possible that subsequent presidential successions would have been more difficult, with efforts by the defeated to contest the results, or by later presidents to retain office indefinitely, much as was to happen in Latin America. But Washington never even entertained the possibility of staying in office, for he knew that he had to set an example and step down, lest people think that "having tasted the sweets of office, he could not do without them." His reputation and his understanding of the requirements for a stable republic required that he withdraw.

The charismatic aspects of Washington's appeal were consciously used by U.S. political leaders to create a character, an identity for the young nation. In 1800, shortly after Washington's death, the British ambassador to the United States discussed the functions of tributes to Washington in a report to the Foreign Office:

> The leading men in the United States appear to be of the opinion that these ceremonies tend to elevate the spirit of the people, and contribute to the formation of a national character, which they consider as much wanting in this country. And assuredly, if self-opinion is (as perhaps it is) an essential ingredient in that character which promotes the prosperity and dignity of a nation, the Americans will be the gainers by the periodical recital of the feats of their Revolutionary War, and the repetition of the praises of Washington. The hyperbolical amplifications, the Panegyricks in question have an evident effect especially among the younger parts of the community, in fomenting the growth of that vanity, which to the feelings of a stranger have already arrived at a sufficient height.

The "near-apotheosis" of Washington characterized almost all that was written and said about him for the first few generations of the new nation.

WASHINGTON'S IMPORTANCE

The importance of Washington's role for the institutionalization of democracy in the early United States can be summarized as follows:

1) In a small, fragile, and new political entity riven by serious cleavages, he singlehandedly provided a basis for unity. His enormous prestige commanded the loyalty of the leaders of the different factions as well as of the general populace.

2) He was strongly committed to constitutional government in both principle and practice, and provided paternal guidance to those involved in developing the machinery of deliberation and administration. He stayed in power long enough to permit the crystallization of factions into embryonic parties, a development that dismayed him greatly.

3) By voluntarily retiring from office, he set a precedent exemplifying a proper republican approach to the problem of succession.

In most new nations that have had them, charismatic leaders have only fulfilled the first of these tasks, acting as symbols to help prolong the feelings of unity that develop prior to the achievement of independence. The neglect of the other two results in "charismatic personalities . . . [who do] not ordinarily build . . . the institutions which are indispensable for carrying on the life of a political society." And when such personalities leave the scene, there arises again, as there did after the achievement of independence, the difficult problem of maintaining national unity among a conglomeration of groups and interests.

Jefferson, even as he worried that Washington's prestige would undermine efforts to develop an opposition party, understood what Washington was doing by epitomizing virtue. As Jefferson emphasized, Washington had been "scrupulously obeying the laws through the whole of his career, civil and military," a model "of which the history of the world furnishes no other example." The first president's great biographer, James Flexner, concludes: "Washington had given the United States an unheard-of boon: charisma with hardly any cost."

Philadelphia's Yellow Fever Epidemic

Samuel Breck

Epidemics were a recurring feature of American life for much of its history. One of the most devastating epidemics struck Philadelphia in 1793. The city, then the nation's capital and its largest city, lost five thousand people to yellow fever. The following firsthand account is by Samuel Breck, a young merchant who later became a noted philanthropist and public servant.

I had scarcely become settled in Philadelphia when in July, 1793, the yellow fever broke out, and, spreading rapidly in August, obliged all the citizens who could remove to seek safety in the country. My father took his family to Bristol on the Delaware, and in the last of August I followed him. Having engaged in commerce, and having a ship at the wharf loading for Liverpool, I was compelled to return to the city on the 8th of September, and spend the 9th there. My business took me down to the Swedes' church and up Front street to Walnut street wharf, where I had my counting-house. Everything looked gloomy, and forty-five deaths were reported for the 9th. In the afternoon, when I was about returning to the country, I passed by the lodgings of the Vicomte de Noailles, who had fled from the Revolutionists of France. He was standing at the door, and calling to me, asked me what I was doing in town. "Fly," said he, "as soon as you can, for pestilence is all around us." And yet it was noth-

Samuel Breck, "Yellow Fever in Philadelphia (1793)," *Recollections*, edited by H.E. Scudder, Philadelphia: Porter & Contes, 1877.

ing then to what it became three or four weeks later, when from the first to the twelfth of October one thousand persons died. On the twelfth a smart frost came and checked its ravages.

The horrors of this memorable affliction were extensive and heartrending. Nor were they softened by professional skill. The disorder was in a great measure a stranger to our climate, and was awkwardly treated. Its rapid march, being from ten victims a day in August to one hundred a day in October, terrified the physicians, and led them into contradictory modes of treatment. They, as well as the guardians of the city, were taken by surprise. No hospitals or hospital stores were in readiness to alleviate the sufferings of the poor. For a long time nothing could be done other than to furnish coffins for the dead and men to bury them. At length a large house in the neighborhood was appropriately fitted up for the reception of patients, and a few pre-eminent philanthropists volunteered to superintend it. At the head of them was Stephen Girard, who has since become the richest man in America.

In private families the parents, the children, the domestics lingered and died, frequently without assistance. The wealthy soon fled; the fearless or indifferent remained from choice, the poor from necessity. The inhabitants were reduced thus to one-half their number, yet the malignant action of the disease increased, so that those who were in health one day were buried the next. The burning fever occasioned paroxysms of rage which drove the patient naked from his bed to the street, and in some instances to the river, where he was drowned. Insanity was often the last stage of its horrors.

ONE PERSON'S STORY

In November, when I returned to the city and found it repeopled, the common topic of conversation could be no other than this unhappy occurrence; the public journals were engrossed by it, and related many examples of calamitous suffering. One of these took place on the property adjacent to my father's. The respectable owner, counting upon the comparative security of his remote residence from the heart of the town, ventured to brave the disorder, and fortunately escaped its attack. He told me that in the height of the sickness, when death was sweeping away its hundreds a week, a man applied to him for leave to sleep one night on the stable floor. The gentleman, like every one else, inspired with fear and caution, hesitated. The stranger pressed his request, assuring him that he had avoided the infected parts of the city, that his health was very good, and promised to go away at sunrise the next day. Under these circumstances he admitted him into his stable for that night. At peep of day the gentleman went to see if the man was gone. On opening the door he found him lying on the floor delirious and in a burning fever. Fearful of alarming his family, he kept it a secret from them, and went to the committee of health to ask to have the man removed.

That committee was in session day and night at the City Hall in Chestnut street. The spectacle around was new, for he had not ventured for some weeks so low down in town. The attendants on the dead stood on the pavement in considerable numbers soliciting jobs, and until employed they were occupied in feeding their horses out of the coffins which they had provided in anticipation of the daily wants. These speculators were useful, and, albeit with little show of feeling, contributed greatly to lessen, by competition, the charges of interment. The gentleman passed on through these callous spectators until he reached the room in which the committee was assembled, and from whom he obtained the services of a quack doctor, none other being in attendance. They went together to the stable, where the doctor examined the man, and then told the gentleman that at ten o'-clock he would send the cart with a suitable coffin, into which he requested to have the dying stranger placed. The poor man was then alive and begging for a drink of water. His fit of delirium had subsided, his reason had returned, yet the experience of the *soi-disant* doctor enabled him to foretell that his death would take place in a few hours; it did so, and in time for his corpse to be conveyed away by the cart at the hour appointed. This sudden exit was of common occurrence. The whole number of deaths in 1793 by yellow fever was more than four thousand. Again it took place in 1797, '98 and '99, when the loss was six thousand, making a total in these four years of ten thousand.

FREED SLAVES PETITION CONGRESS

JACOB NICHOLSON, JUPITER NICHOLSON, JOB ALBERT, AND THOMAS PRITCHET

Following the American Revolution, the population of free blacks rose sharply as the northern states ended slavery, while in the south thousands of slaves were freed (manumitted) by their owners. The first U.S. census in 1790 counted roughly sixty thousand free blacks; by 1800 the number rose to 110,000. However, for many blacks, the line between slavery and freedom was perilously thin. In North Carolina, for example, a state law empowered anyone to recapture and resell manumitted slaves. The 1793 federal Fugitive Slave Law empowered slaveowners or their agents to capture and return runaway slaves, but failed to provide any penalties for kidnapping and selling free blacks back into slavery.

In 1797 four freed slaves sent the following petition to the U.S. Congress. They were all residents of North Carolina but were forced to flee the state to avoid being sold into slavery again. They tell of how they were compelled to flee from their homes and farms in North Carolina. Historians have argued that the document's probable author was Absalom Jones, the pastor of the St. Thomas's African Episcopal Church of Philadelphia and an important figure of that city's African American community. Congress refused to accept the petition.

---

*T*o *the President, Senate, and House of Representatives.*
  The Petition and Representation of the under-named Freemen, respectfully showeth:—
That, being of African descent, late inhabitants and natives of

Jacob Nicholson, Jupiter Nicholson, Job Albert, and Thomas Pritchet, "Petition of North Carolina Blacks to Congress, January 23, 1797," *Annals of Congress*, 4th Congress, 1855.

North Carolina, to you only, under God, can we apply with any hope of effect, for redress of our grievances, having been compelled to leave the State wherein we had a right of residence, as freemen liberated under the hand and seal of humane and conscientious masters, the validity of which act of justice in restoring us to our native right of freedom, was confirmed by judgment of the Superior Court of North Carolina, wherein it was brought to trial; yet, not long after this decision, a law of that State was enacted, under which men of cruel disposition, and void of just principle, received countenance and authority in violently seizing, imprisoning, and selling into slavery, such as had been so emancipated; whereby we were reduced to the necessity of separating from some of our nearest and most tender connexions, and of seeking refuge in such parts of the Union where more regard is paid to the public declaration in favor of liberty and the common right of man, several hundreds, under our circumstances, having, in consequence of the said law, been hunted day and night, like beasts of the forest, by armed men with dogs, and made a prey of as free and lawful plunder. Among others thus exposed, I, Jupiter Nicholson, of Perquimans county, North Carolina, after being set free by my master, Thomas Nicholson, and having been about two years employed as a seaman in the service of Zachary Nickson, on coming on shore, was pursued by men with dogs and arms; but was favored to escape by night to Virginia, with my wife, who was manumitted by Gabriel Cosan, where I resided about four years in the town of Portsmouth, chiefly employed in sawing boards and scantling; from thence I removed with my wife to Philadelphia, where I have been employed, at times, by water, working along shore, or sawing wood. I left behind me a father and mother, who were manumitted by Thomas Nicholson and Zachary Dickson; they have been since taken up, with a beloved brother, and sold into cruel bondage.

STORIES OF THREE PETITIONERS

I, Jacob Nicholson, also of North Carolina, being set free by my master, Joseph Nicholson, but continuing to live with him till, being pursued day and night, I was obliged to leave my abode, sleep in the woods, and stacks in the fields, &c., to escape the hands of violent men who, induced by the profit afforded them by law, followed this course as a business; at length, by night, I made my escape, leaving a mother, one child, and two brothers, to see whom I dare not return.

I, Job Albert, manumitted by Benjamin Albertson, who was my careful guardian to protect me from being afterwards taken and sold, providing me with a house to accommodate me and my wife, who was liberated by William Robertson; but we were night and day hunted by men armed with guns, swords, and pistols, accompanied with mastiff dogs; from whose violence, being one night apprehensive of immediate danger, I left my dwelling, locked and barred, and fastened with a chain, being at some distance from it, while my wife was by my kind master locked up under his roof. I heard them break into my house, where, not finding their prey, they got but a small booty, a handkerchief of about a dollar value, and some provisions; but, not long after, I was discovered and seized by Alexander Stafford, William Stafford, and Thomas Creesy, who were armed with guns and clubs. After binding me with my hands behind me, and a rope round my arms and body, they took me about four miles to Hartford prison, where I lay four weeks, suffering much for want of provision; from thence, with the assistance of a fellow-prisoner, (a white man,) I made my escape, and for three dollars was conveyed, with my wife, by a humane person, in a covered wagon by night, to Virginia, where, in the neighborhood of Portsmouth, I continued unmolested about four years, being chiefly engaged in sawing boards and plank. On being advised to move Northward, I came with my wife to Philadelphia, where I have labored for a livelihood upwards of two years, in Summer mostly along shore in vessels and stores, and sawing wood in the Winter. My mother was set free by Phineas Nickson, my sister by John Trueblood, and both taken up and sold into slavery, myself deprived of the consolation of seeing them, without being exposed to the like grievous oppression.

I, Thomas Pritchet, was set free by my master Thomas Pritchet, who furnished me with land to raise provisions for my use, where I built myself a house, cleared a sufficient spot of woodland to produce ten bushels of corn; the second year about fifteen, and the third, had as much planted as I suppose would have produced thirty bushels; this I was obliged to leave about one month before it was fit for gathering, being threatened by Holland Lockwood, who married my said master's widow, that if I would not come and serve him, he would apprehend me, and send me to the West Indies; Enoch Ralph also threatening to send me to jail, and sell me for the good of the country: being thus in jeopardy, I left my little farm, with my small stock and utensils, and my corn standing, and escaped by night into Virginia, where shipping myself for Boston, I was, through stress of weather landed in New York, where I served as a waiter for seventeen months; but my mind being distressed on account of the situation of my wife and children, I returned to Norfolk in Virginia, with a hope of at least seeing them, if I could not obtain their freedom; but finding I was advertised in the newspaper, twenty dollars the reward for apprehending me, my dangerous situation obliged me to leave Virginia, disappointed of seeing my wife and children, coming to Philadelphia, where I resided in the employment of a waiter upward of two years.

In addition to the hardship of our own case, as above set forth, we believe ourselves warranted, on the present occasion, in offering to your consideration the singular case of a fellow-black now confined in the jail of this city, under sanction of the act of General Government, called the Fugitive Law, as it appears to us a flagrant proof how far human beings, merely on account of color and complexion, are, through prevailing prejudice, outlawed and excluded from common justice and common humanity, by the operation of such partial laws in support of habits and customs cruelly oppressive. This man, having been many years past manumitted by his master in North Carolina, was under the authority of the aforementioned law of that State, sold again into slavery, and, after having served his purchaser upwards of six years, made his escape to Philadelphia, where he has resided eleven years, having a wife and four children; and, by an agent of the Carolina claimer, has been lately apprehended and committed to prison, his said claimer, soon after the man's escaping from him, having advertised him, offering a reward of ten silver dollars to any person that would bring him back, or five times that sum to any person that would make due proof of his being killed, and no questions asked by whom.

We beseech your impartial attention to our hard condition, not only with respect to our personal sufferings, as freemen, but as a class of that people who, distinguished by color, are therefore with a degrading partiality, considered by many, even of those in eminent stations, as unentitled to that public justice and protection which is the great object of Government. We indulge not a hope, or presume to ask for the interposition of your honorable body, beyond the extent of your Constitutional power or influence, yet are willing to believe your serious, disinterested,

and candid consideration of the premises, under the benign impressions of equity and mercy, producing upright exertion of
what is in your power, may not be without some salutary effect,
both for our relief as a people, and towards the removal of ob-
structions to public order and well-being.

A Plea for Sympathy

If, notwithstanding all that has been publicly avowed as essential principles respecting the extent of human right to freedom;
notwithstanding we have had that right restored to us, so far as
was in the power of those by whom we were held as slaves, we
cannot claim the privilege of representation in your councils,
yet we trust we may address you as fellow-men, who, under
God, the sovereign Ruler of the Universe, are intrusted with the
distribution of justice, for the terror of evil-doers, the encouragement and protection of the innocent, not doubting that you
are men of liberal minds, susceptible of benevolent feelings and
clear conception of rectitude to a catholic extent, who can admit
that black people (servile as their condition generally is
throughout this Continent) have natural affections, social and
domestic attachments and sensibilities; and that, therefore, we
may hope for a share in your sympathetic attention while we
represent that the unconstitutional bondage in which multitudes of our fellows in complexion are held, is to us a subject
sorrowfully affecting; for we cannot conceive their condition
(more especially those who have been emancipated and tasted
the sweets of liberty, and again reduced to slavery by kidnap-
pers and man-stealers) to be less afflicting or deplorable than
the situation of citizens of the United States, captured and enslaved through the unrighteous policy prevalent in Algiers. We
are far from considering all those who retain slaves as wilful oppressors, being well assured that numbers in the State from
whence we are exiles, hold their slaves in bondage, not of
choice, but possessing them by inheritance, feel their minds burdened under the slavish restraint of legal impediments to doing that justice which they are convinced is due to fellow-
rationals. May we not be allowed to consider this stretch of
power, morally and politically, a Governmental defect, if not a
direct violation of the declared fundamental principles of the
Constitution; and finally, is not some remedy for an evil of such
magnitude highly worthy of the deep inquiry and unfeigned
zeal of the supreme Legislative body of a free and enlightened

people? Submitting our cause to God, and humbly craving your best aid and influence, as you may be favored and directed by that wisdom which is from above, wherewith that you may be eminently dignified and rendered conspicuously, in the view of nations, a blessing to the people you represent, is the sincere prayer of your petitioners.

JACOB NICHOLSON,
JUPITER NICHOLSON, his mark,
JOB ALBERT, his mark,
THOMAS PRITCHET, his mark.

PHILADELPHIA, *January 23, 1797.*

YANKEE TRADERS IN THE PACIFIC

FRED DALZELL

Maritime historian Fred Dalzell writes of the experiences of American traders with the people of Hawaii and the Pacific coast in the 1790s. He warns against easy generalizations of whites exploiting native peoples, arguing that written accounts instead reveal an interesting intermingling of cultures in which the indigenous peoples were often shrewd in dealings with Yankee merchants.

O n 27 August 1797, the ship *Neptune* from New Haven, Connecticut, crossing the Pacific on a sealing voyage, made the Island of "Attoi" in the Hawaiian Archipelago. As evening fell the *Neptune* ran in for shore, and the next morning a canoe came off towards the ship, carrying Hawaiians bearing island foodstuffs to trade. As it came alongside, the *Neptune*'s supercargo, Ebenezer Townsend, hailed the canoe, asking "Who are you?" He had not really expected to be understood, but Townsend was astonished to hear one of the Hawaiians reply, "I am General Washington."

This exchange suggests how dramatically and unpredictably contact with Yankee mariners was beginning to rearrange Hawaii and the Pacific. "General Washington," it transpired, had shipped on an earlier Yankee vessel during a voyage to trade for furs along the Northwest Coast of America. His experience had given him a new name, and a new sense of himself and his place in the world. This was becoming more common by the time the *Neptune* reached Hawaii, less than a decade

Fred Dalzell, "Yankee Mariners and Early Contact in the Pacific," *America and the Sea: A Maritime History*, Mystic, CT: Mystic Seaport, 1998. Copyright © 1998 by Mystic Seaport. Reproduced by permission.

since the first American vessel called there. On island archipel-agos like the Marquesas and Hawaii, along the coastlines of Patagonia and northwestern North America, on the edges of the ancient metropolitan civilizations of East Asia; indeed, all across the Pacific, Yankee mariners in pursuit of new enterprise skir-mished, had sex, recruited hands, jumped ship and settled, and even began to ferry missionaries, consuls, and diplomats.

Above all, they traded. At nearly every port of call, markets sprang up and an array of new goods began making their way into the material lives and folkways of Pacific peoples. The ships shed parts of their cargoes and pieces of themselves as they went, and acquired parts and pieces of the peoples among whom they moved. Take the *Jefferson*, a Boston fur- and China-trader that plied the Pacific in the early 1790s. At the Marque-sas the Yankees bartered with nails and bits of iron hoop for breadfruit and other island foodstuffs (and meanwhile lost glass lamps, a compass, and other loose parts of the ship to theft). At Hawaii the Yankees swapped more iron pieces and tools, as well as muskets and powder, for sweet potatoes and hogs.

TRADE ALONG THE NORTHWEST COAST

But it was along the Northwest Coast of North America that the *Jefferson*'s hold opened most widely. The ship cruised along the coastline for several trading seasons, from May 1793 to August 1794, seeking sea-otter pelts to carry to market in Canton, China. In the course of this business the *Jefferson* off-loaded a rich stock of goods. Among the Nootkans on Vancouver Island the Yankees traded iron towes (chisel heads), copper sheets (as well as copper hats and pans), cloth, muskets, powder, iron swords and collars (forged onboard by the blacksmith), great coats, jackets, and trousers. As they moved north to the Queen Charlotte Islands, where Haida traders offered an especially rich supply of sea-otter pelts, the men of the *Jefferson* found they had overstocked on iron tools and pieces, and soon exhausted their other trading stock. For a time they stayed in business by trading leather war armor made of elk hides ("clemmons," ac-quired in trade with Native Americans further down the coast), supplemented by clothing cut from spare sailcloth and wooden trunks manufactured by the ship's carpenter. And then, as Haida traders continued to bring more canoe-loads of sea-otter skins, Captain Roberts and his crew began to strip the vessel of whatever they could do without, whatever they could sell.

"Every thing that could be spaired on board were purchass'd
up by the natives with the greatest Evidity," James Magee
recorded in his journal; the Indians "seemed in want of Every
thing they got thire Eye on." In trade the Haida obtained the
ship's longboat, jolly boat, spare sails and rope, sea line, rock-
ets, fishing seines, "old Clothes of the Captn." and his trunk, the
ship's tablecloth and sheets, oil skins and clothing from the
lockers of the officers and crew, the main cabin looking-glass
and much of the ship's crockery. By the time it left the Queen
Charlotte Islands, no small part of the *Jefferson* itself was sink-
ing into the material, social, and spiritual lives of the Haida.

At the same time, trading with natives drew the Yankees, at
least temporarily, semi-wittingly, into native patterns of society
and culture. After trading with the *Jefferson* for a month, the powerful Haida "cheef" Cumeah approached the captain for help
raising a totem pole—a "sepulture of a daughter of Cumeah's,"
the ship's journal recorded. As the captain complied, sending
crew members ashore with tackles and several spare topmasts to
use as sheers, he entered a train of ritual events that carried him
to the core of Haida folkways. The next day Cumeah's family invited the ship's officers to a celebratory feast, where Cumeah
"adressed his Cheeffs & people . . . urging the propriety of thire
making such acknowledgement to [Captain] Roberts for his service & assistance in setting up the monument as they saw fit, &
by which they would shew they considered him as thire frend,
& by whose frendship they might hope to create mutel advantages &c. or in words to that affect." The captain promised to
paint the totem, and Haida clan leaders sent him back to his ship
with ceremonial gifts of several more skins to add to the hold.
The affair climaxed several weeks later when the *Jefferson*'s officers were invited back to shore for a second ceremony in which
an elaborate distribution of presents commemorated the erection
of the totem and the incision of several young women for labrets
(discs worn by high-ranking Haida women in their lips). Roberts
and company were impressed with the solemnity of the proceeding, but they only vaguely sensed its meanings; what the
Yankees were participating in was a potlatch, a complex ceremony in which Northwest Native Americans articulated, or val-
idated, or negotiated the finely calibrated rankings that under-
girded their societies.

The protocols of trade on voyages like the *Jefferson*'s (at least,
before they reached Canton, which had a very strict trading pro-

tocol) were often improvised. In order to do business with each other, Yankee and native had to piece together workable components of trade: sign languages and pidgin trading vocabularies, interpreters and brokers, prices and exchange rates, and procedures for giving and receiving. The Yankees commonly found themselves negotiating on the natives' terms, which they only dimly understood. Local chiefs, who controlled access to most furs, demanded ceremonial gifts before opening trade with a vessel. Trade at a particular anchorage tended to start slowly, as the Indians examined the Yankees' offerings, retreated to shore, returned, often went back and forth for several visits, testing the market, waiting for the Yankees to put favorable rates of exchange on the table. In this waiting period, the natives held a good deal of leverage, for if they did not like the goods or prices offered, they could always hold their furs for the next vessel to come along. Once actual trading commenced, the Northwest Indians proved to be sharp, skillful traders, who haggled stubbornly, applied their leverage shrewdly, avidly exacted maximum profit—so stubbornly, so shrewdly, so avidly, in fact, that they drove Yankee ship captains and supercargoes to distraction. "The people of these isles in general possess a truly mercantile spirit," Joseph Ingraham remarked after several days of trading while the brigantine *Hope* was anchored off Washington's Island in the Queen Charlotte group, "for they will not part with a single skin til they have exerted their utmost to obtain the best price for it."

The structure of the fur trade along the Northwest Coast warns against making easy generalizations about early Yankee-native contacts in the Pacific. Native Americans like the Haida and the Nootkans managed to take fur traders like the *Jefferson* on largely their own terms. These first Yankee mariners of the 1790s came well in advance of later, more intrusive settlers, missionaries, and conquerers. From the first, contact with Americans and Europeans did carry pernicious, destructive consequences: exposure to new diseases like smallpox and venereal disease, for example, and in the case of native North Americans, overhunting of local fur animal populations. And by definition, Yankee-native trade drew previously isolated peoples into a commercial network of exchange and influence that expanded across the globe. But contact, especially early contact, created new opportunities as well, and in many cases indigenous peoples (and people) responded resourcefully, resiliently.

THE HAWAIIAN ISLANDS

The next stage of the *Jefferson*'s voyage was especially revealing in this regard. From the Northwest Coast, the ship sailed to Hawaii, where the Yankees stopped over for reprovisioning. Lying directly athwart developing sea-lanes, the Hawaiian islands were receiving the full brunt of contact. Captain James Cook's third voyage of exploration had revealed the islands to Europeans and Americans in 1778. By the time the *Jefferson* made Hawaii less than twenty years later, Yankee merchantmen crossing the Pacific were regularly stopping at the islands, islanders were starting to ship out on Yankee and British vessels in substantial numbers, and Yankee and European mariners were, in smaller numbers, beginning to settle on the islands. With all of these exchanges, these border meetings and crossings, intercultural give-and-take accelerated rapidly. When the men aboard the *Jefferson* opened trade, they found a ready market for iron tools, as well as a strong demand for muskets, swivel cannon, and powder—armaments fueling heated military expansion and a campaign of conquest by Kamehameha, *ali'i*, or king, of the "Big Island." On the Hawaiian side, business negotiations were handled by two western mariners, John Young and Isaac Davis, whom Kamehameha had drawn into his retinue to administer relations with visiting ships, to train his army in musket and cannon tactics, and to oversee a modest but growing fleet of royal schooners and brigs.

But the Hawaiians' striking capacity of assimilation, for advantageously adapting to contact, manifested itself most fully when the *Jefferson* ran up on a reef about fifteen leagues off Maui. Over the next several weeks, the Hawaiians offered invaluable assistance to the beleaguered Yankees. Canoes came off from shore bearing teams of islanders to man pumps, dive to inspect the hull, and shift the hold to work the vessel off the rocks—a highly organized relief operation administered not only by the officers of the *Jefferson*, but also by local Hawaiian leaders as well as a polyglot cadre of foreigners who had settled on the islands. As the ship's log recorded, "Besides our own company, we were assisted by Messrs. Howel, Davis, Evans, Boyd, Cox, Dinsdale (a lone American, the rest are Europeans), Kelly, Baptist (an Italian), and Hoppo (a Chinese)." And meanwhile, one of Kamehameha's schooners arrived and hovered alongside the ship, receiving her cargo. James Magee observed from on board the *Jefferson:* "she was navigated altogether by natives & Commanded by Capt Caheira, & no man could entertain a higher idea of this important station, than himself, by the many airs that he had been taught to assume, on account of his rank, as first commander of the Kings schooner, & of which his display was highly diverting in many respects." The Yankees' condescension notwithstanding, the Hawaiians here were clearly, actively incorporating western technologies into indigenous island life, taking contact into their own hands, molding and fitting its offerings into distinctively Hawaiian forms.

HAWAII IN TRANSITION

So the rescue and refitting of the *Jefferson* becomes an intriguing, revealing look at Hawaii in transition. Already the islands were becoming a major maritime crossroads and a rich intermingling of peoples and cultures. The *Jefferson* itself carried on this process of cross-pollination, entering on its lists and bearing away "Moses Montcalm & William Collett for the remainder of the voyage, Hoppo the Chinese for Macao, Sam, a young chief, nephew to Tahoomoto, & 10 other natives, young lads, also engag'd to visit America with us." So the ship bore off with new "General Washingtons," agents of change who would be even more revolutionary than their namesake.

Hawaiian adaptation to these new circumstances was uneven, sometimes brutal, jarring. But contact was not simply unilateral victimization; it took on more organic forms of assimilation and adaptation. Hawaii, it is worth noting, would manage to retain its sovereignty for more than one hundred years after the *Jefferson* sailed away, skillfully playing one would-be imperial conqueror off against another, even as tightening commercial and diplomatic ties drew the islands further into the orbit of the United States.

SOCIAL AND CULTURAL DEVELOPMENTS OF THE 1790S

RAYMOND H. ROBINSON

Historian Raymond H. Robinson describes some of the leading demographic, cultural, and artistic developments of the last decade of the 1700s and how the United States had changed in the first years of its existence. The leading artists of this period included Charles Willson Peale and Gilbert Stuart, while leading writers included Charles Brockden Brown and Susanna Rowson. A striking development was the proliferation of newspapers. By 1801 about two hundred were operating in the United States. Robinson is a history professor at Northeastern University in Boston.

T he changing of the guard [when Thomas Jefferson became president in 1801] provided an opportunity for the nation to take stock of itself, especially since the change came as a new century was dawning. The national boundaries had changed not at all since 1783 when the Treaty of Paris had fixed the outside limits of the newly independent place. But other changes were evident. Where there had been thirteen states in the original Union, there were at century's end sixteen. To the seven states north of the Mason-Dixon line and the six states south of it had been added one northern state, Vermont, in 1791 and two southern ones, Kentucky and Tennessee, in 1792 and 1796. These admissions brought to the Union for the

Raymond H. Robinson, *The Growing of America: 1789–1848*, Boston: Allyn and Bacon, 1973. Copyright © 1973 by Allyn and Bacon. Reproduced by permission.

first time states not contiguous with the Atlantic. Where states of the East faced eastward to focus directly on the ocean and, in a sense, the world, the newer states, especially Kentucky and Tennessee, had to turn westward to seek the ocean, the world, and even the eastern United States via the Ohio-Mississippi River system. To residents of Kentucky and Tennessee there was no more central question than the right to use the river artery all the way to its mouth.

Tennessee's admission brought a North-South sectional balance to the American Senate for the first time, if the Mason-Dixon line is taken as dividing those two sections. Already, however, the North dominated the lower house of Congress, for though the two sections were roughly equal in total population, only three-fifths of the slaves were counted for apportionment of representatives. The result in 1800 in a House of Representatives of 141 was 76 seats for northern states and 65 for southern, about one-third of which were assigned to the most populous state of all, Virginia.

POPULATION TRENDS

Observers north and south could take pride in a handsome increase in the nation's population in the ten years since the first census. In 1790 nearly 4,000,000 persons were counted while about 5,300,000 were registered ten years later. Census takers in 1800 provided more information about whites than blacks and more about men than women. Their records revealed a rough numerical equality between white men and women, with males predominating slightly. Statistics of age showed a median age of 16 for the white population; white women were slightly older than white men. Black men and women comprised nearly 20 percent of the total population, and most of them were slaves. Of a total of just over 1,000,000 blacks in 1800, almost 900,000 were unfree.

Not until 1820 did the government begin to keep immigration statistics, and census takers failed to distinguish between native and foreign-born until 1850. But scholars have attempted to make estimates about national origins on the basis of nomenclature. Using the first census, one study claimed that 60 percent of the population was English; 14 percent Scotch or Scotch-Irish; 3.6 percent Irish; 8.6 percent German; 3.1 percent Dutch; and 2.3 percent French. Pennsylvania was the least English of the states and the most German. The Dutch, as would be expected, were strongest in New York. Some of the cities seemed quite cosmopolitan, but even in those places English language and law predominated.

The nation's population was overwhelmingly rural, with nearly 5,000,000 people listed as such and only 322,371 classified as urban; most of the urban dwellers lived in smallish places, with those with populations between 5,000 and 10,000 claiming nearly one-third of the urban people.

RURAL AND URBAN LIFE

Rural life varied considerably from section to section, and to a lesser extent within the sections. New England farmers rarely lived as they had in an earlier time in village clusters with fields some distance from the house; by 1800 their buildings and fields were all part of a "farm" more or less isolated from the nearest neighbor. Their rocky soil yielded stones for picturesque fences but relatively little in the form of commercial crops. Since they consumed much of what they raised, New England farmers commonly operated at a subsistence level. The German farmers of eastern Pennsylvania lived more abundantly. Their rich soil and longer season produced excellent wheat crops and a reputation as bread basket for the nation. South of Pennsylvania, farmers were beginning to grow cotton fiber, but the most important commercial crop was still tobacco. Diversity among farmers was especially pronounced in the South, where farms ranged all the way from large and rich plantations worked by slaves to grubby and impoverished plots that made New England austerity seem grand by comparison.

Though large cities claimed only a tiny fraction of the nation's population in 1800, the most impressive economic and social activity was carried on in big urban places. The nation's political affairs were conducted in a small capital only lately built, but state capitals were older and bigger, and to the extent that state politics was significant, urban places were important political centers as well.

New York City was the nation's largest city in 1800, having left behind the colonial leader, Philadelphia. Slightly more than 60,000 people lived in New York as compared with about 41,000 in Philadelphia. Baltimore was third with more than 26,000, while Boston, the former hub of the American universe, was fourth with nearly 25,000 souls inhabiting the tiny, ragged peninsula. No other place approached these four in size or significance.

All four had good harbors and access to the ocean, and three of them had good river connections to the interior. Boston's Charles River was not unimportant, but it did not compare with New York's Hudson, Philadelphia's Delaware, or Baltimore's Susquehanna. Down the rivers came products of the back country to be consumed by those who lived in the major cities or processed and packaged for shipment to other American places or foreign ports. Up river as far as the "fall lines" and beyond by road went manufactured items produced or imported by those who lived in the cities. Bostonians, unendowed by nature with a major river to the interior, built a canal—the Middlesex—out from the town to tap the better waters of the Merrimac. The canal corporation made Boston in effect the artificial mouth of the Merrimac.

Both New York and Philadelphia owed part of their position as urban centers to the fact that they each had been at one time the national capital. The Confederation headquartered in New York City, and the national government under the Constitution had organized there, only to remove to Philadelphia late in 1790. During their sojourn in those cities, the national government had operated in converted city halls or state houses that remained monuments to political activity.

AMERICAN ARCHITECTURE AND ART

Of the four principal urban places, only Boston was a state capital in 1800, for Philadelphia had surrendered the role to Lancaster the year before. In spite of similar pressure to move the capital farther west, Massachusetts retained the political center in the old town (for Boston did not become a city until 1822). Boston's political activity necessitated public buildings that became outstanding examples of American architecture. The Old State House, an eighteenth-century structure, had given way to a brand new building atop Beacon Hill where once Governor Hancock had pastured cows. Architect of the new capitol was Bostonian Charles Bulfinch, who had toured in Europe after graduation from Harvard in 1781 and returned to his home town to become the nation's leading architect in the 1790s. His first executed design was the new Hollis Street Church to replace one destroyed by fire. Other commissions in the decade of the 1790s included the Tontine Crescent, sixteen connected three-story houses built along a curve in the street. Individual dwellings were built for such Boston worthies as Harrison Gray

Otis, first on Cambridge Street and just a few years later another on Beacon Hill. Bulfinch also designed a cathedral for the French priest, Father Cheverus, who became the first Catholic bishop of Boston. But no building in the decade matched the State House, which was occupied in 1798. For thirty years into the new century Bulfinch continued to be active as an architect, leaving behind his contribution to America's quest for culture in the form of Georgian or Federal buildings.

All cities had painters who brought glory to the places where they did their work, but no city in the 1790s had more to boast of than Philadelphia where Charles Willson Peale worked and where Gilbert Stuart had settled. The principal work of both artists was portraiture, and each painted worthies during the decade.

Peale, born in Maryland in 1741, began his career as a saddler, but that business bored him, and he branched out into upholstery, carriage-building, clock-making, and sign-painting. His talent for painting attracted attention, and friends funded a trip to England where he studied in the studio of Benjamin West, a Pennsylvania artist who spent nearly the last six decades of his life in England where George III patronized him and Americans sought his advice. After a few years with West, Peale returned to America and finally settled in Philadelphia in 1776. A man of scientific as well as artistic interest, he named his many children after famous artists and scientists and founded a museum where art and science were exhibited. His artistic forte was portraiture, and many notable Americans, including George Washington, sat for him. Peale did Washington first in 1772 at Mount Vernon, then several times during the Revolution, and finally in Philadelphia in 1795. On that occasion other members of the Peale family sketched the president too, and a visitor, artist Gilbert Stuart, reported that the family was "peeling" the president.

The most famous portrait of Washington was done by Stuart, a Rhode Islander who lived in England and Ireland until his return to America in 1792. Stuart moved with the capital to Philadelphia, then to Washington and finally, seeking other than political clients, to Boston. Washington sat twice for Stuart, and each time the artist made numerous replicas that he sold for $100. He copied the so-called Athenaeum portrait so often that he was able to reproduce the president's image in two hours. That painting created the face of Washington known to all who pause to examine the one dollar bill.

Like Bulfinch, who copied English models to produce his Federal buildings, Peale and Stuart and other portraitists relied on English tradition in painting. While they did not establish an American school of portraiture, their work deserved recognition as strong example of what English artists were doing.

LITERARY DEVELOPMENTS

Philadelphia was the birthplace and New York the residence of America's leading novelist in the decade of the 1790s. Born in 1771 Charles Brockden Brown loved the solitude and ruggedness of the land along the Schuylkill River, and the place provided the setting for some of his novels. Beginning his literary activity in the 1790s, he quickly established a reputation as the most important American novelist of the day or at least as the first American brave enough to attempt to live from his literary output. By 1801 he had published *Alcuin,* a treatise that preached William Godwin's ideas of women's liberation; three Gothic romances, *Wieland, Arthur Mervyn,* and *Ormond; Edgar Huntly,* the first American detective story; and finally, two love stories, *Clara Howard* and *Jane Talbot.* The chilling Gothic romances were considered his best works, and while they were heavily derivative from English works, they added a fresh dimension, the exploration of the inner mind. Brown thought a trip to the mind of an ordinary ploughman was of greater value than a geographical trip to the recesses of Africa. Later American authors paid homage to him. Poe borrowed images for his tales and poems; Cooper said that he would never forget the impact of *Wieland,* which remained fresh in his mind though crowded by thousands of later pictures; and Hawthorne ranked him with Shakespeare and Scott. Indeed, Scott himself, as well as other English writers, admired his work. Shelley was so impressed that he borrowed the heroine of *Ormond* for one of his poems. Other American writers would soon outdistance Brown, but for the nonce he had few peers.

Two potential rivals were Susanna Rowson and Hugh Brackenridge. Mrs. Rowson, born in England and brought to Massachusetts as a young girl, published *Charlotte, A Tale of Truth,* first in England in 1791 and then in Philadelphia three years later. The sentimental love story was the best seller in American fiction until *Uncle Tom's Cabin* appeared. Mathew Carey, the Philadelphia publisher of the novel, had his first notable success with the tale of Charlotte Temple. Mrs. Rowson achieved fame in a second career as a playwright and actress in the 1790s, and before the decade was out she had turned to a third as operator of a school near Boston.

Western fiction appeared in 1792 when Hugh Henry Brackenridge, a Princeton classmate of James Madison and Philip Freneau, began the serial publication of *Modern Chivalry*. A Democratic-Republican, Brackenridge was not unable to see the dangers of democratic excess and described these in his novel. A resident of Pittsburgh at the time of the writing, Brackenridge had earlier lived in Philadelphia where he edited for a brief period the outstanding *United States Magazine*. He established Pittsburgh's first newspaper, the *Gazette*, in 1786.

Apart from fiction, the leading literary production of the 1790s was historical. Not yet ready to write of the nation as a whole, historians focused on the states. The most important work to appear was the Reverend Jeremy Belknap's history of New Hampshire. Belknap published the first volume in 1784 while resident in that state and the next two in the 1790s after he moved to Boston. The third volume was of special importance for its discussion of social and economic matters at a time when most historians were narrowly political. Belknap, one of the founders of the Massachusetts Historical Society, the first of its kind in America, also published two volumes of *American Biography* during the decade.

Another New England state, Connecticut, had Benjamin Trumbull for its historian during the decade. A clergyman like Belknap and a host of other historians, Trumbull spent a lifetime gathering material and published his first of two volumes of state history in 1797. He knew the history of the Nutmeg State by heart, and he felt the need to tell all that he knew. Later, in the nineteenth century, he undertook to write the history of all of America, but the work was not completed.

Toward the end of the decade the history of Pennsylvania came from the pen of Robert Proud, who differed from Belknap and Trumbull in many ways. His birth abroad, his occupation as a schoolmaster (he had been Brockden Brown's teacher), and his Toryism during the Revolution contrasted sharply with their ministerial calling and patriotic pride in their native place. Proud's volumes were best for the earliest and latest years and especially for their printing of documents hitherto scattered to the four winds.

Philadelphia was the home of the nation's two most out-standing magazines at the time of Washington's first inaugura-tion. *The Columbian Magazine* was begun in 1786 by five part-ners, including Mathew Carey, a newspaperman newly arrived in America from Ireland, and John Trenchard, an engraver who supplied copperplates for the periodical. Another owner was a printer and a fourth was a bookseller. Specializing in agricul-tural and mechanical articles and in fiction, the magazine reor-ganized as the *Philadelphia Magazine and Universal Asylum* and continued publication until 1792.

Cary remained active in the *Columbian* for only three months before withdrawing to publish his own magazine, *The American Museum.* Like the *Columbian,* the *Museum* lasted until 1792 when both periodicals closed as a result of the Post Office Act of that year, which forced magazines to pay letter rates. Unable to meet the expense, publications closed their doors, and people waited for reform that came in 1794 when a new postal act provided lower rates. The new legislation encouraged publishers to start up, and more magazines were begun in the last six years of the eighteenth century than in all the years back to 1741, when the first American magazine appeared. But commencement did not guarantee duration, for most periodicals died after brief lives. By the close of the century there were only twelve magazines published in the entire country. Charles Brockden Brown, the novelist who edited *The Monthly Magazine and American Review,* felt that population dispersed over a wide space was one of the principal burdens faced by magazine publishers.

AN EXPLOSION OF NEWSPAPERS

Newspapers, smaller in size and less costly to produce, fared better than magazines. In 1790 there were 92 newspapers in the United States, of which 70 were weeklies and only 8, dailies.

The least objective and most exciting newspapers of the 1790s were the political organs. The Federalists had John Fenno's *Gazette of the United States,* which began publication in New York on the eve of Washington's inauguration and followed the government to Philadelphia the next year. Outspoken criticism of Fenno appeared in the pages of the opposition paper, the *National Gazette,* edited by the "poet of the Revolution," Philip Fre-neau. Neither paper had mass circulation, but Federalist money enabled Fenno to continue while Freneau's *Gazette* died in 1793. It was replaced as Democratic-Republican spokesman by the

Aurora, edited by Benjamin Franklin's grandson and namesake, B.F. Bache, until his death in 1798 when William Duane succeeded him.

Less political and more brilliant was the *American Minerva,* founded by Noah Webster in 1793. Though Webster ceased to be editor after five years, the paper continued a successful career as the *Commercial Advertiser.*

By 1801 there were about two hundred newspapers in the country of which about twenty were dailies. The United States had become in the view of one commentator "a nation of newspaper readers." Charles Brockden Brown agreed. He believed newspapers more "widely diffused and read" in America "than in any other part of the world."

Expansion, War, and Nationalism, 1800–1824

CHAPTER 2

THOMAS JEFFERSON'S FIRST INAUGURAL ADDRESS

THOMAS JEFFERSON

In his Farewell Address, George Washington warned against "the baneful effects of the Spirit of Party." However, even before Washington retired in 1797 and was succeeded by John Adams, American politics was becoming increasingly defined by the rise of two recognizable political parties. The Federalists, whose primary leaders were Adams and Alexander Hamilton, tended to support a strong national government and to favor the merchant and financial interests that were strongest in New England. The Republicans, led by Thomas Jefferson and James Madison, advocated limited government (especially at the national level) and favored agrarian interests; they were strongest in Virginia and other southern states.

The 1800 presidential election between incumbent John Adams and Thomas Jefferson was marked by extreme charges on both sides. Federalists charged Jefferson and other Republicans with being anarchists, atheists, and political radicals, while Adams and other Federalists were accused of being elitists plotting to overturn the American Revolution and establish a monarchy. Jefferson ended up winning a very close election. Historian Robert Kelley notes that Jefferson's victory has been called a second revolution "because for the first time in world history a ruling party had been removed from power *by use of the ballot box alone.*"

In his inaugural address, delivered on March 4, 1801, in the

Thomas Jefferson, "Inaugural Address," *The Life and Selected Writings of Thomas Jefferson*, edited by Adrienne Koch and William Peden, New York: Macmillan, 1972.

partially built Capital building in Washington, D.C., Jefferson sought to reach out to his political opponents and to assure them that rights of political minorities would be respected. He also summarized some of his fundamental principles of government and his vision for America's future.

F riends and Fellow Citizens:—
    Called upon to undertake the duties of the first executive office of our country, I avail myself of the presence of that portion of my fellow citizens which is here assembled, to express my grateful thanks for the favor with which they have been pleased to look toward me, to declare a sincere consciousness that the task is above my talents, and that I approach it with those anxious and awful presentiments which the greatness of the charge and the weakness of my powers so justly inspire. A rising nation, spread over a wise and fruitful land, traversing all the seas with the rich productions of their industry, engaged in commerce with nations who feel power and forget right, advancing rapidly to destinies beyond the reach of mortal eye—when I contemplate these transcendent objects, and see the honor, the happiness, and the hopes of this beloved country committed to the issue and the auspices of this day, I shrink from the contemplation, and humble myself before the magnitude of the undertaking. Utterly, indeed, should I despair, did not the presence of many whom I here see remind me, that in the other high authorities provided by our constitution, I shall find resources of wisdom, of virtue, and of zeal, on which to rely under all difficulties. To you, then, gentlemen, who are charged with the sovereign functions of legislation, and to those associated with you, I look with encouragement for that guidance and support which may enable us to steer with safety the vessel in which we are all embarked amid the conflicting elements of a troubled world.

REFLECTIONS ON THE 1800 ELECTION

During the contest of opinion through which we have passed, the animation of discussion and of exertions has sometimes worn an aspect which might impose on strangers unused to think freely and to speak and to write what they think; but this being now decided by the voice of the nation, announced according to the rules of the constitution, all will, of course, arrange themselves under the will of the law, and unite in common efforts for the common good. All, too, will bear in mind this sacred principle, that though the will of the majority is in all cases to prevail, that will, to be rightful, must be reasonable; that the minority possess their equal rights, which equal laws must protect, and to violate would be oppression. Let us, then, fellow citizens, unite with one heart and one mind. Let us restore to social intercourse that harmony and affection without which liberty and even life itself are but dreary things. And let us reflect that having banished from our land that religious intolerance under which mankind so long bled and suffered, we have yet gained little if we countenance a political intolerance as despotic, as wicked, and capable of as bitter and bloody persecutions. During the throes and convulsions of the ancient world, during the agonizing spasms of infuriated man, seeking through blood and slaughter his long-lost liberty, it was not wonderful that the agitations of the

Thomas Jefferson

billows should reach even this distant and peaceful shore; that this should be more felt and feared by some and less by others; that this should divide opinions as to measures of safety. But every difference of opinion is not a difference of principle. We have called by different names brethren of the same principle. We are all republicans, we are all federalists. If there be any among us who would wish to dissolve this Union or to change its republican form, let them stand undisturbed as monuments of the safety with which error of opinion may be tolerated where reason is left free to combat it. I know, indeed, that some honest men fear that a republican government cannot be strong; that this government is not strong enough. But would the honest patriot, in the full tide of successful experiment, abandon a government which has so far kept us free and firm, on the theoretic and visionary fear that this government, the world's best hope, may by possibility want energy to preserve itself? I trust not. I believe this, on the contrary, the strongest government on earth. I believe it is the only one where every man, at the call of the laws, would fly to the standard of the law, and would meet invasions of the public order as his own personal concern. Sometimes it is said that man cannot be trusted with the government of himself. Can he, then, be trusted with the government of others? Or have we found angels in the forms of kings to govern him? Let history answer this question.

Let us, then, with courage and confidence pursue our own federal and republican principles, our attachment to union and representative government. Kindly separated by nature and a wide ocean from the exterminating havoc of one quarter of the globe; too high-minded to endure the degradations of the others; possessing a chosen country, with room enough for our descendants to the hundredth and thousandth generation; entertaining a due sense of our equal right to the use of our own faculties, to the acquisitions of our industry, to honor and confidence from our fellow citizens, resulting not from birth but from our actions and their sense of them; enlightened by a benign religion, professed, indeed, and practiced in various forms, yet all of them including honesty, truth, temperance, gratitude, and the love of man; acknowledging and adoring an overruling Providence, which by all its dispensations proves that it delights in the happiness of man here and his greater happiness hereafter; with all these blessings, what more is necessary to make us a happy and prosperous people? Still one thing more, fellow citizens—a wise and frugal government, which shall restrain men from injuring one another, which shall leave them otherwise free to regulate their own pursuits of industry and improvement, and shall not take from the mouth of labor the bread it has earned. This is the sum of good government, and this is necessary to close the circle of our felicities.

ESSENTIAL PRINCIPLES OF GOVERNMENT

About to enter, fellow citizens, on the exercise of duties which comprehend everything dear and valuable to you, it is proper that you should understand what I deem the essential principles of our government, and consequently those which ought to shape its administration. I will compress them within the narrowest compass they will bear, stating the general principle, but not all its limitations. Equal and exact justice to all men, of whatever state or persuasion, religious or political; peace, commerce, and honest friendship, with all nations—entangling alliances with none; the support of the state governments in all their rights, as the most competent administrations for our domestic concerns and the surest bulwarks against anti-republican tendencies; the preservation of the general government in its whole constitutional vigor, as the sheet anchor of our peace at home and safety abroad; a jealous care of the right of election by the people—a mild and safe corrective of abuses which are lopped by the sword of revolution where peaceable remedies are unprovided; absolute acquiescence in the decisions of the majority—the vital principle of republics, from which there is no appeal but to force, the vital principle and immediate parent of despotism; a well-disciplined militia—our best reliance in peace and for the first moments of war, till regulars may relieve them; the supremacy of the civil over the military authority; economy in the public expense, that labor may be lightly burdened; the honest payment of our debts and sacred preservation of the public faith; encouragement of agriculture, and of commerce as its handmaid; the diffusion of information and the arraignment of all abuses at the bar of public reason; freedom of religion; freedom of the press; freedom of person under the protection of the habeas corpus; and trial by juries impartially selected—these principles form the bright constellation which has gone before us, and guided our steps through an age of revolution and reformation. The wisdom of our sages and blood of our heroes have been devoted to their attainment. They should be the creed of our political faith—the text of civil instruction—the touchstone by which to try the services of those we trust; and should we wander from them in moments of error or alarm, let us hasten to retrace our steps and to regain the road which alone leads to peace, liberty, and safety.

A PLEA FOR SUPPORT

I repair, then, fellow citizens, to the post you have assigned me. With experience enough in subordinate offices to have seen the difficulties of this, the greatest of all, I have learned to expect that it will rarely fall to the lot of imperfect man to retire from this station with the reputation and the favor which bring him into it. Without pretensions to that high confidence reposed in our first and great revolutionary character [George Washington], whose preeminent services had entitled him to the first place in his country's love, and destined for him the fairest page in the volume of faithful history, I ask so much confidence only as may give firmness and effect to the legal administration of your affairs. I shall often go wrong through defect of judgment. When right, I shall often be thought wrong by those whose positions will not command a view of the whole ground. I ask your indulgence for my own errors, which will never be intentional; and your support against the errors of others, who may condemn what they would not if seen in all its parts. The approbation implied by your suffrage is a consolation to me for the past; and my future solicitude will be to retain the good opinion of those who have bestowed it in advance, to conciliate that of others by doing them all the good in my power, and to be instrumental to the happiness and freedom of all.

Relying, then, on the patronage of your good will, I advance with obedience to the work, ready to retire from it whenever you become sensible how much better choice it is in your power to make. And may that Infinite Power which rules the destinies of the universe, lead our councils to what is best, and give them a favorable issue for your peace and prosperity.

THE LOUISIANA PURCHASE

ALISTAIR COOKE

The Louisiana Purchase has long been regarded as one of the greatest presidential achievements of Thomas Jefferson. For $15 million, the United States acquired most of the land between the Mississippi River and the Rocky Mountains, doubling the size of its territory. Many historians have noted certain ironies about Jefferson's achievement. The president professed adherence to frugality, limited executive powers, and a strict interpretation of the Constitution, but stretched all three principles to the breaking point when France's ruler Napoléon unexpectedly offered to sell Louisiana.

In the following selection, Alistair Cooke tells of the foreign policy crisis Jefferson faced in 1800, when he learned that France had secretly acquired Louisiana from Spain, and the subsequent chain of events that led to the American acquisition. Napoléon's decision to sell was influenced by France's costly effort to quell a slave uprising in Santo Domingo (Haiti). Cooke also briefly describes the Lewis and Clark expedition that reached the Pacific Ocean in 1805. Cooke is a British-born journalist and television and radio commentator who has written several popular books on American society and history.

E ven at the beginning of the nineteenth century, the many great rivers, running ultimately north and south, sustained a flourishing trade between Canada and the Gulf of Mexico. And, for the enterprising pioneer with no family to worry about, there were careers opening up in the marketing of

Alistair Cooke, *Alistair Cooke's America*, New York: Alfred A. Knopf, 1973. Copyright © 1973 by Alfred A. Knopf. Reproduced by permission of Random House, Inc.

furs, skins, turpentine, tar, lead, grains, rum, and whiskey. The Missouri, the Illinois, the Wabash, the Ohio, all flowed into the vast current of the Mississippi down through the glamorous abstraction of Louisiana into the port of New Orleans. And we should recall that in 1803 Louisiana was not the compact little state of the Deep South that we know today. In 1803 Louisiana was an unmanned, undefended empire embracing the whole watershed of the Mississippi and comprising the present states of Louisiana, Arkansas, Oklahoma, Missouri, both Dakotas, Iowa, Nebraska, Kansas, Minnesota, Colorado, Wyoming, and Montana—a third of North America.

It will be remembered that the British had acquired everything east of the Mississippi after the French and Indian Wars, and in turn the Americans had won it from the British in the Revolution. Nobody ruled the huge territories to the west, but in 1801 the paper title belonged to Spain. There was an irregular chain of trading posts and a few garrisons hundreds of miles apart. Only a tiny percentage of settlers had chosen to go to Louisiana, even the sophisticated back East had only the blankest or most romantic notion of how it looked and what was there.

JEFFERSON'S FEARS

In 1801 Spain ceded Louisiana, for protective services rendered, to Napoleon in a secret treaty. Jefferson, now the third President of the United States, got wind of it. He knew that Napoleon was busy with plans to invade Britain and crush the old enemy once for all, but when he heard that a French expeditionary force had landed at Santo Domingo to suppress a native revolt, he divined a sinister connection between this move and Napoleon's designs on the American continent. Jefferson, indeed, was throughout his life a fascinating combination of a true *naïf* and a shrewdly paranoid lawyer. Left to himself with his gadgets and his gardens and the superb view he enjoyed around his circle of mountains, he could dream up the most chivalrous fate for the human race. Confronted with an enemy, a talebearer, or the odd movement of a fleet, and he could leap like a foxy lawyer to the protection of his client. He followed the battles in Santo Domingo on a map, and he learned without wincing overmuch that the flower of the French infantry was either wilting under heat and malaria or being cut down by a black general who was also a master of guerrilla warfare, Toussaint L'Ouverture.

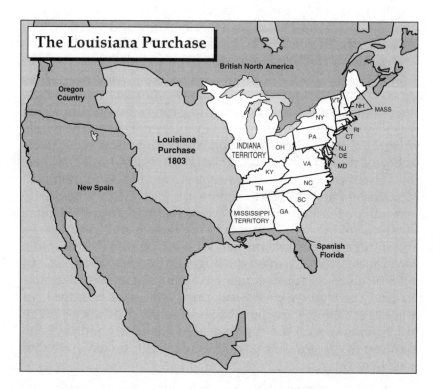

In January 1803, Jefferson sent precise instructions to Robert Livingston, then Minister to France, to make a deal with Napoleon. Then he shipped off James Monroe as an envoy extraordinary (of the Harry Hopkins–Henry Kissinger type) to help him. Offer Napoleon $10,000,000 for New Orleans and Florida, or $7,500,000 for New Orleans alone. If he refused, secure a guarantee of perpetual navigation rights. If he would not go even so far, then Monroe was to "open confidential communication with the ministers of the British government," a threat that Jefferson ostentatiously advertised for the benefit of the French minister in Washington. In April Livingston, who had been making regular calls on the unyielding French Minister of Foreign Affairs, went along to the Ministry. Old Talleyrand came limping in on his club foot and said: "What would you give for the *whole* of Louisiana?" The staggered Livingston blurted out an off-the-cuff price of $4,000,000. It was much too low, and Livingston retired to wait for Monroe to sail in.

Jefferson had suspected that the Santo Domingo campaign was meant to be the rehearsal for a grander exercise—for nothing less than the physical conquest of the Louisiana Territory and, in time, of the United States. "The day that France takes possession of New Orleans," Jefferson wrote to Livingston, "we must marry ourselves to the British fleet and nation." Luckily, there was no need. Napoleon had sent thirty-five thousand of the crack infantrymen of Europe to put down a rabble of unorganized natives, and he had lost twenty-four thousand of them. What hope, then, for crushing a continent of savages *and* the Americans, who fought with similar guile? Santo Domingo was Napoleon's Vietnam. He withdrew and decided against any further adventures three thousand miles from home. And before Monroe was off the boat, he had sold Louisiana to Livingston for the ridiculously low price of $16,000,000.

CONGRESS AND THE TREATY

There is a cheerful-looking bust of Jefferson in the Cabildo in New Orleans, where the territorial transfer was signed. It ought to bear the inscription, "Thomas Jefferson chuckled here." For although a President cannot conclude a treaty with a foreign nation without the "advice and consent of the Senate," Jefferson had advised and consented with nobody. He never mentioned a word of the Louisiana Purchase to Congress until it was settled. His comment on why he kept it secret is a wonderfully barefaced bit of gall, worthy of Franklin Roosevelt at his blandest:

> This Treaty must of course be laid before both Houses.
> ... They, I presume, will see their duty to their country
> in ratifying and paying for it ... the Executive, in seiz-
> ing the fugitive occurrence which so much advances
> the good of their country, have done an act beyond the
> Constitution. ... It is the case of the guardian investing
> the money of his ward in purchasing an important ad-
> jacent territory, and saying to him when of age, I did
> this for your good!

Of course it was unconstitutional. It was outrageous. But, in the end, even a majority of Jefferson's enemies accepted it for the most reliable of American reasons: it worked. Jefferson had more than doubled the existing territory of the United States (a one hundred and forty percent increase, to be exact). And for four cents an acre! He decided at once to measure and survey the Purchase with a military expedition led by his secretary, a veteran of several Indian campaigns named Meriwether Lewis, and a soldier friend, William Clark, the younger brother of General George Rogers Clark, the "Washington of the West." They had the luck to pick up as a guide an Indian girl, a sixteen-year-old Shoshone named Sacajawea; her husband, a French-Canadian, would be guide, interpreter, and go-between. In the only threatening encounter they had with Indians, Sacajawea herself literally got between Lewis and a menacing chief, who, astoundingly, turned out to be her brother.

LEWIS AND CLARK REACH THE PACIFIC

They started from St. Louis, in the spring of 1804, in a long flat-boat, and by the time they got through North Dakota were threading their way in six canoes and two keelboats into country totally unknown to white men, except possibly to lone and unsung French-Canadian rovers. Jefferson's orders were, as always, crisp and all-embracing. They were to open up a river route for a continental fur trade, to study the Indian tribes, their languages and customs, to be nice to them on all occasions, but to convey the message that they now belonged to the Great White Father back in Washington. Lewis and Clark were blithely required to do for the whole lateral stretch of the continent what Jefferson had done for his familiar Virginia. To list and describe all the birds, trees, plants, flowers, fish, weather systems, geology along the way. To map all the interior river systems, march over the single range (as Jefferson imagined) of the Rockies, to come to the headwaters of the Columbia River, formally claim the whole continent for the United States, and so float sweetly in triumph to the Pacific. When they saw it, at the end of November 1805, after eighteen exhausting months, it was as if the first two men had landed on the moon.

Lewis died only four years later, and Clark in 1838. Neither of them could have doubted the blessing they had bestowed on their countrymen. But Sacajawea lived into her nineties, and must have been a very embittered old lady—for the great expedition had doomed the hope that her people would keep their native land.

MARBURY V. MADISON

JOHN MARSHALL

The U.S. Constitution left several questions unanswered regarding its application. One was what would happen if Congress passed a law that exceeded its Constitutional powers. When Congress passed the Alien and Sedition Acts in 1798, for example, Thomas Jefferson and James Madison argued that state governments could ignore federal laws if they believed them unconstitutional, but their views were not shared by all Americans.

In 1803, this question was answered in the historic case of *Marbury v. Madison*. William Marbury was appointed by President John Adams in the closing hours of his administration to a minor federal post. Before his commission could be officially delivered, however, Thomas Jefferson had taken office as president, and Jefferson's secretary of state, James Madison, refused to accept Marbury's commission. (Both Marbury and Adams were Federalists, political opponents of the Jefferson-led Republicans.) Marbury sued, arguing that the Judiciary Act of 1789 authorized the Supreme Court to issue a legal order (called a writ of mandamus) to compel Madison to receive his commission.

The chief justice of the Supreme Court, John Marshall, authored the opinion on behalf of an unanimous court and presented it on February 24, 1803. In his opinion, excerpts of which appear here, Marshall concluded that while Marbury had a legal right to his commission, the 1789 law authorizing the Supreme Court to force Madison to accept Marbury's appointment was an unconstitutional delegation of power by Congress to the Court. Marshall declared the law to be void and thus established that the power of judicial review—the right and duty to overrule unconstitutional laws—over acts of Congress was lodged in the Supreme Court. In subsequent cases, he extended

Supreme Court of the United States, "Marbury v. Madison," www.lib.drake.edu, February 1803.

the Supreme Court's power of judicial review to state laws as well. In doing so, he helped to make the Supreme Court an equal partner in the national government along with the legislative and executive branches.

I n the order in which the court has viewed this subject, the following questions have been considered and decided.

1st. Has the applicant a right to the commission he demands?

2dly. If he has a right, and that right has been violated, do the laws of his country afford him a remedy?

3dly. If they do afford him a remedy, is it a mandamus issuing from this court?

The first object of enquiry is,

1st. Has the applicant a right to the commission he demands? . . .

It is . . . decidedly the opinion of the court, that when a commission has been signed by the President, the appointment is made; and that the commission is complete, when the seal of the United States has been affixed to it by the secretary of state. . . .

Mr. Marbury, then, since his commission was signed by the President, and sealed by the secretary of state, was appointed; and as the law creating the office, gave the officer a right to hold for five years, independent of the executive, the appointment was not revocable; but vested in the officer legal rights, which are protected by the laws of his country.

To withhold his commission, therefore, is an act deemed by the court not warranted by law, but violative of a vested legal right.

SEARCHING FOR A REMEDY

This brings us to the second enquiry; which is,

2dly. If he has a right, and that right has been violated, do the laws of his country afford him a remedy?

The very essence of civil liberty certainly consists in the right of every individual to claim the protection of the laws, whenever he receives an injury. . . .

The government of the United States has been emphatically termed a government of laws, and not of men. It will certainly cease to deserve this high appellation, if the laws furnish no remedy for the violation of a vested legal right. . . .

It is . . . the opinion of the court,

1st. That by signing the commission of Mr. Marbury, the president of the United States appointed him a justice of peace, for the county of Washington in the district of Columbia; and that the seal of the United States, affixed thereto by the secretary of state, is conclusive testimony of the verity of the signature, and of the completion of the appointment; and that the appointment conferred on him a legal right to the office for the space of five years.

2dly. That, having this legal title to the office, he has a consequent right to the commission; a refusal to deliver which, is a plain violation of that right, for which the laws of his country afford him a remedy.

It remains to be enquired whether,

3dly. He is entitled to the remedy for which he applies. . . .

This . . . is a plain case for a mandamus, either to deliver the commission, or a copy of it from the record; and it only remains to be enquired,

Whether it can issue from this court.

EXAMINING THE 1789 JUDICIARY ACT

The act to establish the judicial courts of the United States authorizes the supreme court "to issue writs of mandamus, in cases warranted by the principles and usages of law, to any courts appointed, or persons holding office, under the authority of the United States."

The secretary of state, being a person holding an office under the authority of the United States, is precisely within the letter of the description; and if this court is not authorized to issue a writ of mandamus to such an officer, it must be because the law is unconstitutional, and therefore absolutely incapable of conferring the authority, and assigning the duties which its words purport to confer and assign.

The constitution vests the whole judicial power of the United States in one supreme court, and such inferior courts as congress shall, from time to time, ordain and establish. This power is expressly extended to all cases arising under the laws of the United States; and consequently, in some form, may be exercised over the present case; because the right claimed is given by a law of the United States.

In the distribution of this power it is declared that "the supreme court shall have original jurisdiction in all cases affecting ambassadors, other public ministers and consuls, and those in which a state shall be a party. In all other cases, the supreme court shall have appellate jurisdiction.". . .

If it had been intended to leave it to the discretion of the legislature to apportion the judicial power between the supreme and inferior courts according to the will of that body, it would certainly have been useless to have proceeded further than to have defined the judicial powers, and the tribunals in which it should be vested. The subsequent part of the section is mere surplusage, is entirely without meaning, if such is to be the construction. If congress remains at liberty to give this court appellate jurisdiction, where the constitution has declared their jurisdiction shall be original; and original jurisdiction where the constitution has declared it shall be appellate; the distribution of jurisdiction, made in the constitution, is form without substance. . . .

It cannot be presumed that any clause in the constitution is intended to be without effect; and therefore such a construction is inadmissible, unless the words require it. . . .

The authority, therefore, given to the supreme court, by the act establishing the judicial courts of the United States, to issue writs of mandamus to public officers, appears not to be warranted by the constitution; and it becomes necessary to enquire whether a jurisdiction, so conferred, can be exercised.

WHAT SHOULD BE DONE ABOUT UNCONSTITUTIONAL LAWS?

The question, whether an act, repugnant to the constitution, can become the law of the land, is a question deeply interesting to the United States; but, happily, not of an intricacy proportioned to its interest. It seems only necessary to recognize certain principles, supposed to have been long and well established, to decide it.

That the people have an original right to establish, for their future government, such principles as, in their opinion, shall most conduce to their own happiness, is the basis, on which the whole American fabric has been erected. The exercise of this original right is a very great exertion; nor can it, nor ought it to be frequently repeated. The principles, therefore, so established, are deemed fundamental. And as the authority, from which they proceed, is supreme, and can seldom act, they are designed to be permanent.

This original and supreme will organizes the government,

and assigns, to different departments, their respective powers. It may either stop here; or establish certain limits not to be transcended by those departments.

The government of the United States is of the latter description. The powers of the legislature are defined, and limited; and that those limits may not be mistaken, or forgotten, the constitution is written. To what purpose are powers limited, and to what purpose is that limitation committed to writing, if these limits may, at any time, be passed by those intended to be restrained? The distinction, between a government with limited and unlimited powers, is abolished, if those limits do not confine the persons on whom they are imposed, and if acts prohibited and acts allowed, are of equal obligation. It is a proposition too plain to be contested, that the constitution controls any legislative act repugnant to it; or, that the legislature may alter the constitution by an ordinary act.

Between these alternatives there is no middle ground. The constitution is either a superior, paramount law, unchangeable by ordinary means, or it is on a level with ordinary legislative acts, and like other acts, is alterable when the legislature shall please to alter it.

If the former part of the alternative be true, then a legislative act contrary to the constitution is not law: if the latter part be true, then written constitutions are absurd attempts, on the part of the people, to limit a power, in its own nature illimitable.

Certainly all those who have framed written constitutions contemplate them as forming the fundamental and paramount law of the nation, and consequently the theory of every such government must be, that an act of the legislature, repugnant to the constitution, is void.

This theory is essentially attached to a written constitution, and is consequently to be considered, by this court, as one of the fundamental principles of our society. It is not therefore to be lost sight of in the further consideration of this subject.

If an act of the legislature, repugnant to the constitution, is void, does it, notwithstanding its invalidity, bind the courts, and oblige them to give it effect? Or, in other words, though it be not law, does it constitute a rule as operative as if it was a law? This would be to overthrow in fact what was established in theory; and would seem, at first view, an absurdity too gross to be insisted on. It shall, however, receive a more attentive consideration.

THE DUTY OF THE COURTS

It is emphatically the province and duty of the judicial department to say what the law is. Those who apply the rule to particular cases, must of necessity expound and interpret that rule. If two laws conflict with each other, the courts must decide on the operation of each.

So if a law be in opposition to the constitution; if both the law and the constitution apply to a particular case, so that the court must either decide that case conformably to the law, disregarding the constitution; or conformably to the constitution, disregarding the law; the court must determine which of these conflicting rules governs the case. This is of the very essence of judicial duty.

If then the courts are to regard the constitution; and the constitution is superior to any ordinary act of the legislature; the constitution, and not such ordinary act, must govern the case to which they both apply. Those then who controvert the principle that the constitution is to be considered, in court, as a paramount law, are reduced to the necessity of maintaining that courts must close their eyes on the constitution, and see only the law.

This doctrine would subvert the very foundation of all written constitutions. It would declare that an act, which, according to the principles and theory of our government, is entirely void; is yet, in practice, completely obligatory. It would declare, that if the legislature shall do what is expressly forbidden, such act, notwithstanding the express prohibition, is in reality effectual. It would be giving to the legislature a practical and real omnipotence, with the same breath which professes to restrict their powers within narrow limits. It is prescribing limits, and declaring that those limits may be passed at pleasure.

That it thus reduces to nothing what we have deemed the greatest improvement on political institutions—a written constitution—would of itself be sufficient, in America, where written constitutions have been viewed with so much reverence, for rejecting the construction. But the peculiar expressions of the constitution of the United States furnish additional arguments in favor of its rejection.

The judicial power of the United States is extended to all cases arising under the constitution.

Could it be the intention of those who gave this power, to say that, in using it, the constitution should not be looked into? That a case arising under the constitution should be decided without examining the instrument under which it arises?

This is too extravagant to be maintained.

In some cases then, the constitution must be looked into by the judges. And if they can open it at all, what part of it are they forbidden to read, or to obey?

EXAMINING PARTS OF THE CONSTITUTION

There are many other parts of the constitution which serve to illustrate this subject.

It is declared that "No tax or duty shall be laid on articles exported from any state." Suppose a duty on the export of cotton, of tobacco, or of flour; and a suit instituted to recover it. Ought judgment to be rendered in such a case? Ought the judges to close their eyes on the constitution, and only see the law?

The constitution declares that "no bill of attainder or ex post facto law shall be passed."

If, however, such a bill should be passed and a person should be prosecuted under it; must the court condemn to death those victims whom the constitution endeavors to preserve?

"No person," says the constitution, "shall be convicted of treason unless on the testimony of two witnesses to the fame overt act, or on confession in open court." Here the language of the constitution is addressed especially to the courts. It prescribes, directly for them, a rule of evidence not to be departed from. If the legislature should change that rule, and declare one witness, or a confession out of court, sufficient for conviction, must the constitutional principle yield to the legislative act?

From these, and many other selections which might be made, it is apparent, that the framers of the constitution contemplated that instrument, as a rule for the government of courts, as well as of the legislature.

Why otherwise does it direct the judges to take an oath to support it? This oath certainly applies, in an especial manner, to their conduct in their official character. How immoral to impose it on them, if they were to be used as the instruments, and the knowing instruments, for violating what they swear to support!

The oath of office, too, imposed by the legislature, is completely demonstrative of the legislative opinion on the subject. It is in these words, "I do solemnly swear that I will administer justice without respect to persons, and do equal right to the poor and to the rich; and that I will faithfully and impartially discharge all the duties incumbent on me as according to the best of my abilities and understanding, agreeably to the constitution, and laws of the United States."

Why does a judge swear to discharge his duties agreeably to the constitution of the United States, if that constitution forms no rule for his government? if it is closed upon him, and cannot be inspected by him?

If such be the real state of things, this is worse than solemn mockery. To prescribe, or to take this oath, becomes equally a crime.

It is also not entirely unworthy of observation, that in declaring what shall be the supreme law of the land, the constitution itself is first mentioned; and not the laws of the United States generally, but those only which shall be made in pursuance of the constitution, have that rank.

Thus, the particular phraseology of the constitution of the United States confirms and strengthens the principle, supposed to be essential to all written constitutions, that a law repugnant to the constitution is void; and that courts, as well as other departments, are bound by that instrument.

STRUGGLES AND RENEWAL OF THE IROQUOIS NATION

DEAN R. SNOW

The Iroquois was a powerful confederacy of six Indian tribes in what is now the state of New York. Influential for hundreds of years both before and after the arrival of European colonists, the confederacy was divided over the American Revolution, with some tribes aligned with the British, others with the Americans. During the war itself many Iroquois settlements and crops were destroyed. Following America's victory, many Iroquois fled to Canada; those who remained were compelled to sell much of their traditional lands. Many succumbed to alcoholism.

In the early 1800s, an Iroquois leader, Handsome Lake, urged his people to revitalize their society by adapting white farming techniques and technologies while retaining some traditional cultural values and ceremonies. His efforts are described in the following selection by Dean R. Snow, a professor of anthropology at Pennsylvania State University.

The departure of the French, and then the American Revolution against English rule, were disastrous for the Iroquois. These events were a disaster in political terms, but their significance went much deeper than that. The Senecas retained fractured holdings of eleven reservations after 1797, only four of them sizeable. The Allegany band retained a reservation 42 square miles in size along both sides of the Allegheny River

Dean R. Snow, *The Iroquois*, Cambridge, MA: Blackwell, 1994. Copyright © 1994 by Blackwell Publishing. Reproduced by permission.

in southwestern New York. Part of the band lived on the adjacent Cornplanter grant just to the south in Pennsylvania, under the leadership of Cornplanter himself.

The new reservation system might have worked well. The Iroquois regarded the reservations as secure home bases from which they could hunt, travel, or gather food over unoccupied lands they had ceded. The Indians sold splint baskets and beadwork to non-Indians, or even secured employment among them. Cornplanter hired non-Indians to operate smithies and mills on his grant. Quakers moved into this optimistic setting, intent to show the Senecas the way to civilization. They did not necessarily seek to convert the Indians to their faith, but rather to teach them literacy, mathematics, modern farming, and various arts and crafts. Despite these good intentions, the reservations slid into deplorable wilderness slums. Iroquois men no longer ruled the world beyond the edge of the woods, abroad for months on end to deal with hunting, diplomacy, and warfare. Rather, they found themselves confined to a woman's world of farming and village affairs. Hunting was restricted and villages could not relocate easily when soil declined, so the Iroquois had to adopt plow agriculture and domesticated animals that provided fertilizer. At a time when the Plains Indians were approaching the apogee of their new equestrian adaptation, oxen become more important than horses to the Iroquois.

Fueled by alcoholism, families fragmented, the mechanism of reciprocal condolence came apart, and Indian society fell into a darkness of mutual suspicion and rumors of witchcraft. The cycle of endless offense and revenge, which the Peacemaker had ended within Iroquoia centuries earlier, began anew. Families that had previously been parts of extended matrilineal households had to survive on their own at the very moment at which stress on the traditionally weak marriage link reached its maximum. The traditional ceremonies, with their emphasis on thanksgiving, solidarity, and catharsis, did little to relieve the general hostility. By the end of the century, Iroquois culture was near death.

HANDSOME LAKE'S DREAMS

Cornplanter had a half-brother, a man named Handsome Lake (Skanyadariyoh) who had been raised up to the office of the Turtle clan League sachem in about 1795. Handsome Lake was living with Cornplanter in 1799, bedridden by prolonged alcoholism. In June of that year Handsome Lake collapsed and appeared to die, at the end of a stressful spring during which a suspected witch had been executed. Blacksnake, his nephew, discovered that he was still alive, but in a coma. It was while he was in his coma that Handsome Lake had the first of a series of visions in which the Creator spoke to him. Three people in traditional Iroquois dress appeared to him and instructed him to give up alcohol or die. They also warned that witches must repent and confess their sins. Handsome Lake was commanded to spread these words and to ensure that the Strawberry Ceremony was held that year and each year from then on.

On his recovery, Handsome Lake conveyed these messages in council and to the local Quaker schoolmaster. In a vision a few weeks later, Handsome Lake was taken on a tour of heaven and hell. He met George Washington and Jesus, neither of whom appeared to be in ideal circumstances. These features surely reflect the long contact the Iroquois had experienced with Christians. He was also shown vignettes having to do with drunkenness, witchcraft, promiscuity, wife abuse, quarreling, and gambling. All of these led to the definition of an explicit moral code, which Handsome Lake was compelled to take to his people. The code was called the *Gai'wiio*, "The Good Message."

The Iroquois put much stock in dreams, and have traditionally maintained a relatively modern view of their significance. While the Algonquian shamans of New England saw dreams as out-of-body experiences, the Iroquois thought them to be the expressions of suppressed desires. Dreams not acted upon would cause the dreamer to suffer a disruptive imbalance that could lead to personal illness or death, or even misfortune for the entire community. The higher the rank of the dreamer, the more likely it was that a dream had far-reaching significance. So it was that the visions of Handsome Lake came to have wider significance.

CEREMONIES, DANCES, AND GAMES

During the following winter, Handsome Lake had a third vision. In it he was instructed to ensure that the traditional ceremonies were continued, especially the Midwinter Ceremony. The consequence of not doing so, he believed, would be the destruction of the world by fire. He revived the Midwinter Ceremony by adding four sacred rituals as a second segment. These were the

Feather Dance, Thanksgiving Dance, Rite of Personal Chant, and Bowl Game, which added as many as four days to the ceremony.

Most games are just that. However, the Bowl Game was elevated to sacred status by its inclusion in the Midwinter Ceremony as one of the four sacred rituals. The Bowl Game (called the Peach Stone Game after the introduction of that fruit) is played with flat fruit pits. The pits, which are colored black on one side, are tossed six at a time in a shallow bowl by thumping the bowl against the ground. Players collect counters by turning up five or six pits of the same color. The length of the game depends upon the number of counters used.

The central themes of revived Iroquois ceremony remained the traditional ones. They were and are thanksgiving and appreciation for the goodwill of the supernatural, and attention to the meaning of the dreams. Iroquois dances are regarded as either sacred or social. Sacred dances are usually performed in the longhouse as part of a ceremony. Social dances are for fun and relaxation. These are also the dances that are performed outside the longhouse, at powwows, and at festivals attended by non-Iroquois. The most sacred of dances are the Feather Dance and the Thanksgiving Dance (sometimes called the Drum or Skin Dance), which Handsome Lake added to the Midwinter Ceremony. Other less sacred dances include the Women's Dance, Corn Dance, Stomp Dance (also called Trotting or Standing Quiver), Bean Dance (also called Hand-in-Hand or Linking Arms), Striking-the-Pole Dance, and War Dance.

Social dances, which are most likely to be performed in more public settings today, are numerous. They have names like Fish, Raccoon, Chicken, Sharpening a Stick, Choose a Partner, Shake the Pumpkin, Garter, Pigeon, Duck, Robin, Skin Beating, Cherokee, Grinding the Arrow, Knee Rattle, Alligator, and Rabbit. There is also a new Women's Dance, which is in addition to the sacred dance of the same name and can be performed socially. As may be clear from their names, several of these were borrowed from other Indian nations. The Eagle Dance began as a war dance derived from the Calumet Dance of western Indians. Over the last two centuries it has evolved into a curing society dance. Most dances are round dances, with people alone or paired according to the requirements of each dance. Except for certain dances for the dead, movement is almost always counterclockwise. Every dance has its own specific steps, and everyone participates regardless of proficiency.

A NEW PROPHET

Handsome Lake's health improved. He began spreading the word as a new Iroquois prophet. He even went to Washington to solicit the support of President Jefferson. Visions and periods of meditation led to more revelations, and over the course of the next 15 years, Handsome Lake gradually compiled a complex code of behavior. He did not argue that witchcraft did not exist, but rather that it should be given up. While Handsome Lake lived, the *Gai'wiio* was called the New Religion by some Iroquois in order to distinguish the movement from the Old Religion of the Iroquois. This distinction was not very important to many traditional Iroquois at the time or for many decades later, but it would be revived by some late in the twentieth century.

For a while Handsome Lake was obsessed with witch hunting. He came to believe that the traditional medicine societies were covens of witches, and he demanded that they be disbanded. Some members pretended to comply, but continued to practice their rituals in private. It was for this reason that a century later [ethnographer Arthur] Parker would refer to them as secret medicine societies. Handsome Lake ordered people to confess to witchcraft, and those that refused were sometimes killed. Inevitably, he eventually began throwing such accusations at the famous Seneca Pine Tree Chief known as Red Jacket and other political rivals, nearly precipitating a war in one instance. But overall, his code began to have some positive effects. Handsome Lake realized that the Quakers had some things right. Iroquois men could no longer afford to insist that farming was women's work. Nor could the tradition of easy divorce continue to work in the absence of extended matrilineal households. He realized that the strong matrilocal extended family was a thing of the past, and argued that gossip and family meddling (especially by women's mothers) had to end. These points became first principles in Handsome Lake's evolving code, which he preached as an extended oral tradition in a classically Iroquois manner.

Handsome Lake opposed any further land sales. He also opposed the participation of Iroquois men in the United States military, particularly in the case of the War of 1812. In these and other things, his code was conservative. He was calling the Iroquois to revive and adapt the best of traditional Iroquois belief. His teaching sought to reinforce the old myths and ceremonies, not replace them. But he also sought to replace the catharsis of acting out dreams with therapeutic confession and the repression of illicit desires. Whether he realized it himself or not, Handsome Lake was helping traditional Iroquois belief to adapt to the realities of reservation life.

Handsome Lake deliberately struck at the central link in Iroquois society as a means of reinforcing the new nuclear family unit. He realized that the bond between husband and wife was more important than that between mother and daughter now that the longhouse residence was gone. He did not threaten the clan system or the rights of clan matrons to appoint chiefs, but he did everything he could to subvert the authority of matriliny at its root. It may well be that the Iroquois survived the nineteenth century because Handsome Lake made it acceptable for men to work the fields, and made it difficult for women to accuse their sons-in-law of adultery. Quaker-inspired technology and handsome Lake's religious revival gave new spirit to the Iroquois. Like all nativistic movements, this one claimed to revive traditional religious values while it was in reality carefully selective of those values and inventive in finding innovative solutions to new problems.

THE WAR OF 1812

REGINALD HORSMAN

Less than thirty years after America won independence from Great Britain, the two nations found themselves again at war. Reginald Horsman, a professor at the University of Wisconsin at Milwaukee, provides a brief overview of the causes and events of the War of 1812. He places the conflict in the context of England's war against France in the early nineteenth century in which America struggled to remain neutral. England's actions on the high seas against American ships and seamen, as well as Indian uprisings in the Great Lakes region that many believed were incited by the British, led President James Madison to call for and Congress to issue a declaration of war.

The war itself was marked by more American defeats than victories. A low point came in 1814, when Great Britain (having defeated France and thus able to bring more forces to the United States) invaded and burned the nation's capital. However, subsequent American victories in Baltimore and Lake Champlain in New York caused Great Britain to lose interest in fighting. In December 1814 the two countries signed a peace treaty that resolved almost none of the issues that had officially caused the war. However, America's victory in New Orleans (under General Andrew Jackson), which ironically occurred in January 1815 after the peace treaty was signed but before it could be communicated, left many Americans celebrating the War of 1812 as a national triumph. Horsman is the author of numerous works of history including *The Causes of the War of 1812* and *The New Republic: The United States of America, 1789–1815*.

Reginald Horsman, "The War of 1812," *The Reader's Companion to American History*, edited by Eric Foner and John A. Garraty, Boston: Houghton Mifflin, 1991. Copyright © 1991 by Houghton Mifflin Company. Reproduced by permission.

T he War of 1812, sometimes called "the Second War of Independence," was fought between the United States and Great Britain from 1812 to 1815. Relations between the two countries had often been strained after the United States won its independence in 1783, but the greatest problems developed during the war between England and France that broke out in 1793. To prevent American neutral shipping from helping the French, the British instituted extensive maritime blockades of European ports. The resulting seizures of American merchant shipping quickly brought demands for retaliation in the United States. From 1794 on, however, tensions eased as the administrations of George Washington and John Adams worked to avoid diplomatic difficulties with the British.

RISING TENSIONS

In the years between 1803 and 1812 relations between the United States and Great Britain again deteriorated sharply. France was now ruled by Napoleon, and the European struggle became more widespread. Beginning in 1805 the British imposed much stricter maritime blockades, culminating in the Orders in Council of 1807. These orders severely restricted neutral trade with Europe. The effect of these blockades was compounded by the British practice of impressment. The British navy claimed the right to stop neutral vessels on the high seas to look for "deserters." In the course of searching American ships, mistakes were often made, and as a result many American seamen were impressed into the British navy.

From 1807 to 1811 the Democratic-Republican administrations of Thomas Jefferson and James Madison attempted to change British policies by economic coercion, restricting British imports as well as American exports to Great Britain. The most severe of these measures was the Embargo Act, passed in December 1807, which banned all exports and confined American shipping to the coastal trade. When neither economic coercion nor negotiation changed British policies, war sentiment built in the United States.

Beginning in 1810 young Democratic-Republican "War Hawks" from the West and the South argued that the right to export American products without losing ships and men had to be defended. They also objected to the British inciting the Indians along the Great Lakes frontier and argued that the British would be forced to change their policies if the United States attacked Canada. Some believed that the future of republican government was in danger if the United States could not successfully defend its rights. Others hoped that if Canada was conquered it could be retained after the war.

MILITARY CAMPAIGNS

In spite of bitter opposition from the Federalist party, centered in New England, the United States declared war against Great Britain on June 18, 1812. General American strategy called for an invasion of Canada on three fronts: along Lake Champlain toward Montreal, across the Niagara frontier, and from Detroit into upper Canada. The campaigns of the summer and fall of 1812 were disasters. Detroit surrendered to the British on August 18, and the Americans were defeated on the Niagara frontier at the Battle of Queenston Heights in October. The year ended with American forces on the Lake Champlain front withdrawing from an attempted invasion of Canada without seriously engaging the enemy.

The main consolation in the first year of the war was the unexpected performance of the small American navy. In a single-ship engagement the frigate *Constitution* defeated the *Guerriere* in August 1812. Later in the year the *United States* captured the British frigate *Macedonian* and brought it into port as a prize of war. Later the *Constitution* defeated the *Java* in a battle off the coast of Brazil. This run of successes came to an end in June 1813 when the *Chesapeake* lost to the *Shannon* in a bitterly fought engagement. But in spite of the morale-boosting victories of the frigates and successful forays by American privateers, the British navy effectively blockaded the American coast and laid it open to hit-and-run raids.

American attempts to invade Canada failed again in 1813. Although Capt. Oliver Hazard Perry's ships won the Battle of Lake Erie in October and Gen. William Henry Harrison defeated the British and the Indians at the Battle of the Thames in Canada in the same month, the Americans were unable to make major inroads into Canada.

In 1814, with France collapsing, the British were able to launch major attacks against the United States. In July, American forces resisted the British at the Battles of Chippawa and Lundy's Lane on the Niagara frontier, but in the next month the United States suffered a severe blow. When Washington was occupied in August, President Madison and Congress were forced to flee, and the White House and other public buildings were burned. American morale was at a low ebb: the country faced bankruptcy as a result of the British blockade and the Federalists of New England were in open opposition to the war.

But in the following months American fortunes suddenly revived. The British force that had occupied Washington failed in an attempt to take Baltimore, and on September 11 Thomas Macdonough's naval force won a decisive victory at the Battle of Plattsburg Bay on Lake Champlain. This victory forced an invading British army to retreat into Canada.

PEACE AND A FINAL BATTLE

Since August 1814 the two sides had been negotiating a settlement at Ghent in Belgium. When the British heard of the retreat of their army in the Battle of Plattsburg Bay, they lost interest in continuing the war. On December 24 the Treaty of Ghent was signed. It provided for the mutual restoration of territory captured by both sides. With the ending of the European war, the problem of American neutral rights was no longer an issue.

One battle was still to be fought, however, for the British force proceeding against the Gulf coast could not be informed of the peace in time. On January 8, 1815, the American forces commanded by Andrew Jackson inflicted a crushing defeat on the British at New Orleans. Americans heard of Jackson's great victory and the Treaty of Ghent at about the same time. Once again the British had been successfully resisted, and a surge of national self-confidence swept the United States. A war that had begun with the object of defending American commerce and vindicating republican independence was viewed in the end as a victory only because British attacks on the United States had failed.

WESTERN SETTLEMENT AND EUROPEAN IMMIGRATION

PAUL JOHNSON

In the early nineteenth century the United States experienced an enormous growth in its population, which was propelled both by high birth rates and by immigration from Europe. British historian and journalist Paul Johnson examines how European immigration influenced the development of America following the War of 1812, a trend that was slowed but not extinguished by a financial panic in 1819. He describes the social and political conditions in Europe that led many people to emigrate and factors that drew them to the United States. Many immigrants, he asserts, came in the hopes of obtaining farmland that the U.S. government was making available at bargain prices. Johnson has written a number of popular histories, including *A History of the American People*, from which the following is excerpted.

R ight at the end of his life, Benjamin Franklin wrote a pamphlet giving advice to Europeans planning to come to America. He said it was a good place for those who wanted to become rich. But, he said, it was above all a haven for the industrious poor, for 'nowhere else are the laboring poor so well fed, well lodged, well clothed and well paid as in the United States of America.' It was a country, he concluded, where 'a general happy mediocrity prevails.' It is important for

Paul Johnson, *A History of the American People*, New York: HarperCollins, 1997. Copyright © 1997 by HarperCollins. Reproduced by permission.

those who wish to understand American history to remember this point about 'happy mediocrity.' The historian is bound to bring out the high points and crises of the national story, to record the doings of the great, the battles, elections, epic debates, and laws passed. But the everyday lives of simple citizens must not be ignored simply because they were uneventful. This is particularly true of America, a country specifically created by and for ordinary men and women, where the system of government was deliberately designed to interfere in their lives as little as possible. The fact that, unless we investigate closely, we hear so little about the mass of the population is itself a historical point of great importance, because it testifies by its eloquent silence to the success of the republican experiment.

Early in the 19th century, America was achieving birthrates never before equaled in history, in terms of children reaching adulthood. The 1800 census revealed a population of 5,308,843, itself a 35 percent increase over ten years. By 1810 it had leaped to 7,239,881, up another 36.4 percent. By 1820 it was 9,638,453, close to doubling in twenty years, and of this nearly 80 percent was natural increase. As one Congressman put it: 'I invite you to go to the west, and visit one of our log cabins, and number its inmates. There you will find a strong, stout youth of eighteen, with his Better Half, just commencing the first struggles of independent life. Thirty years from that time, visit them again; and instead of two, you will find in that same family twenty-two. That is what I call the American Multiplication Table.'

AN IMMIGRATION BOOM

But with the end of the world war in 1815 high American birthrates were compounded by a great flood of immigrants. It is a historical conjunction of supreme importance that the coming of the independent American republic, and the opening up of the treasure-house of land provided by the Louisiana Purchase and the destruction of Indian power by Andrew Jackson, coincided with the beginnings of the world's demographic revolution, which hit Europe first. Between 1750 and 1900 Europe's population rose faster than anywhere else in the world (except North America), from 150 million to over 400 million. This, in turn, produced a huge net outflow of immigration: to South America, Russia, Australasia, Canada, South Africa, and above all the United States. The rush to America began after the Battle of Waterloo in June 1815 and continued right through the autumn and winter, the immigrant ships braving gales and ice. It accelerated in 1816, which in Europe was 'the year without a summer,' with torrential rain and even sleet and snow continuing into July and August and wrecking harvests, sending poor and even starving people to the coast to huddle in the transports. Ezekiah Niles (1777–1839), who ran *Niles's Weekly Register* from 1811 onwards, in many ways America's best journal of record at the time, calculated that 50,000 immigrants reached America in the year, though this figure was later revised downwards. His more careful calculation for 1817, based on shipping lists (the federal government, though it took censuses, did not yet publish statistics), produced a figure of 30,000 up to the end of the main season in September. Of this half went to New York and Philadelphia, though some went straight over the Appalachians into the Ohio Valley.

No authority on either side of the Atlantic was bothered with who was going where or how, though the British limited ship-carrying capacity to one passenger to every 2 tons of registry in their own ships. The sheer freedom of movement was staggering. An Englishman, without passport, health certificate or documentation of any kind—without luggage for that matter—could hand over £10 at a Liverpool shipping counter and go aboard. The ship provided him with water, nothing else, and of course it might go down with all hands. But if it reached New York he could go ashore without anyone asking him his business, and then vanish into the entrails of the new society. It was not even necessary to have £10, as the British provided free travel to Canada, whence the emigrants could bum rides on coastal boats to Massachusetts or New York. There was no control and no resentment. One of them, James Flint from Scotland, recorded in 1818: 'I have never heard of another feeling than good wishes to them.' In the five years up to 1820, some 100,000 people arrived in America without having to show a single bit of paper.

THE PANIC OF 1819

The first check of this inflow—the end of innocence if you like—came with the catastrophic bank crash of 1819, the first financial crisis in America's history. . . .

The result . . . was a crisis in manufacturing industry. The Philadelphia cotton mills employed 2,325 in 1816; by autumn 1819 all but 149 had been sacked. In New England the crisis was mitigated by sound banking but it was still acute and unem-

ployment shot up. John Quincy Adams, always quick to strike
a note of gloom, recorded in his diary on April 24, 1819: 'In the
midst of peace and partial prosperity we are approaching a crisis which will shake the Union to its center.' The news of trouble reached Europe too late to affect the 1819 sailings, so tens of
thousands of immigrants continued to arrive, to find no work
and rising hostility. One observer, Emanuel Howitt, wrote that
'the Yankees now [1819] regard the immigrant with the most
sovereign contempt . . . a wretch, driven out of his own wretched
country, and seeking a subsistence in this glorious land.' It
would 'never be glad confident morning again.' In March 1819
Congress, in a panic attempt to stop ships arriving at New York
and other ports, slapped a two-persons-for-5-tons rule on in-
coming ships, effective from September—the beginning of control. The State Department, in a prescript published in *Niles's
Weekly Register,* announced its policy-lines: 'The American Republic invites nobody to come. We will keep out nobody. Arrivals will suffer no disadvantages as aliens. But they can expect
no advantages either. Native-born and foreign-born face equal
opportunities. What happens to them depends entirely on their
individual ability and exertions, and on good fortune.'

There is something magnificent about this declaration, penned
by John Quincy Adams himself. It epitomizes the spirit of
laissez-faire libertarianism which pervaded every aspect of
American life at this time—though, as we shall see, there were
state interventionists at large too. Libertarianism was, of course,
based upon an underlying, total self-confidence in the future of
the country. There was something magnificent too about the
speed and completeness with which America recovered from
this crisis, which within a year or two seemed a mere mishap, a
tiny blip on a rising curve of success. Mass immigration soon re-
sumed, thanks this time to Ireland. Hitherto, America had taken
in plenty of Ulster Protestants, but few from the Catholic south.
But in 1821, when the Irish potato crop failed, one in an ominous
series of failures culminating in the catastrophe of the mid–1840s,
the British government tried to organize a sea-lift to Canada.
There was panic in Mayo, Clare, Kerry, and Cork, where rumor
had it the ships would transport them to convict bondage in
Australia. But, once the truth was known, the idea of going to
America, at virtually no cost, caught on in the poorest parts of
Ireland. When the first letters reached home in 1822, explaining
how easy it was to slip from Canada into America, and how the

United States, albeit Protestant, gave equal rights to Catholics, the transatlantic rush was on. In 1825, 50,000 Southern Irish applied for a mere 2,000 assisted places on a government scheme. It was a foretaste of the exodus which was to transport one-third of the Irish nation to America. This, in turn, was part of the process whereby the continuing English (and Welsh and Scottish) immigration to the United States was now balanced by new arrivals from outside Britain. The number of Continental Europeans rose from 6,000 to 10,000 a year in the early 1820s to 15,000 in 1826 and 30,000 in 1828. In 1832 it passed the 50,000-a-year mark and thereafter fell below it only twice. An Anglicized United States was gradually becoming Europeanized.

WHY AMERICA WAS ATTRACTIVE TO IMMIGRANTS

Why did the immigrants come? One reason was increasingly cheap sea-passages. Another was food shortages, sometimes widening into famines. The bad weather of 1816, and the appalling winters of 1825–6, 1826–7, and 1829–30, the last one of the coldest ever recorded, produced real hunger. The demographic-catastrophe theories of Thomas Malthus filtered downwards to the masses, in horrifyingly distorted form, and men wanted to get their families out of Europe before the day of wrath came. Then there was the tax burden. At the end of the Bonapartist Wars, all Europe groaned under oppressive taxation. A parliamentary revolt in 1816 abolished income tax in Britain, and in the 1820s duties were gradually reduced too. But in Europe it was the same old story of the state piling the fiscal burdens on the backs of poor peasants and tradespeople. This was compounded, on the Continent, by tens of thousands of internal customs barriers, imposing duties on virtually everything which crossed them.

By comparison, America was a paradise. Its army was one-fiftieth the size of Prussia's. The expense of government per capita was 10 percent of that in Britain, itself a country with a small state by Continental standards. There were no tithes because there was no state church. Nor were there poor rates—there were virtually no poor. An American farm with eight horses paid only $12 a year in tax. Europeans could scarcely believe their ears when told of such figures. Not only were American wage-rates high, but you kept your earnings to spend on your family. Then there were other blessings. No conscription.

No political police. No censorship. No legalized class distinctions. Most employers ate at the same table as their hands. No one (except slaves) called anyone 'Master.' Letters home from immigrants who had already established themselves were read aloud before entire villages and acted as recruitment-propaganda for the transatlantic ships. So, interestingly enough, did the President's annual messages to Congress, which were reprinted in many Continental newspapers until the censors suppressed them. As the *Dublin Morning Post* put it: 'We read this document as if it related purely to our concerns.'

THE LURE OF LAND

But the most powerful inducement was cheap land. Immigrants from Europe were getting cheap land from all the old hunting grounds of the world's primitive peoples—in Australia and Argentina especially—but it was in the United States where the magic was most potent because there the government went to enormous trouble to devise a system whereby the poor could acquire it. In the entire history of the United States, the land-purchase system was the single most benevolent act of government. The basis of the system was the Act of 1796 pricing land at $2 an acre. It allowed a year's credit for half the total paid. An Act of 1800 created federal land offices as Cincinnati, Chillicothe, Marietta, and Steubenville, Ohio, that is, right on the frontier. The minimum purchase was lowered from 640 acres, or a square mile, to 320 acres, and the buyer paid only 25 percent down, the rest over four years. So a man could get a big farm—indeed, by Continental standards, an enormous one—for only about $160 cash. Four years later, Congress halved the minimum again. This put a viable family farm well within the reach of millions of prudent, saving European peasants and skilled workmen. During the first eleven years of the 19th century, nearly 3,400,000 acres were sold to individual farmers in what was then the Northwest, plus another 250,000 in Ohio. These land transfers increased after 1815, with half a million acres of Illinois, for instance, passing into the hands of small- and medium-scale farmers every year. It was the same in the South. In Alabama, government land sales rose to 600,000 acres in 1816 and to 2,280,000 in 1819. In western Georgia the state gave 200-acre plots free to lottery-ticket holders with lucky numbers. In the years after 1815, more people acquired freehold land at bargain prices in the United States than at any other time in the history of the world.

Individual success-stories abounded. Daniel Brush and a small group of Vermonters settled in Greene County, Illinois, in spring 1820. 'A prairie of the richest soil,' Brush wrote, 'stretched out about four miles in length and one mile wide . . . complete with pure springs of cold water in abundance.' Once a cabin, 16 by 14 feet, had been built, they began the hard task of breaking up the prairie. This done, Brush wrote, 'No weeds or grass sprung up upon such ground the first year and the corn needed no attention with plough or hoe. If got in early, good crops were yielded, of corn and fodder.' He added: 'Provisions in abundance was the rule . . . no one needed to go supperless to bed.' The Ten Brook family moved to what became Parke County, Indiana, in autumn 1822. There were twenty-seven of them altogether—three interrelated families, three single men, two teamsters, thirteen horses, twenty-one cows, two yoke-oxen, and four dogs. Their first priority was to build a strong cabin. The soil was rich but virgin. Working throughout the winter, they had cleared 15 acres by the spring and fashioned 200 fence-rails. They had 100 bushels of corn for winter-feed and spring planting. They put two more acres under potatoes and turnips. The spring brought seven calves, and that first summer they made forty 12-pound cheeses, sold at market for a dollar each. The harvest was good. They not only ground their own corn but made 350 pounds of sugar and 10 gallons of molasses from the same soil they cleared for corn. Their leader, Andrew Ten Brook, recounted: 'After the first year, I never saw any scarcity of provisions. The only complaint was that there was nobody to whom the supplies could be sold.'

The sheer fertility of the soil made all the backbreaking work of opening it up worth while. In the Lake Plains—parts of Indiana, Illinois, and Michigan—a vast glacier known as the Wisconsin Drift had in prehistoric times smoothed off the rocks and laid down a deep layer of rich soil containing all the elements needed for intensive agriculture. The settlers, steeped in the Old Testament, called it Canaan, God's Country, because it yielded a third more than the rest, known as 'Egypt.' Some of the settlements in the years after 1815 became celebrated for quick prosperity. One was Boon's Lick, a belt 60 miles wide on each side of the Missouri River which became Howard County in 1816. It boasted superb land, pure water, as much timber as required, and idyllic scenery. By 1819 the local paper, the *Missouri*

Intelligence, produced at the little town of Franklin, offered a spring toast: 'Boon's Lick—two years since, a wilderness. Now—*rich in cotton and cattle!*' It was widely reputed to be the best land in all the West.

SQUATTERS AND SPECULATORS

Moreover, the tendency was for the land price to come down— in the 1820s it was often as low as $1.25 an acre. The modern mind is astonished that, even so, it was regarded as too high and there was a clamor for cheaper or even free land. Many settlers were termed 'squatters.' This simply signified they had got there first, paid over money immediately after the survey but before the land was 'sectionalized' for the market. They risked their title being challenged by non-resident purchasers-speculators. By the end of 1828 two-thirds of the population of Illinois were squatters. Their champion was Thomas Hart Benton (1782– 1858), Senator 1821–51. He sensibly argued against a minimum price for Western lands, proposing grading by quality, and he insisted that settlers pay compensation for improvements, passing a law to this effect. In frontier areas, speculators were naturally hated and took a risk if they showed their faces. A Methodist preacher recorded at Elkhorn Creek, Wisconsin: 'If a speculator should bid on a settler's farm, he was knocked down and dragged out of the [land] office, and if the striker was prosecuted and fined, the settlers paid the fine by common consent among themselves. [But] no jury would find a verdict against a settler in such a case because it was considered self-defense. [So] no speculator dare bid on a settler's land, and as no settler would bid on his neighbor, each man had his land at Congress price, $1.25 an acre.'

All the same, speculation and land dealing were the foundation of many historic fortunes at this time. And powerful politicians (and their friends) benefited too. . . . Of course some land speculation was parasitical and downright antisocial. But large-scale speculators were indispensable in many cases. They organized pressure on Congress to put through roads and they invested capital to build towns like Manchester, Portsmouth, Dayton, Columbus, and Williamsburg. . . .

There is an important historical and economic point to be noted here. Men always abuse freedom, and 19th-century land speculators could be wicked and predatory. But Congress, true to its origins, was prepared to take that risk. It laid down the ground rules by statute and then, in effect, allowed an absolutely free market in land to develop. It calculated that this was the best and quickest way to get the country settled. And it was proved right—freedom worked. In South Africa, Australia, New Zealand, and Canada, the British authorities interfered in the land market in countless ways and from the highest of motives, and as a result these countries—some of which had even bigger natural advantages than the United States—developed far more slowly. One British expert, H.G. Ward, who had witnessed both systems, made a devastating comparison before a House of Commons committee in 1839. In Canada, the government, fearing speculators, had devised a complex system of controls which actually played straight into their hands. By contrast, the American free system attracted multitudes who quickly settled and set up local governments which soon acted as a restraining force on antisocial operators. The system worked because it was simple and corresponded to market forces. 'There is one uniform price at $1.25 an acre [minimum]. No credit is given [by the federal government]. There is a perfect liberty of choice and appropriation at this price. Immense surveys are carried on, to an extent strangers have no conception of. Over 140 million acres have been mapped and planned at a cost of $2,164,000. There is a General Land Office in Washington with 40 subordinate district offices, each having a Registrar and Receiver. . . . Maps, plans and information of every kind are accessible to the humblest persons. . . . A man if he please may invest a million dollars in land. If he miscalculates it is his own fault. The public, under every circumstance, is the gainer.'

He was right and the proof that the American free system worked is the historic fact—the rapid and successful settlement of the Mississippi Valley. This is one of the decisive events in history. By means of it, America became truly dynamic, emerging from the eastern seaboard bounded by the Appalachians and descending into the great network of river valleys beyond. The Mississippi occupation, involving an area of 1,250,000 square miles, the size of western Europe, marked the point at which the United States ceased to be a small, struggling ex-colony and turned itself into a major nation.

ROADS AND GOVERNMENT

The speed with which representative governments were set up was an important part of this dynamism. In addition to Kentucky and Tennessee, the first trans-Appalachian states, Ohio became a state in 1803, Louisiana in 1812, Indiana in 1816, Mississippi in 1817, Illinois in 1818, Alabama in 1819, Missouri in 1821, Arkansas in1836, Michigan in 1837. Insuring rapid progress from territory to state was the best way Washington could help the settlement, though under the Constitution it could also build national roads. The first national road, a broad, hardened thoroughfare across the Appalachians, was open in 1818 as far as Wheeling, whence settlers could travel along the Ohio River. By the early 1830s the road had reached Columbus, Ohio. Further south, roads were built by state and federal government in collaboration or by thrusting military men like General Jackson, who in 1820, as commander of the Western Army, strung a road between Florence, Alabama, and New Orleans, the best route into the Lower Mississippi area. There were also the Great Valley Road, the Fall Line Road, and the Upper Federal Road. They were rough by the standards of the new McAdam–Telford roads in Britain but far superior to anything in Latin America, Australasia, or trans-Ural Russia, other vast territories being settled at this time. In addition there were the rivers, most of them facing in the direction of settlement. Even before the steamers came, there were hundreds, then thousands, of flatboats and keelboats to float settlers and their goods downriver. By 1830 there were already 3,000 flatboats floating down the Ohio each year. In 1825 the completion of the Erie Canal, which linked the Atlantic via the Hudson River to the Great Lakes, made easy access possible to the Great Plains. It also confirmed New York's primacy as a port, especially for immigrants, as they could then proceed, via the Canal, straight to new towns in the Midwest. From that point on steamboats were ubiquitous in the Mississippi Valley, not only bringing settlers in but taking produce out to feed and clothe the people of America's explosive cities—only 7 percent of the population in 1810, over a third by mid-century.

A CALL FOR THE HIGHER EDUCATION OF WOMEN

EMMA HART WILLARD

In the early nineteenth century the United States poured a significant amount of public resources into improving its educational institutions and raising educational standards. However, male students were the sole beneficiaries; women were not admitted to colleges or high schools, and the boarding or finishing schools that did exist for (mostly upper class) women concentrated on such subjects as painting and embroidery. During this time Emma Hart Willard became one of the most prominent voices for women's education. In 1814 she founded Middlebury Female Academy at her home in Vermont, where she taught her students geometry, classical philosophy, and other topics that previously had only been taught to men. A few years later, she wrote a pamphlet, *An Address to the Public; Particularly to the Members of the Legislature of New York, Proposing a Plan for Improving Female Education*, in which she called for the establishment of publicly supported schools ("seminaries") for women. The pamphlet gained the favorable attention of, among others, New York governor DeWitt Clinton, who invited her to move her academy to New York. The following is taken from her 1819 speech before the New York state legislature, in which she pleads for their support in establishing public educational institutions for women. Willard later moved to Troy, New York, where she founded and led the Troy Female Seminary. Among that school's early graduates was American feminist Elizabeth Cady Stanton.

Emma Hart Willard, "Education and the Weaker Sex," *Woman and the Higher Education*, edited by Anna C. Brackett, New York: Harper, 1893.

L et us now proceed to inquire what benefits would result from the establishment of female seminaries.

They would constitute a grade of public education superior to any yet known in the history of our sex; and through them, the lower grades of female instruction might be controlled. The influence of public seminaries over these would operate in two ways: first by requiring certain qualifications for entrance; and second by furnishing instructresses initiated in these modes of teaching and imbued with their maxims. Female seminaries might be expected to have important and happy effects on common schools in general; and in the manner of operating on these would probably place the business of teaching children into hands now nearly useless to society; and take it from those whose services the state wants in many other ways.

That nature designed for our sex the care of children, she has made manifest by mental as well as physical indications. She has given us, in a greater degree than men, the gentle arts of insinuation to soften their minds and fit them to receive impressions; a greater quickness of invention to vary modes of teaching to different dispositions; and more patience to make repeated efforts. There are many females of ability to whom the business of instructing children is highly acceptable; and who would devote all their faculties to their occupation. For they would have no higher pecuniary object to engage their attention; and their reputation as instructors they would consider as important. Whereas, whenever able and enterprising men engage in this business, they consider it merely as a temporary employment to further some object, to the attainment of which their best thoughts and calculations are all directed. If, then, women were properly fitted by instruction, they would be likely to teach children better than the other sex; they could afford to do it cheaper; and those men who would otherwise be engaged in this employment might be at liberty to add to the wealth of the nation, by any of those thousand occupations from which women are necessarily debarred.

But the females who taught children would have been themselves instructed either immediately or indirectly by the seminaries. Hence through these, the government might exercise an intimate and most beneficial control over common schools. Anyone who has turned his attention to this subject must be aware that there is great room for improvement in these, both as to the modes of teaching and the things taught; and what method could be devised so likely to effect this improvement as to prepare by instruction a class of individuals whose interest, leisure, and natural talents would combine to make them pursue it with ardor! Such a class of individuals would be raised up by female seminaries. And therefore they would be likely to have highly important and happy effects on common schools.

PRESERVING OUR GOVERNMENT

It is believed that such institutions would tend to prolong or perpetuate our excellent government.

An opinion too generally prevails that our present form of government, though good, cannot be permanent. Other republics have failed, and the historian and philosopher have told us that nations are like individuals; that at their birth, they receive the seeds of their decline and dissolution. Here, deceived by a false analogy, we receive an apt illustration of particular facts for a general truth. The existence of nations cannot, in strictness, be compared with the duration of animate life; for by the operation of physical causes, this, after a certain length of time, must cease. But the existence of nations is prolonged by the succession of one generation to another, and there is no physical cause to prevent this succession's going on, in a peaceable manner, under a good government, till the end of time. We must then look to other causes than necessity for the decline and fall of former republics. If we could discover these causes and seasonably prevent their operation, then might our latest posterity enjoy the same happy government with which we are blessed; or if but in part, then might the triumph of tyranny be delayed, and a few more generations be free.

Permit me, then, to ask the enlightened politician of any country whether, amid his researches for these causes, he cannot discover one in the neglect which free governments, in common with others, have shown to whatever regarded the formation of the female character.

In those great republics which have fallen of themselves, the loss of republican manners and virtues has been the invariable precursor of their loss of the republican form of government. But is it not the power of our sex to give society its tone, both as to manners and morals? And if such is the extent of female influence, is it wonderful that republics have failed when they calmly suffered that influence to become enlisted in favor of luxuries and follies wholly incompatible with the existence of freedom?

PREVENTING THE CORRUPTIONS OF WEALTH

It may be said that the depravation of morals and manners can be traced to the introduction of wealth as its cause. But wealth will be introduced; even the iron laws of Lycurgus could not prevent it. Let us then inquire if means may not be devised to prevent its bringing with it the destruction of public virtue. May not these means be found in education? in implanting in early youth habits that may counteract the temptations to which, through the influence of wealth, mature age will be exposed? and in giving strength and expansion to the mind, that it may comprehend and prize those principles which teach the rigid performance of duty? Education, it may be said, has been tried as a preservative of national purity. But was it applied to every exposed part of the body politic? For if any part has been left within the pestilential atmosphere of wealth without this preservative, then that part, becoming corrupted, would communicate the contagion to the whole; and if so, then has the experiment, whether education may not preserve public virtue, never yet been fairly tried. Such a part has been left in all former experiments.

Females have been exposed to the contagion of wealth without the preservative of a good education; and they constitute that part of the body politic least endowed by nature to resist, most to communicate it. Nay, not merely have they been left without the defense of a good education, but their corruption has been accelerated by a bad one. The character of women of wealth has been, and in the old governments of Europe now is, all that this statement would lead us to expect. Not content with doing nothing to promote their country's welfare, like pampered children they revel in its prosperity and scatter it to the winds with a wanton profusion. And still worse, they empoison its source, by diffusing a contempt for useful labor. To court pleasure their business, within her temple in defiance of the laws of God and man, they have erected the idol fashion; and upon her altar they sacrifice, with shameless rites, whatever is sacred to virtue or religion. Not the strongest ties of nature, not even maternal love can restrain them! Like the worshiper of Moloch, the mother, while yet yearning over the newborn babe, tears it from the bosom which God has swelled with nutrition for its support, and casts it remorseless from her, the victim of her unhallowed devotion!

But while with an anguished heart I thus depict the crimes of my sex, let not the other stand by and smile. Reason declares that you are guiltier than we. You are our natural guardians, our brothers, our fathers, and our rulers. You know that our ductile minds readily take the impressions of education. Why then have you neglected our education? Why have you looked with lethargic indifference on circumstances ruinous to the formation of other characters which you might have controlled?

But it may be said the observations here made cannot be applied to any class of females in our country. True, they cannot yet; and if they could, it would be useless to make them; for when the females of any country have become thus debased, then is that country so corrupted that nothing but the awful judgments of heaven can arrest its career of vice. But it cannot be denied that our manners are verging toward those described; and the change, though gradual, has not been slow; already do our daughters listen with surprise when we tell them of the republican simplicity of our mothers. But our manners are not as yet so altered, but that throughout our country they are still marked with republican virtues.

WHAT FEMALE EDUCATION CAN ACCOMPLISH

The inquiry to which these remarks have conducted us is this: what is offered by the plan of female education here proposed, which may teach or preserve among females of wealthy families that purity of manners which is allowed to be so essential to national prosperity, and so necessary to the existence of a republican government?

1. Females, by having their understandings cultivated, their reasoning powers developed and strengthened, may be expected to act more from the dictates of reason and less from those of fashion and caprice.

2. With minds thus strengthened they would be taught systems of morality, enforced by the sanctions of religion; and they might be expected to acquire juster and more enlarged views of their duty, and stronger and higher motives to its performance.

3. This plan of education offers all that can be done to preserve female youth from a contempt of useful labor. The pupils would become accustomed to it in conjunction with the high objects of literature and the elegant pursuits of the fine arts; and it is to be hoped that, both from habit and association, they might in future life regard it as respectable.

To this it may be added that if housewifery could be raised to a regular art, and taught upon philosophical principles, it would become a higher and more interesting occupation; and ladies of fortune, like wealthy agriculturists, might find that to regulate their business was an agreeable employment.

4. The pupils might be expected to acquire a taste for moral and intellectual pleasures, which would buoy them above a passion for show and parade, and which would make them seek to gratify the natural love of superiority, by endeavoring to excel others in intrinsic merit, rather than in the extrinsic frivolities of dress, furniture, and equipage.

5. By being enlightened in moral philosophy and in that which teaches the operations of the mind, females would be enabled to perceive the nature and extent of that influence which they possess over their children, and the obligation which this lays them under, to watch the formation of their characters with unceasing vigilance, to become their instructors, to devise plans for their improvement, to weed out the vices from their minds, and to implant and foster the virtues. And surely, there is that in the maternal bosom which, when its pleadings shall be aided by education, will overcome the seductions of wealth and fashion, and will lead the mother to seek her happiness in communing with her children and promoting their welfare, rather than in a heartless intercourse with the votaries of pleasure: especially when, with an expanded mind, she extends her views to futurity, and sees her care to her offspring rewarded by peace of conscience, the blessings of her family, the prosperity of her country, and finally with everlasting pleasure to herself and to them. . . .

NATIONAL GLORY

In calling on my patriotic countrymen to effect so noble an object, the consideration of national glory should not be overlooked. Ages have rolled away; barbarians have trodden the weaker sex beneath their feet; tyrants have robbed us of the present light of heaven, and fain would take its future. Nations calling themselves polite have made us the fancied idols of a ridiculous worship, and we have repaid them with ruin for their folly. But where is that wise and heroic country which has considered that our rights are sacred, though we cannot defend them? That though a weaker, we are an essential part of the body politic, whose corruption or improvement must effect the whole; and which, having thus considered, has sought to give us by education that rank in the scale of being to which our importance entitles us?

History shows not that country. It shows many whose legislatures have sought to improve their various vegetable productions and their breeds of useful brutes; but none whose public councils have made it an object of their deliberations to improve the character of their women. Yet though history lifts not her finger to such a one, anticipation does. She points to a nation which, having thrown off the shackles of authority and precedent, shrinks not from schemes of improvement because other nations have never attempted them; but which, in its pride of independence, would rather lead than follow in the march of human improvement: a nation, wise and magnanimous to plan, enterprising to undertake, and rich in resources to execute. Does not every American exult that this country is his own? And who knows how great and good a race of men may yet arise from the forming hand of mothers, enlightened by the bounty of that beloved country, to defend her liberties, to plan her future improvement, and to raise her to unparalleled glory.

SLAVERY AND THE MISSOURI QUESTION

DONALD R. WRIGHT

Historian Donald R. Wright describes how the issue of slavery, which had been submerged during the War of 1812, threatened to divide the nation following that war. Many northerners grew alarmed at the rapid growth of the U.S. slave population as cotton growers and planters settled in western lands and established the states of Alabama and Mississippi. When the territory of Missouri applied for statehood in 1819, its admission threatened to give the slave states a twelve-to-eleven edge and thus strengthen slaveowners' control of Congress. For months national leaders debated the "Missouri Question" before finally settling on a compromise that admitted Missouri as a slave state, Maine as a free state, and established a dividing line between free and slave territory in the rest of the land bought in the Louisiana Purchase. Wright also notes how the Missouri Compromise dismayed free African Americans, who were virtually prohibited from entering the new state. Wright teaches history at the State University of New York at Cortland, and has done historical research and writing in both African and African American history.

T he years following the War of 1812 were good ones for many Americans. International peace was at hand for the first time in years, a spirit of rapprochement was descending on Anglo-American relations, Spain agreed to a southern border favorable to the United States, the country seemed more united than ever before, and its economy was

Donald R. Wright, *African Americans in the Early Republic, 1789–1831*, Arlington Heights, IL: Harlan Davidson, 1993. Copyright © 1993 by Harlan Davidson, Inc. Reproduced by permission.

prospering. Following the unsettled quarter-century since the nation's beginning, the period after the War of 1812 seemed especially tranquil, and the tranquility showed in the American people's outlook and demeanor. Historians refer to the two-term presidency of James Monroe, between 1817 and 1825, as the Era of Good Feelings.

But the period of Monroe's presidency and the half dozen years that followed were not full of good feelings all around. This was a time when stormy national issues drew the public's attention to the very existence of slavery and to the future of the institution in the United States. The disagreement over these issues brought out fundamental differences between various elements of the white population, but between northerners and southerners generally, with frightening portents for the future. In the Era of Good Feelings lay some of the early groundwork for the disruption of the Union that ultimately would end slavery.

THE MISSOURI QUESTION

If slavery had been removed from the public eye during the years of the war, it came back into sharp focus after 1815. With the war's end and the annihilation or forced removal of most of the major Indian groups in the South, new lands for cotton growing opened and the domestic slave trade began to operate at unprecedented levels. It did not take long for the inhumane treatment of black men and women through their sale and relocation to catch humanitarians' attention. Then, with the rapid movement of planters and slaves into the Deep South, Mississippi and Alabama entered the Union as slave states in 1817 and 1819. Northerners, who had come to consider the Ohio River as the unofficial northern limit of slavery in the West, did not object. But when Missouri Territory petitioned for statehood as a slave state, a controversy arose first in Congress and then across the nation that awakened many persons, as it did Thomas Jefferson, "like a fire bell in the night." The Missouri question, Jefferson wrote to Massachusetts Congressman John Holmes, ". . . filled me with terror. I considered it at once the knell of the Union."

Whites in the North were alarmed at the rapid growth of the slave population—a dangerous, inassimilable element in the country's core, or so many of them believed, and a cheap labor force that might give the southern economy an advantage—and were still annoyed by the three-fifths compromise of the Constitution, which allowed a slave state to count 60 percent of its slave population in determining its due number of representatives in Congress. Once Alabama became part of the Union in 1819, there were eleven free and eleven slave states. Admission of Missouri as a slave state would give slave interests control of the Senate and still more disproportional weight in the House of Representatives. Who knew where the trend would stop?

It was with these matters in mind that New York Representative James Tallmadge, in February 1819, introduced an amendment to the Missouri Enabling Act to cease the further importation of slaves into the territory and to free all slaves in the new state once they reached the age of twenty-five. The amendment frightened and angered most southern congressmen, who were wary of losing their political influence and fearful of racial conflict that might occur if the South's fast-growing African-American population was confined to the present slave states. Some were probably concerned as well over what restricting slavery would do to slave prices over the long run. The House passed the act with Tallmadge's amendment, but the Senate, where southern influence was stronger, did not. Arguments in each chamber grew heated; congressmen and senators recklessly tossed about threats of disunion and civil war.

Then, between March and December 1819, while Congress was out of session, the "Missouri Question" became a national cause. State legislatures, counties and towns, antislavery groups, and southern apologists sent memorials to Congress, pressing one or another point of view. When the lawmakers reconvened in December, the tone of debate grew angrier still. Senator Rufus King of New York went beyond discussion of slavery's extension; he attacked the institution itself as "contrary to the law of nature, which is the law of God." (John Quincy Adams wrote in his diary that "the great slaveholders of the House gnawed their lips and clenched their fists as they heard him.") New Hampshire's Arthur Livermore showed how the Missouri debates prompted some of slavery's opponents to bring to full boil their long-simmering thoughts on the Constitution, slavery, and its extension into new territories. "Slavery is not established by our Constitution," Livermore argued. Instead he asserted, "a part of the States are indulged in the commission of a sin from which they could not at once be restrained, and which they would not consent to abandon." Congress had to allow slavery to continue where it existed, Livermore concluded, "for our boasted Constitution connives at it." But, he concluded, "liberty and equal rights are the end and aim of all our institutions, and . . . to tolerate slavery beyond the Constitution, is a perversion of them all."

Southerners rose to the occasion, defending their Constitutional guarantees of property rights and insisting that Congress lacked the authority to prohibit slavery's extension. The debates raged for months at unprecedented levels of intensity and employing language seldom heard before in either chamber.

FASHIONING A COMPROMISE

Eventually, congressmen worked out a compromise that, as we now know, served to put off the question of slavery's extension into new territories for a generation. (Jefferson recognized that the compromise was "a reprieve only, not a final sentence.") When Maine petitioned to enter the Union as a free state in 1820, the possibility of a compromise was apparent. Maine and Missouri could enter as free and slave states respectively, preserving the balance in the Senate. To make the compromise more palatable for House members and to prevent further conflict, Congress adopted Illinois Senator Jesse B. Thomas's proposal to prohibit slavery forever in all of the Louisiana Purchase north of Missouri's southern boundary (thirty-six degrees, thirty minutes north latitude). President Monroe signed the compromise legislation on March 6, 1820.

But that was not the end. The compromise nearly fell apart when Missourians drafted a state constitution that called for laws prohibiting free blacks from entering the state. This made for particularly thorny debate in Congress, because some northern states had laws that virtually did the same thing. More argument and delay ensued until, in an act that defied logic, Congress permitted Missouri to keep its constitutional clause excluding blacks so long as it would "never be construed to authorize the passage of any law discriminating against the citizens of another state" as Article IV, Section 2 of the federal Constitution prohibited. Thus did Missouri enter the Union in August 1821.

The Missouri question gave long pause to many thoughtful Americans. John Quincy Adams called it the "title page to a great tragic volume." Southerners had gained admission of Missouri and with it the extension of slavery into land that stretched northward to the same latitude as New York City— precisely where many northerners did not want it to go. Also, southerners had agreed to keep slavery out of a vast hunk of unorganized Indian territory that many thought impractical for slavery anyway. The only thing, then, that northerners gained was reinforcement of the principle, set down in the Northwest Ordinance of 1787, that Congress could prohibit slavery in the territories.

But the Missouri controversy had effects beyond the most obvious. For the first time since the country was formed, slavery was the topic of open, national debate. Although Congress focused only tangentially on the morality of slavery or the institution's right to exist where it was already established, persons away from the capitol did not limit their discussion. Budding abolitionists leaped into the debate; opinions on slavery filled newspaper columns across the country; and common people discussed it wherever they met—in general stores, livery stables, along the docks, or in drinking establishments. It turned out that southerners were right about one issue—such open questioning of slavery could indeed "contaminate" the minds of slaves. Denmark Vesey read about the Missouri debates and spoke his approval of King's strong speech before the Senate. Vesey began conspiring with Charleston blacks within months of the time Missouri had become a new slave state.

FREE BLACKS QUESTION THEIR PLACE IN SOCIETY

Moreover, the Missouri debates gave free blacks further reason to question their position in society. Free African Americans in the North were generally dismayed by approval of slavery's extension in Missouri. The compromise not only gave slavery new life in their eyes, but it practically prohibited any of their number from entering the state. And could they help but to recognize the hypocrisy of all the northerners who wished to prohibit slavery's extension but cared little for African Americans as people and for the rights of free blacks as citizens in the country?

The Missouri issue had a way of lingering, too. It seemed to convulse the internal politics of other states and to lie not far in the background when additional sectional matters caught the nation's attention. It clearly influenced happenings in Illinois. The state, whose southern half lay just east of Missouri, had entered the Union in 1818. A good portion of its population had proslavery leanings. Although the Northwest Ordinance forbade slavery in Illinois, the state's constitution contained elements that fairly defied that prohibition. The Illinois Constitution freed not one of the nine hundred slaves already there when the state entered the Union, leaving open the possibility of a future amendment to legalize slavery. With the debate over Missouri fresh in their minds, slave interests in Illinois in 1822 attempted to call a state legislative convention to make slavery legal. For nearly two years, proslavery and antislavery advocates from inside and outside Illinois fought over the effort. In the end a popular vote defeated the convention proposal by a margin of almost two thousand votes out of 11,500 cast. By the middle of the 1820s, while Illinois was no bastion of sentiment for black rights—it still carried "Black Codes" on its books that required free African Americans to register and carry certificates—it would not join the group of southern states that allowed slavery.

AMERICAN NATIONALISM AFTER THE WAR OF 1812

DON E. FEHRENBACHER

Historian Don E. Fehrenbacher provides an overview of the decade following the signing of the Treaty of Ghent in 1815, which ended the War of 1812 between the United States and Great Britain. He describes it as an era of nationalism in which Americans, given greater freedom from interference from Great Britain and other European powers, turned their energies inward into occupying a growing area in the North American continent. In foreign affairs, the United States acquired Florida from Spain and recognized the young Latin American republics that had declared independence from Spain. President James Monroe in an 1823 message to Congress expressed American opposition to all European colonization in the Western Hemisphere. His pronouncement became known as the Monroe Doctrine. In domestic affairs, the Federalist Party faded from the scene, even as tariffs, a national bank, and other ideas originally proposed by Federalist leader Alexander Hamilton became accepted national policy. Fehrenbacher concludes that much of the national unity celebrated in the so-called "era of good feelings" was superficial and contained seeds of future conflict. Fehrenbacher was a longtime Stanford University history professor and the author of several books on American history, including *The Dred Scott Case: Its Significance in American Law and Politics.*

Don E. Fehrenbacher, *The Era of Expansion: 1800–1848*, New York: John Wiley & Sons, 1969. Copyright © 1969 by Don E. Fehrenbacher. Reproduced by permission.

Indecisive though the War of 1812 had been, its conclusion introduced a new period of American history. The Treaty of Ghent, coinciding with the end of the long conflict in Europe, signaled the release of powerful internal forces from the restraints previously imposed by external dangers. In addition, the mood of the country was being set more and more by a generation born since the Declaration of Independence and less responsive to European influences. "Nationalism," the word commonly used to characterize the postwar years, is accurate within limits and appropriate in more than one sense.

After 1815, the attention of the American people turned inward to domestic matters and the work of occupying a continent. Disentanglement from the political fortunes of the Old World had been an unattainable objective during the preceding decades, but now there began a century of comparative isolation and security for the United States, paralleled by a century of comparative peace in Europe. Against threats from abroad, the nation was protected by the same Atlantic Ocean that had been the scene of so much conflict. At the same time, dangers nearer home were progressively reduced by the elimination or neutralization of European power in the Western Hemisphere. The critical factor in both cases was the benevolent influence, only partly intended, of British strength and British foreign policy.

The Treaty of Ghent left Britain and the United States facing each other across a long border, but with increased mutual respect and a pronounced willingness to settle disputes by negotiation. Canada was still British and still vulnerable to American attack—a virtual hostage to peace that offset the supremacy of the Royal Navy in times of stress. The Rush-Bagot agreement of 1817, limiting the number of armed vessels on the Great Lakes, proved to be the first step in the establishment of an "unguarded frontier." A convention signed the following year redrew the northwestern boundary along the 49th parallel from the Lake of the Woods to the Rocky Mountains and provided for joint occupation of the Oregon country beyond. Disagreements and occasional crises continued to disturb Anglo-American relations throughout the century, but the disposition to negotiate instead of fight became a fixed habit.

To the south, meanwhile, the vast Spanish empire was falling apart. During the years 1810 to 1813, while Spain struggled in the grasp of Napoleon and revolution spread through Latin America, the United States had seized West Florida. Spanish control of East Florida was also precarious, and American acquisition seemed to be only a matter of time. Indian troubles along the border led to an invasion of the colony in 1818 by federal troops under Andrew Jackson. This aggressive action helped to convince officials in Madrid that they could no longer resist American demands. In the Adams-Onis Treaty of 1819, Spain surrendered Florida, together with her claims to the Pacific Northwest. The United States, in return, agreed to assume as much as $5 million of private American claims against the Spanish government, and it also renounced a dubious claim to Texas as part of the Louisiana Purchase. Spanish procrastination delayed ratification of the treaty until 1821. By that time, Mexico had won its fight for independence, and the flag of Spain no longer flew anywhere on the North American continent.

The belief that America's destiny was different from Europe's destiny dated back to colonial times, but in the setting of the postwar years it acquired added relevance and force. National confidence was resurgent, the national domain had been extended, and many parts of the New World were imitating the United States in throwing off European rule. The American government formally recognized the young Latin American republics in 1822. Then, one year later, President James Monroe gave classic expression to the concept of separate hemispheres.

THE MONROE DOCTRINE

The famous Monroe Doctrine originated as nothing more than several paragraphs in the President's annual message to Congress of December 2, 1823. Written in collaboration with Secretary of State John Quincy Adams, it dealt with two distinct problems. One was the threat of Russian expansion on the Northwest Coast. More important were the indications that Spain might receive help from certain other European powers in reconquering some of her lost colonies. The British government, desiring to keep the new Latin American markets open, offered to join the United States in a declaration opposing such intervention, but Adams argued successfully for an independent pronouncement. With Russia in mind, Monroe first asserted that the American continents were "henceforth not to be considered as subjects for future colonization by any European powers." Then, maintaining that the political systems of the Old and New Worlds were "essentially different" from each other, he warned that any attempt by European monarchies to subdue the Latin American

republics would be regarded as "the manifestation of an un-
friendly disposition toward the United States." At the same time,
the American government would continue to refrain from in-
terfering in the "internal concerns" of European nations.

These bold words amounted to a statement of unilateral policy without much effective force, and the immediate practical
effects were relatively slight. Negotiations with Russia, already
well advanced, soon produced a treaty fixing the southern
boundary of Alaska at 54°40´. As for the Latin American republics, it was primarily the sea power of a hostile Britain that
compelled Spain and her allies to abandon their vague schemes
of reconquest. Not until many years later would the Monroe
Doctrine be translated into action. Furthermore, despite its un-
selfish tone and hemispheric scope, the document was essentially a manifestation of ebullient nationalism. Here, something
not said in Monroe's message is especially significant. Nowhere
did he bind the United States itself to the principles of noncol-
onization and nonintervention in Latin America. The British
government had included a self-denying provision in its general proposal for joint action, but American leaders, with their
eyes on Cuba and Texas, were not to be caught in such a trap.
Thus the Monroe Doctrine extended the horizons of American
ambition and served as a preface to Manifest Destiny.

Nationalism in the form of disengagement from Europe can
also be seen in postwar efforts to obtain a larger measure of economic self-sufficiency and in appeals for cultural independence.
Yet the United States continued to be, in many respects, a colonial society, still heavily dependent upon the Old World for
markets, manufactured goods, capital, people, ideas, and tastes.
The reorientation that began in 1815 was more a shift of attention than a renunciation. Indeed, it may be regarded as the natural sequel of the Revolution, delayed for two decades by the
abnormal condition of world affairs.

TRANSITIONAL YEARS

In its internal aspect, the nationalism of this period seemed to
confirm [Alexander] Hamilton's design for the Republic. With
patriotism vindicated at New Orleans and sectional feeling dis-
credited at Hartford, the country was apparently ready to accept vigorous leadership from the federal government. Congress responded by enacting a protective tariff, establishing a
new national bank, and proposing to subsidize construction of

inland transportation facilities. Thus the Jeffersonians continued to appropriate the old Federalist program. Yet this change
of attitude, which had begun before the war, fell far short of being a complete surrender to the Hamiltonian ideal of a consol-
idated state. The decade after 1815 was a time of contradictory
tendencies and shifting allegiances in which nationalism as the
equivalent of centralization actually made little headway.

The responsibilities of power had caused the Jeffersonians to
set aside their worst fears of the central government and to compromise some of their old constitutional principles. They had
even come eventually to a grudging acceptance of the Bank of
the United States. [President James] Madison and his Secretary
of the Treasury, Albert Gallatin, recommended renewal of the
Bank's charter when it expired in 1811, but a combination of
hostile groups in Congress defeated the necessary legislation.
The lack of a fiscal agent severely handicapped the government
during the War of 1812. Accordingly, Congress reversed itself in
1816 by establishing a second Bank of the United States, with
authorized capitalization of $35 million and the government a
one-fifth shareholder. Enemies of the institution were not si-
lenced, however. The battle merely shifted to the state level,
where the various branches of the Bank often met fierce opposition from local enterprise, As an expression of nationalism, the
revival of the Bank was a very limited victory at best.

Expediency also governed the tariff legislation of 1816. In-
dustries, stimulated by the long interruption of normal trade
with Europe, suddenly faced ruinous competition from abroad
after the war. In setting the rates on dutiable goods at 15 to 30
percent ad valorem, Congress was meeting an obvious need
and making only a moderate concession to the principle of protection. The act consequently received support from all parts of
the nation—even from many Southerners, like John C. Calhoun,
who expected their section to share in the benefits. Circumstances soon produced dramatic changes, however. In spite of
the tariff, imports from Europe continued to flood the United
States, and the Panic of 1819 introduced a period of widespread
economic distress. Western farmers and urban workers now
joined the manufacturing interests in demanding higher duties
to protect their respective products. Meanwhile, with the cotton
kingdom expanding rapidly and depending more and more
upon the foreign market, Southerners closed ranks in bitter hostility to protection. Thus feelings on both sides were sharply in-

tensified, and the tariff became an explosive sectional issue in the 1820s.

INTERNAL IMPROVEMENTS AND THE SUPREME COURT

More nationalistic in its implications than the Bank or the tariff was Calhoun's Bonus Bill of 1817, earmarking certain government funds for internal improvements. As a precedent, supporters of the measure could point to the Cumberland Road, authorized during [President Thomas] Jefferson's administration and still under construction. Jefferson, in fact, had recommended an extensive system of federal roads and canals, but with the assumption that it would require an amendment to the Constitution. Calhoun's argument that such expenditures were permissible under the general welfare clause did not convince Madison, who vetoed the Bonus Bill, even though he approved of its purpose. His successor, Monroe, displayed the same constitutional scruples. Internal-improvements legislation also met persistent opposition from New England and the Old South, sections that had little to gain from rapid development of the West. A comprehensive federal program therefore never materialized, and the task of providing transportation facilities was left, for the most part, to the states and private enterprise.

It was the Supreme Court that gave the most emphatic expression to the spirit of nationalism during the postwar decade. John Marshall's decision in *McCulloch v. Maryland* (1819) upheld the constitutionality of the Bank of the United States and rescued it from excessive state taxation. More than that, in ringing phrases Marshall asserted the Hamiltonian doctrine of implied powers and broad construction of the Constitution. In *Cohens v. Virginia* (1821), the Court reaffirmed its authority to review decisions of state courts, and in *Gibbons v. Ogden* (1824), it laid down a broad definition of federal power under the commerce clause. The Dartmouth College decision (1819) extended the meaning of "contract" to include a corporate charter, thus interposing a clause of the Constitution as a protective screen between the authority of a state government and the private rights of its own citizens. The general effect of this judicial nationalism was to place immediate restraints upon the states and to lay the foundation for later expansion of federal power. The posture of the Court is commonly attributed to Marshall's success in imposing Federalist principles upon his Republican colleagues, but it also reflected the significant changes in Jeffersonian thinking that had occurred since 1800.

AN APPEARANCE OF NATIONAL CONSENSUS

In politics after the War of 1812, there was a deceptive appearance of national consensus. With Madison's second term drawing to a close in 1816, the Republican congressional caucus nominated Secretary of State James Monroe for the presidency. Monroe won an easy victory in what proved to be the last stand, nationally, of the Federalist party. Four years later, he was reelected with just one dissenting vote in the electoral college. Republican ascendancy had become complete and therefore much less meaningful. The disappearance of organized Federalist opposition put an end, temporarily, to party politics and left faction as the only vehicle of partisanship. Underneath the semblance of unity in the so-called "era of good feelings," a process of fragmentation was erasing the Republican synthesis and introducing a political revolution.

Indeed, the almost unanimous presidential election of 1820 took place during the later stages of a violent controversy that had cut an angry and ominous gash across the nation. Early in 1819, when the application of Missouri for admission to statehood came before Congress, an antislavery amendment to the enabling act aligned Northerners against Southerners in a legislative struggle that lasted two years. Here was the very issue that would eventually disrupt the Union. It aroused Federalist hopes and revealed the thinness of the Republican consensus, but sectional loyalties were not yet strong enough to transform politics. This first great conflict over slavery ended in compromise. Congress admitted Missouri as a slave state and Maine (separated from Massachusetts) as a free state, thus preserving the sectional balance. More important for the future, slavery was forbidden north of 36°30′ in the remainder of the Louisiana Purchase. These arrangements seemed to settle the dangerous issue completely and permanently. The sectional confrontation therefore ceased, and politics returned to familiar channels.

Monroe presided over a period of such change, complexity, and contradiction that it cannot be summed up with a label or descriptive phrase. The glow of postwar nationalism, for instance, was never universal, and it soon began to fade. Yet sectional rivalry did not dominate the scene, except in the Missouri episode. The interests of each section were shifting rapidly, and attitudes had only partly congealed. For political parties, too, it was a time of transition. The superficial harmony of Monroe's presidential tenure signified the inadequacy of old alignments and issues, not a decline of partisanship. This, the election of 1824 would clearly reveal. In a republic of free men, as the Jeffersonians had demonstrated, one party was not enough.

The Jacksonian Age, 1824–1840

CHAPTER 3

ANDREW JACKSON AND JACKSONIAN DEMOCRACY

JOHN E. FINDLING AND FRANK W. THACKERAY

Historians John E. Findling and Frank W. Thackeray provide an overview of the political career of Andrew Jackson, a presidential candidate in 1824 and president from 1829 to 1837 whose name came to signify the era. Jackson, a folk hero who rose from an impoverished childhood in the Tennessee frontier to become a noted military commander and landowner, personified the growing democratization of American government. His election in 1828 involved a far greater number of voters than previous elections as states extended the right to vote to men without property (females and minorities were still excluded). As president, Jackson instituted the "spoils system" by which he replaced numerous federal workers with his own political supporters. He also became involved in a bitter conflict with the Bank of the United States and its president, Nicholas Biddle. Jackson's handpicked successor, Martin van Buren, lacked Jackson's personal charisma and endured a troubled administration after a economic depression swept the nation in 1837—a depression caused in part by the closing of the Bank of the United States. Findling and Thackeray are both professors of history at Indiana University Southeast at New Albany.

N amed for Andrew Jackson, the noted War of 1812 veteran and Indian fighter from Tennessee who served as president from 1829 to 1837, Jacksonian democracy rep-

John E. Findling and Frank W. Thackeray, "Jacksonian Democracy, 1828–1840," *Events That Changed America in the Nineteenth Century*, Westport, CT: Greenwood Press, 1997. Copyright © 1997 by Greenwood Press. Reproduced by permission.

resented a new and different concept of the nature and responsibilities of the federal government. Jacksonian democracy was
seen primarily in a greater sense of democratic participation in
the government and in a reduction of federal responsibility, particularly with respect to the nation's economic system.

Andrew Jackson had lost the 1824 presidential election to
John Quincy Adams in a close and controversial contest that
was decided in the House of Representatives. Although Jackson had received a plurality of electoral votes in the general
election, he had fallen short of a majority, and when third-place
finisher Henry Clay shifted his support to Adams in the House
of Representatives vote, it was sufficient to vault the former secretary of state into the White House. Although many at the time
thought a secret deal had been made between Adams and Clay,
especially since Clay became Adams's secretary of state, no hard
evidence has ever been found to prove what was called a "corrupt bargain."

THE 1828 ELECTION

Jackson was not a man to forget or forgive, however, and he
came back with a vengeance in the election of 1828. This campaign was the first in which personal attacks played a role. Jackson's campaign spread the word that Adams had installed a bil-
liards table and a chess set in the White House and claimed that
the White House now contained "gaming tables and gambling
furniture." Adams's campaign retaliated with tales about Jackson's frontier brawls and, worse, Jackson's alleged premarital
relations with the woman he later married. Possibly because of
the stress of these personal attacks, Jackson's wife died soon after the election and never lived in the White House.

Adams had not had a very successful presidency, and that,
combined with Jackson's heroic military exploits, was enough
to carry the day. Jackson won states in every region of the country and, to use the present-day term, clearly won a national
"mandate" to govern. And with Jackson's highly personalized
presidency came that which is known as Jacksonian democracy.

The process of democratization that is central to Jacksonian
democracy was clear in the election itself. Between 1810 and
1820, six new states had entered the union with constitutions
that contained no property qualifications for voting; other states
liberalized their qualifications. The result was that the number
of voters increased from just 355,000 in 1824 to 1.16 million in

1828. Over the next 20 years, the number voting jumped to nearly 3 million, an increase far greater than can be accounted for by population growth.

In more general terms, other changes were accomplished in the political system. The increase in population in the West, along with the economic distress that followed the panic of 1819, showed the need for electing officials who would represent the true interests of the majority. Through the growth of free public education and a cheap press during this time, the common man became much more aware of the political system and what it could do to protect or advance his opportunities in society.

Andrew Jackson

One immediate result was the scrapping of the old system of nominating presidential candidates through a congressional caucus, a process that the public now viewed as remote and aristocratic. Additionally growing sectional conflicts made it more difficult for the caucus to achieve consensus on a single candidate. Consequently, parties turned to the national party convention during this time, a move that allowed far more democratic participation and deliberation. By the time Jackson left office, all parties were holding conventions on a regular basis.

Although Jackson was not nominated at a party convention, he nevertheless personified the democratic movement. He was the first president from outside the Virginia or Massachusetts aristocracy. Born on the Tennessee frontier, he was of humble origins, and the people loved him for it. His military victory at the Battle of New Orleans in 1815, moreover, had made him a kind of folk hero, a symbol of American valor and nationalism. And he looked the part—tall and lean, with a hawklike frontier face and a thatch of thick white hair. He was quick to anger and slow to forgive, and he had been in more than one duel. He was known for his chivalrous attitude toward "the fair," and his excellent manners, provided he kept his temper.

Jacksonian democracy would not allow for class distinction, so all were invited to the White House inauguration party, and some 10,000 people showed up, standing on chairs with muddy boots, fighting for the limited refreshments, and breaking glass and porcelain. Jackson escaped the mob by climbing out a window, and the guests were induced to leave the White House by the ploy of placing large tubs of punch out on the lawn.

THE SPOILS SYSTEM

More serious events during the early months of Jackson's presidency contributed to the idea of Jacksonian democracy. One issue was the nature of bureaucratic appointments and the spoils system, the process of replacing public servants from the previous administration with loyal supporters of the new administration. Although the spoils system had been common practice at the state level for some time, Jackson is particularly identified with it. He was the first to discard bureaucrats on a wide scale at the national level for no other reason than to reward deserving Democrats, and the haste with which he did it was alarming. In the end, he removed only 252 of 612 presidential appointments, but the Adams people were shocked, and Adams charged that it made government "a perpetual and unintermitting scramble for office."

Jackson, however, considered it a positive good—a reform. To him, it was the rooting out of a permanent office-holding class. He felt that most bureaucratic jobs were simple and routine enough that any citizen with average intelligence could adequately perform them and that the country gained more from the rotation of bureaucrats than it did from having experienced people in the offices. Thus, old and able Jeffersonians were replaced by young and often disreputable Jacksonians, the worst of whom was one Samuel Swartout, who became the collector of customs of the port of New York. He managed to steal over $1 million before he was caught. The spoils system endured on a large scale until the 1880s, when civil service reform was introduced, and it still continues to some degree.

Jackson's belief in greater democracy became apparent in his dealings with Congress. He conceived of himself as a national leader responsible to the people as a whole. Presidents before him had been content simply to administer laws Congress passed; Jackson, however, vetoed more legislation in his two terms than all his predecessors combined. He was also the first to take advantage of the pocket veto: the provision that permits a president to kill a measure passed fewer than ten days before the adjournment of Congress simply by withholding his signature. In reply to charges of presidential usurpation of power, Jackson maintained that he needed to use his office as a bulwark against aristocratic establishments and powerful monopolies. He favored what he called a "plain system" of government, "void of pomp—protecting all and granting favors to none—dispensing its blessings, like the dews of heaven, unseen and unfelt save in the freshness and beauty they contribute to produce."

THE BANK CONTROVERSY

In the 1832 presidential election that matched Jackson, running for his second term, against Henry Clay, the Bank of the United States was the major issue. The bank had been chartered in 1816 for a 20-year period to handle federal finances, issue national bank notes, and maintain financial stability in the country, but many were critical of the bank for its refusal to honor the paper money of state banks, which often was overissued relative to the real value of the bank's assets. Jackson had at first favored the Bank of the United States, but by 1832, he had come to doubt both its constitutionality and its value to the country. He believed it operated in the spirit of monopoly, and he hated monopolies. Nevertheless, he was reluctant to attack the bank because several of its supporters sat in his cabinet and because the bank did provide certain useful services for the country. Jackson instead contented himself with pressuring Nicholas Biddle, the bank's president, to place more administration people on the bank's payroll. Biddle resisted, fearing that the bank would fall under the spoils system, and instead he tried to influence key members of Congress by offering them advances on their salaries or low-interest loans. Among the bank's friends in Congress were Henry Clay, who saw political advantage in siding with the institution, and Daniel Webster, who earned a handsome fee serving as the bank's legal adviser.

Biddle's lobbying efforts only made the stubborn Jackson more determined to get rid of the bank when its charter came up for renewal in 1836. In early 1832, the bank's supporters in Congress decided to make the renewal of its charter a central campaign issue by bringing forward a bill for renewal four years early. They reasoned that the bank was so popular in the country that Jackson would have no choice but to sign the renewal if he expected to be reelected. But Jackson told his vice president, Martin Van Buren, "The Bank, Mr. Van Buren, is trying to kill me, but I will kill it." And so he vetoed the renewal bill, concluding in his veto message that the bank was neither necessary, nor proper, nor constitutional. Biddle thought Jackson's message was so outrageous that he circulated it as pro-bank propaganda during the campaign, but Jackson was an easy winner in the election, which he took as a mandate to carry on against Biddle's "Hydra of corruption."

Over the next four years, Jackson and Biddle battled over the status of the bank. Biddle thought that Jackson might withdraw government funds from it and so used a good part of those already on deposit to make even more loans and publicize the bank's virtues in the press. Jackson became convinced that federal funds were not safe in the bank and, after some political infighting with his cabinet, succeeded in placing most government money in selected state banks.

Biddle responded by launching a campaign to restrict credit and create enough financial distress in the country to force the president to change his policies. Although Biddle did manage to create some distress, Jackson was able to turn the blame on Biddle, who in 1834 was forced to retreat from his campaign at the urging of his friends in the business community. But by this time, it was too late; the battle between Biddle and Jackson had caused irreparable damage to the economy. Two years of unrestrained land speculation on the part of the state banks, fat with federal funds, followed. To try to halt this, Jackson issued the Specie Circular in 1836, requiring that all land payments to the government be in specie, or gold and silver. This decision made the paper money that state banks issued virtually worthless, and almost overnight land sales collapsed, followed in 1837 by a disastrous fall in stock and commodity prices and the worst economic downturn of the century. Jackson left office two months before the onset of the economic crisis and thus escaped most of the blame for the troubles, which fell on the administration of his handpicked successor, Martin Van Buren. Hoping to lead people out of oppression, Jackson led them into depression.

JACKSON'S SUCCESSOR

Van Buren entered office in March 1837 riding the crest of Jackson's popularity, but the depression that began later in the year dominated his single term. Van Buren's solution to restore confidence in the banking system and the crippled economy was something called the Independent Treasury System, whereby federal funds would be taken from banks and placed in subtreasuries around the country. Receipts from customs duties and federal land sales would also be deposited in the subtreasuries, and government expenditures would be made in cash. The idea would have protected government funds and discouraged speculation, but it would have taken much specie out of circulation, which would have hurt business. Still, Van Buren managed to push the measure through Congress in 1840, and it, along with the depression, cost him reelection in November of that year. The next administration did away with the Independent Treasury System, the economy recovered mostly on its own, and one of Jackson's legacies passed from the scene. Not until the Civil War would the nation see another centralized national banking system.

Jackson's was a flawed presidency, but it was a significant one. He reshaped the whole character of the office by his belief in greater democracy and by his own autocratic and imperious style. As Van Buren and many others who followed him discovered, Jackson was a hard act to follow.

Jackson's Inauguration

Margaret Bayard Smith

Margaret Bayard Smith was for many years one of the leading
social figures of Washington, D.C. The wife of a journalist and
government official, she frequently entertained prominent public officials at her home. Smith was also a prolific writer whose
works included novels, magazine articles, and personal letters.
The following excerpt from one of her letters (which were collected and published posthumously) describes the events surrounding the presidential inauguration of Andrew Jackson. She
notes how thousands of people gathered "without distinction
of rank" at both the inauguration and subsequent reception at
the White House. While the inauguration itself was an inspir-
ingly reverent affair, she writes, the following reception soon
degenerated into a riot.

I left the rest of this sheet for an account of the inauguration.
It was not a thing of detail of a succession of small incidents.
No, it was one grand whole, an imposing and majestic spectacle and to a reflective mind one of moral sublimity. Thousands
and thousands of people, without distinction of rank, collected
in an immense mass round the Capitol, silent, orderly and tranquil, with their eyes fixed on the front of that edifice, waiting
the appearance of the President in the portico. The door from
the Rotunda opens, preceded by the marshals, surrounded by
the Judges of the Supreme Court, the old man with his grey
locks, that crown of glory, advances, bows to the people, who
greet him with a shout that rends the air, the Cannons, from the

Margaret Bayard Smith, *The First Forty Years of Washington Society*, edited by Gaillard
Hunt, New York: Charles Scribner's Sons, 1906.

heights around, from Alexandria and Fort Warburton proclaim the oath he has taken and all the hills reverberate the sound. It was grand,—it was sublime! An almost breathless silence, succeeded and the multitude was still,—listening to catch the sound of his voice, tho' it was so low, as to be heard only by those nearest to him. After reading his speech, the oath was administered to him by the Chief Justice. The Marshal presented the Bible. The President took it from his hands, pressed his lips to it, laid it reverently down, then bowed again to the people— Yes, to the people in all their majesty. And had the spectacle closed here, even Europeans must have acknowledged that a free people, collected in their might, silent and tranquil, restrained solely by a moral power, without a shadow around of military force, was majesty, rising to sublimity, and far surpassing the majesty of Kings and Princes, surrounded with armies and glittering in gold. But I will not anticipate, but will give you an account of the inauguration in mere detail. The whole of the preceding day, immense crowds were coming into the city from all parts, lodgings could not be obtained, and the newcomers had to go to George Town, which soon overflowed and others had to go to Alexandria. I was told the Avenue and adjoining streets were so crowded on Tuesday afternoon that it was difficult to pass.

A RIOTOUS RECEPTION

A national salute was fired early in the morning, and ushered in the 4th of March. By ten oclock the Avenue was crowded with carriages of every description, from the splendid Barronet and coach, down to waggons and carts, filled with women and children, some in finery and some in rags, for it was the people's President, and all would see him. . . . Some one came and informed us the crowd before the President's house, was so far lessen'd, that they thought we might enter. This time we effected our purpose. But what a scene did we witness! *The Majesty of the People* had disappeared, and a rabble, a mob, of boys, negros, women, children, scrambling, fighting, romping. What a pity what a pity! No arrangements had been made no police officers placed on duty and the whole house had been inundated by the rabble mob. We came too late. The President, after having been *literally* nearly pressed to death and almost suffocated and torn to pieces by the people in their eagerness to shake hands with Old Hickory, had retreated through the back way or south front and had escaped to his lodgings at Gadsby's. Cut glass and china to the amount of several thousand dollars had been broken in the struggle to get the refreshments, punch and other articles had been carried out in tubs and buckets, but had it been in hogsheads it would have been insufficient, ice-creams, and cake and lemonade, for 20,000 people, for it is said that number were there, tho' I think the estimate exaggerated. Ladies fainted, men were seen with bloody noses and such a scene of confusion took place as is impossible to describe,— those who got in could not get out by the door again, but had to scramble out of windows. At one time, the President who had retreated and retreated until he was pressed against the wall, could only be secured by a number of gentlemen forming round him and making a kind of barrier of their own bodies, and the pressure was so great that Col Bomford who was one said that at one time he was afraid they should have been pushed down, or on the President. It was then the windows were thrown open, and the torrent found an outlet, which otherwise might have proved fatal.

This concourse had not been anticipated and therefore not provided against. Ladies and gentlemen, only had been expected at this Levee, not the people en masse. But it was the People's day, and the People's President and the People would rule. God grant that one day or other, the People, do not put down all rule and rulers.

THE RISE OF THE TWO-PARTY SYSTEM

GEOFFREY C. WARD

In the following essay, Geoffrey C. Ward describes the evolution of American presidential campaigns from 1824 to 1840. Previous elections had been relatively quiet affairs in which the American people played little direct role. This changed as voting became a right of all white men, rather than a privilege of those who owned property. In 1828 supporters of Andrew Jackson organized an unprecedented political effort to turn out votes for their candidate. The campaign formed the basis of the Democratic Party. By 1840 Jackson's opponents—called Whigs—had learned from their previous failures and outdid the Democrats in organizing mass rallies and running a populist campaign for their candidate, William Harrison. Ward is a writer and historian best known for his work in television documentaries, including the 1990 television series *The Civil War*.

"Politicks at the present time are the all-engrossing topic of discourse," wrote a young New Hampshireman named Benjamin Brown French as the presidential election got underway in 1828. "... In the ballroom, or at the dinner table, in the Stagecoach & in the tavern; even the social chitchat of the tea table must yield to the everlasting subject."

There was nothing new in that. Americans had always been intensely interested in how they were governed, even though at first most of them played little direct part in any of it: Candidates for President and Vice President were selected in private by congressional caucuses, and most members of the Electoral

Geoffrey C. Ward, "The Man Who . . . ," *We Americans: Celebrating a Nation, Its People, and Its Past*, edited by Thomas B. Allen and Charles O. Hyman, Washington, DC: National Geographic Society, 1999. Copyright © 1999 by National Geographic Society. Reproduced by permission.

College who chose the winner were themselves picked by state legislators, not by ordinary voters. There were no party conventions, no mass meetings, no catchy slogans. All of the country's first six Presidents had been more or less polished aristocrats—two members of the same distinguished Massachusetts clan and four wealthy Virginia planters. James Monroe was reelected without any opposition at all in 1820, and until 1824 no one even bothered to keep an official count of the popular vote.

But now everything had suddenly changed. What alarmed Benjamin French and a good many others in 1828 was that for the first time in American history two full-fledged national parties were waging what seemed something like an all-out war on one another, a clamorous war of unsubstantiated charges, character assassination, and out-and-out lies. "I . . . tremble with apprehension that our Constitution will not long withstand the current which threatens to overwhelm it . . . ," French wrote. "[T]he rancorous excitement which now threatens our civil liberties and a dissolution of this Union does not emanate from an *honest* difference, but from a determination of an unholy league to trample down an Administration, be it ever so pure, & be its acts ever so just."

THE FOUNDERS' WORST FEARS

French's alarm would have been understood by the Founding Fathers whose worst fears about their republic seemed to be coming true. They had been certain that the growth of political parties or "factions" would lead to demagoguery, mob rule, and dictatorship. It was the task of politics to repress factional division, they argued, and Presidents were meant to be selfless, nonpartisan patriots who embodied the hopes and dreams of the whole people. To help insure the election of such paragons, they hoped the vote would remain a privilege, limited exclusively to men of means, property-owning, taxpaying citizens who had an economic stake in calm and stability. And they assumed the whole business would be conducted in a staid, dignified manner befitting its importance to the country.

But the country grew much faster than its founders had imagined it would, and by the 1820s, beginning with Ohio, the new Western states adopted constitutions that granted the vote to all white males over 21, whatever the contents of their pocketbooks. Older states, worried that the greater freedoms offered in the West would lure away their citizenry, dropped their property ownership requirements, too. By 1828, in every state but one, the people—not the legislature—picked the presidential electors. The vote was fast becoming a right, not a privilege.

Four men had run for President in 1824, all of them at least nominally members of the original Republican Party founded by Thomas Jefferson. One of three Americans then lived west of the Alleghenies. Most of them had favored the candidacy of Andrew Jackson, a blunt, self-taught military hero from Tennessee whom they considered one of their own. Jackson received the largest number—but not a majority—of both the popular and electoral votes, yet lost the Presidency to John Quincy Adams in the House of Representatives. Both Jackson and his supporters were enraged, convinced they had been the victims of a conspiracy among aristocrats seeking power to pursue their own selfish ends.

THE 1828 ELECTION

Charging that a "corrupt bargain" had thwarted the people's will, Jackson's supporters vowed revenge. Organized as a new national Democratic Party, they were determined to turn out an unprecedented popular vote and put their man in the White House four years later. Jackson himself played no active part in their efforts. It was still considered unseemly for a man to appear to want the job too much. "I have no doubt if I was to travel to Boston where I have been invited that would insure my election," he had told a friend during the 1824 race. "But this I cannot do. I would feel degraded the balance of my life." Still, he did now consent to travel by steamboat to New Orleans to commemorate the 13th anniversary of his victory over the British in 1815 on the grounds that this was a purely patriotic occasion. He was rewarded with an outpouring of affection and gratitude.

Then Jackson returned to his plantation home near Nashville, refused all requests for his views on any topic, and let his lieutenants go to work behind the scenes. Perhaps the ablest was a diminutive New York politician named Martin Van Buren, whose air of mystery and shrewd organizing skills earned him the nickname the Little Magician. With his help, the Jackson campaign was launched simultaneously all across the country on July 4, 1827. Americans had never seen anything like it. "The *Hurra Boys* [are] for Jackson . . . ," one disgusted Adams man complained, "and all the noisey *Turbulent Boisterous* politicians are with him." There were torchlight processions and mass meetings that drew thousands to hear orators praise their hero and charge his opponent with everything from being overly fond of "kingly pomp and splendour" to pimping for the czar of Russia. There were free cookouts, too, from which those too fastidious "to grease their fingers with a barbecued pig or twist their mouths away at whisky grog" were urged to stay away.

Jackson's toughness in the face of the enemy had won him the nickname Old Hickory. So local Democratic chapters were Hickory Clubs and steeples, signposts, and street corners all over the country sprouted hickory poles in his honor. "Planting hickory trees!" one New England editor wrote. "Odds nuts and drumsticks! What have hickory trees to do with republicanism and the great contest?"

President Adams and his supporters were caught off guard. Adams considered himself a statesman, not a politician. He hated electioneering. "The fashion of peddling for popularity," he called it, "by travelling around the country gathering crowds together, hawking for public dinners and spouting empty speeches." Adams' men denounced Jackson as a murderer for having executed deserters during his campaign against the Seminole Indians; the legitimacy of his marriage was questioned; posters charged that he was the bastard son of a prostitute.

JACKSON'S VICTORIES

Nothing Adams supporters did seemed to matter. Jackson won an easy victory. To the American people in every part of the country, he had come to seem the living symbol of the self-made, democratic spirit of the age. So many of them surged up the stairs of the Capitol to get close to him at his inauguration that a cable had to be stretched across the staircase to hold them back. And so many more elbowed their way into the White House at the reception afterward, breaking windows and smashing crockery, that some feared the mansion itself would collapse. "I never saw such a mixture," said Associate Supreme Court Justice Joseph Story "The reign of KING MOB seemed triumphant." But Jackson men loved it: "It is beautiful. It is sublime," said Francis Scott Key, composer of "The Star-Spangled Banner." Even Benjamin French, who had been so frightened by the recent presidential race, soon entered politics as an enthusiastic Jacksonian Democrat.

For all its tawdry excess and cynical manipulation, the 1828 campaign had demonstrated the people's resolve to have a more direct voice in the choice of their Presidents. When Jackson ran for reelection four years later, both he and his opponent, Henry Clay, were chosen by the nominating conventions of their respective parties. In 1832, the Jacksonians again out-marched and out-organized and even out-fed the opposition. "If we tell Democrats we have great strength," one Clay champion complained, *they reply by swallowing a pig. If we show them our gains in the Senate, they reply by devouring a turkey. If we point to our two-thirds majority in the House, they reply by pouring off a pint of whiskey or apple-toddy.* There is no withstanding such arguments. We give it up."

Jackson's opponents—they now called themselves Whigs, after members of the British antimonarchist party—failed again in 1836, and Martin Van Buren, the canny but uncharismatic operative who had helped engineer Jackson's first victory, was elected to succeed him. Although the country soon fell into a depression, the Democrats still seemed invincible: By 1839, when Philip Hone, a wealthy, well-connected Whig and former mayor of New York, ran for the state senate, political allies told him to forget it. In the current political climate, they said, "No gentleman can succeed."

Hone's friends were right—he was soundly beaten—but the Whigs were learning. By 1840, the depression had still not lifted, and bitter voters had begun to blame "President van Ruin" for their distress. To run against him, the Whigs nominated an old soldier of their own for President, William Henry Harrison of Ohio, with Senator John Tyler of Virginia as his running mate. Then the Democrats played into their hands. When a Democratic editor airily dismissed Harrison as the kind of man who would be content if given enough hard cider to "sit the remainder of his days in a log cabin," Whig strategists saw a way to turn the Democrats' own tactics against them.

This time, they would present themselves as the party of the plain people. They would paint Van Buren as the pampered son of privilege and their man as the repository of Jacksonian virtues. Harrison was, in fact, a wealthy man who had been born in a handsome brick house, not a log cabin. He was not a notable soldier, either; his victories over the Indians at Tippecanoe and the Battle of the Thames had been due more to overwhelming numbers and able subordinates than to his own tactical skill. And he was distinctly unsteady in his views: At first his handlers forbade him to so much as write a letter, for fear he would inadvertently alienate one group of voters or another. Then, when the Democrats began to ridicule him as "General Mum," he delivered 23 innocuous speeches, the first ones ever made by a presidential candidate. The speeches are remembered best for the ostentatious swig from a barrel labeled "hard cider" he was instructed to take halfway through each one.

Whigs outdid the Democrats this time. They staged more processions and organized bigger rallies, gathering "17 acres of men" on the Tippecanoe battlefield to cheer their hero and putting a mammoth log cabin at the corner of Wall and Prince streets in lower Manhattan. Whigs wrote more campaign songs and slogans, too, and they inundated the country with specially made bric-a-brac—mugs and teapots, handkerchiefs, medals, women's brooches, all emblazoned with Harrison and his supposed cabin. And party spokesmen relentlessly dinned his slogan, "Tippecanoe and Tyler Too," into the voters' ears, day and night.

"The question is not whether Harrison drinks hard cider," complained the poet William Cullen Bryant. ". . . The question is what he and his party will do if they obtain power." But few seemed to care as Whig orators mounted an all-out assault on the unpopular President. Van Buren, whose origins were actually humbler than Harrison's, was denounced as a perfumed dandy who had turned the White House into a "PALACE *as splendid as that of the Caesars*" and wasted "the People's cash in FOREIGN . . . GREEN FINGER CUPS, in which to wash his pretty, tapering, soft, white lily-fingers, after dining on fricandeau de veau and omelette soufflé." It was cheap, inaccurate, unfair—and hugely effective, the most vivid possible evidence, as one Whig editor admitted, that "passion and prejudice, properly aroused and directed, [would] do about as well as principle and reason in a party contest."

Van Buren won more popular votes than he had four years earlier, but many more Americans had gone to the polls this time—some 80 percent of all qualified voters—and they gave Harrison a narrow win, which he did not savor for long. He died of pneumonia within a month of his inauguration, and John Tyler, the first Vice President to succeed to the Presidency, had to endure Democratic jibes as His Accidency. But the Whigs had beaten the Democrats at their own game. "They have at last learned from defeat the art of victory!" the *Democratic Review* lamented. "We have taught them how to conquer us!" For better or worse, the two-party system was here to stay.

JACKSON'S REMOVAL OF NATIVE AMERICANS

STEVEN MINTZ

When Andrew Jackson became president in 1829, more than one hundred thousand Native Americans still lived east of the Mississippi River. By the end of the 1830s, most of them had been forced to leave their homes and move westward to what is now Oklahoma and Arkansas. In this excerpt, historian Steven Mintz describes how Jackson pursued a strategy of forced Indian removal (a policy he inherited from his predecessors) with great vigor despite resistance by some Native American tribes and legal challenges that reached the Supreme Court. Mintz argues that while Jackson's Indian policy is indefensible by modern standards, it should be viewed in the context of its time. During this era many white Americans regarded Native Americans as a threat to national security, and the federal government lacked the means to protect Native Americans from encroaching squatters and settlers. Mintz is a history professor at the University of Houston. His books include *Domestic Revolutions: A Social History of American Family Life, from the Colonial Era to the Present.*

In 1829, at the time Andrew Jackson became president, 125,000 Native Americans still lived east of the Mississippi River. Cherokee, Choctaw, Chickasaw, and Creek Indians—60,000 strong—held millions of acres in what would become the Southern Cotton Kingdom stretching across Georgia, Alabama, and Mississippi. The political question was whether these In-

Steven Mintz, *Native American Voices: A Social History and Anthology*, St. James, NY: Brandywine Press, 1995. Copyright © 1995 by Brandywine Press. Reproduced by permission.

dian tribes would be permitted to block white expansion. By 1840, Jackson and his successor, Martin Van Buren, had answered this question. All Indians east of the Mississippi had been uprooted from their homelands and moved westward, with the exception of rebellious Seminoles in Florida and small numbers of Indians living on isolated reservations in Michigan, North Carolina, and New York.

ASSIMILATION AND REMOVAL

Since Jefferson's presidency, two conflicting Indian policies, assimilation and removal, had governed the treatment of Native Americans. Assimilation encouraged Indians to adopt white American customs and economic practices. The government provided financial assistance to missionaries in order to Christianize and educate Native Americans and convince them to adopt single family farms. Proponents defended the assimilation policy as the only way Indians would be able to survive in a white-dominated society. According to the American Board of Commissioners for Foreign Missions, "There is no place on earth to which they can migrate, and live in the savage and hunter state. The Indian tribes must, therefore, be progressively civilized, or successively perish."

The other policy—removal—was first suggested by Thomas Jefferson as the only way to ensure the survival of Indian cultures. The goal of this policy was to encourage the voluntary migration of Indians westward to tracts of land where they could live free from white harrassment. As early as 1817, James Monroe declared that the nation's security depended upon rapid settlement along the southern coast and that it was in the best interests of Native Americans to move westward. In 1825 he set before Congress a plan to resettle all eastern Indians upon tracts in the West where whites would not be allowed to live. Initially, Jackson followed the dual policy of assimilation and removal, promising remuneration to tribes that would move westward, while offering small plots of land to individual Indians who would operate family farms. After 1830, however, Jackson favored only removal.

APPEALS TO THE SUPREME COURT

The shift in federal Indian policy came partly as a result of a controversy between the Cherokee nation and the state of Georgia. The Cherokee people had adopted a constitution asserting sov-

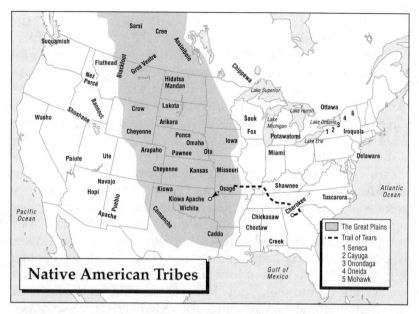

Native American Tribes

The Great Plains
Trail of Tears
1 Seneca
2 Cayuga
3 Onondaga
4 Oneida
5 Mohawk

ereignty over their land, and the state of Georgia responded by abolishing tribal rule and claiming that the Cherokee fell under its jurisdiction. The discovery of gold on Cherokee land triggered a land rush, and the Cherokee nation sued to keep white settlers from encroaching upon their territory. In two important cases, *Cherokee Nation v. Georgia* in 1831 and *Worcester v. Georgia* in 1832, the Supreme Court ruled that states could not pass laws conflicting with federal Indian treaties and that the federal government had an obligation to exclude white intruders from Indian lands. Angered, Jackson is said to have exclaimed: "John Marshall has made his decision; now let him enforce it."

The primary thrust of Jackson's removal policy was to encourage Indian tribes to sell all tribal lands in exchange for new lands in Oklahoma and Arkansas. Such a policy, the President maintained, would open new farmland to whites while offering Indians a haven where they would be free to develop at their own pace. "There," he wrote, "your white brothers will not trouble you, they will have no claims to the land, and you can live upon it, you and all your children, as long as the grass grows and the water runs, in peace and plenty."

Pushmataha, a Choctaw chieftain, called on his people to reject Jackson's offer. Far from being a "country of tall trees, many water courses, rich lands and high grass abounding in games of all kinds," the promised preserve in the West was simply a barren desert. Jackson responded by warning that if the Choctaw refused to move west, he would destroy their nation.

During the winter of 1831, the Choctaw became the first tribe to walk the "Trail of Tears" westward. Promised government assistance failed to arrive and malnutrition, exposure, and an epidemic of cholera killed many members of the nation. In 1836, the Creek suffered the hardships of removal. About 3,500 of the tribes 15,000 members died along the westward trek. Those who resisted removal were bound in chains and marched in double file.

The Cherokee, emboldened by the Supreme Court decisions that declared that Georgia law had no force on Indian territory, resisted removal. Fifteen thousand Cherokee joined in a protest against Jackson's policy: "Little did [we] anticipate, that when taught to think and feel as the American citizen . . . [we] were to be despoiled by [our] guardian, to become strangers and wanderers in the land of [our] fathers, forced to return to the savage life, and to seek a new home in the wilds of the far west, and that without [our] consent." The federal government bribed a faction of the tribe to leave the land in exchange for transportation costs and $5 million, but the majority of the people held out until 1838, when the army evicted them from their land. All totaled, 4,000 of the 15,000 Cherokee died along the trail to Oklahoma.

A number of tribes organized resistance against removal. In the Old Northwest, the Sauk and Fox Indians fought the Black Hawk War to recover ceded tribal lands in Illinois and Wisconsin. At the time that they had signed a treaty transferring title to their land, these people had not understood the implications of their action. "I touched the goose quill to the treaty," said Chief Black Hawk, "not knowing, however, that by that act I consented to give away my village." The United States army and the Illinois state militia ended resistance by wantonly killing nearly 500 Sauk and Fox men, women, and children who were trying to retreat across the Mississippi River. In Florida, the military spent seven years putting down Seminole resistance at a cost of $20 million and 1,500 troops, and even then only after the treacherous act of seizing the Seminole leader Osceola during peace talks.

EVALUATING INDIAN REMOVAL

By twentieth-century standards, Jackson's Indian policy was both callous and inhumane. Despite the semblance of legality—

ninety-four treaties were signed with Indians during Jackson's presidency—Indian migrations to the West usually occurred under the threat of government coercion. Even before Jackson's death in 1845, it was obvious that tribal lands in the West were no more secure than Indian lands had been in the East. In 1851 Congress passed the Indian Appropriations Act, which sought to concentrate the western Native American population upon reservations.

Why were such morally indefensible policies adopted? The answer is that many white Americans regarded Indian control of land and other natural resources as a serious obstacle to their desire for expansion and as a potential threat to the nation's security. Even had the federal government wanted to, it probably lacked the resources or military means to protect eastern Indians from the encroaching white farmers, squatters, traders, and speculators. By the 1830s, a growing number of missionaries and humanitarians agreed with Jackson that Indians needed to be resettled westward for their own protection. But the removal program was doomed from the start. Given the nation's commitment to limited government and its lack of experience with social welfare programs, removal was destined for disaster. Contracts for food, clothing, and transportation were let to the lowest bidders, many of whom failed to fulfill their contractual responsibilities. Indians were resettled on arid lands, unsuited for intensive farming. The tragic outcome was readily foreseeable.

The problem of preserving native cultures in the face of an expanding nation was not confined to the United States. Jackson's removal policy can only be properly understood when it is seen as part of a broader process: the political and economic incorporation of frontier regions into expanding nation-states. During the early decades of the nineteenth century, European nations were penetrating into many frontier areas, from the steppes of Russia to the plains of Argentina, the veldt of South Africa, the outback of Australia, and the American West. In each of these regions, national expansion was justified on the grounds of strategic interest (to preempt settlement by other powers) or in the name of opening valuable land to settlement and development. And in each case, expansion was accompanied by the removal or wholesale killing of native peoples.

SOCIAL CURRENTS AND REFORMS OF THE JACKSONIAN ERA

ROBERT V. REMINI

In the following selection, historian Robert V. Remini provides an overview of the social and cultural developments of the Jacksonian era. He notes that it was a time of rapid economic growth and industrialization—a time when many Americans optimistically worked hard in the belief that they could improve their material place in life. The same spirit of optimism inspired numerous cultural and social movements, he argues. Believers in Transcendentalism—espoused by philosopher and lecturer Ralph Waldo Emerson and his followers—preached the mystical approach to knowledge and a critical appraisal of the materialist values of industrial society. Evangelists such as Charles Grandison Finney traveled the country arguing that humans had the individual ability to achieve personal salvation. Evangelicals were also at the forefront of the many social reform movements of this era. People joined in voluntary organizations to discourage alcohol consumption, improve schools and prisons, and abolish slavery, among other causes. Remini, a professor emeritus of history and the humanities at the University of Illinois at Chicago, is the author of an acclaimed three-volume biography of Andrew Jackson.

P robably the most important development during the Jacksonian era was the powerful urge to reform and improve society and the conditions developing from an increas-

Robert V. Remini, *The Jacksonian Era*, Arlington Heights, IL: Harlan Davidson, 1989. Copyright © 1989 by Harlan Davidson, Inc. Reproduced by permission.

ingly industrial and materialistic nation. "The demon of reform"—to use Ralph Waldo Emerson's phrase—had been
loosed in the land and no one escaped it. Some of the efforts
were feeble and insignificant. Others, like abolitionism, rocked
the nation. All added to the texture of American society in the
Age of Jackson.

IMPROVING ONE'S LOT

The American of the early nineteenth century was a hustler, a
man on the make, invariably alert to any opportunity which
might improve his station in life. Money meant everything. "No
man in America is contented to be poor, or expects to continue
so," remarked one foreign traveler. "Go ahead." "Get ahead."
That was the spirit of the Jacksonian age. "The whole continent
presents a scene of *scrambling* and roars with greedy hurry," was
the comment of one visitor. "Go ahead! is the order of the day."
It is "the real motto of the country." "Our age," agreed Senator
Daniel Webster, "is full of excitement" and rapid change.

It was a materialistic society Americans were building, one
dedicated to business, trade, and the acquisition of wealth. Once
in place it became permanent—the creed to which most Americans in future generations subscribed. The doctrine of the "self-
made man," that is, "rags to riches," became the gospel of
America. The term "self-made man" was invented in the Jacksonian era, and Andrew Jackson himself was its personification.
Americans did not expect "greatness" to be thrust upon them—
although they would have assuredly accepted it under any circumstances. They knew and believed that they had to work for
their success. "Work," lectured one man, "and at eighteen you
shall . . . live in plenty, be well clothed, well housed, and able to
save." All good things necessarily followed. "Be attentive to
your work, be sober and religious, and you will find a devoted
and submissive wife; you will have a more comfortable home
than many of the higher classes in Europe." This Puritan work
ethic had been prevalent in America since the arrival of the first
English settlers, but it now took on a special urgency and new
purpose. "He who is an active and useful member of society,"
declared one, "who contributes his share to augment the national wealth and increase the numbers of the population, he
only is looked upon with respect and favor."

Because they were so economically motivated, Americans at
the beginning of the nineteenth century were able to develop an

extraordinarily successful economy, one which grew rapidly during the first few decades of the century and eventually raised the United States to the highest economic level. All during Jackson's term in office the economy ballooned. Only the Panic of 1837 caused a momentary setback. It was a sharp rebuke to a seemingly unstoppable prosperity. But within a few years the economy was off and running again. The nation had reached the "take off" stage in becoming an industrial society.

In explaining this phenomenal development, an English commission sent to America in 1851 to discover the reasons for this economic success reported: "The extent to which the people of the United States have as yet succeeded in manufactures may be attributed to indomitable energy and an educated intelligence, as also to the ready welcome accorded to the skilled workmen of Europe."

Not only "skilled workmen" but also farmers and laborers were migrating to America in increasing numbers, and they spread out to both cities and rural areas just as the United States was expanding across a continent. In less than fifty years, aided by the acquisition of Texas in 1845 and the acquisition of California, Arizona, New Mexico, and Utah following the Mexican War, a nation that had once been a small collection of British colonies huddled along the Atlantic coastline exploded across a continent. The highways, turnpikes, canals, and railroads built during the first half of the nineteenth century provided arteries to send a constant flow of people and commodities from city to town to remote communities all over the nation, binding them together and pumping economic life into them. Cincinnati, Chicago, St. Louis sprang up virtually overnight, while older cities like New York, Boston, Philadelphia expanded at a rapid pace. "What a country God has given us!" cried Jackson in a moment of spontaneous enthusiasm. "How thankful we ought to be that God has given us such a country to live in."

Much of the enthusiasm and faith in America was based on the fact that the intellectual currency of the Jacksonian era was minted in the Enlightenment and embossed in a Romantic age. Americans were the product of an age which preached the perfectability of man, the inevitability of improvement, and the supremacy of reason in all things. They believed in their own ability to improve their condition in life and to participate in the reform and advancement of society. There was in America a rising tendency, said William Ellery Channing, a New England clergyman, to exalt the people based on a "devotion to the progress of the whole human race."

AN ERA OF SOCIAL REFORM

Although Americans were zealous about improving their economic condition in life—"I know of no country, indeed," wrote Alexis de Tocqueville, in his classic work, *Democracy in America,* "where the love of money has taken stronger hold of the affections of men" than in the United States—nevertheless, they were also intent on improving social conditions generally. They were committed, continued Tocqueville, to the philosophical theory "that man is endowed with an indefinite faculty for improvement." This comes in large measure from American belief in equality, he said. Aristocratic nations tend to narrow the scope of human perfectability, he continued, while democratic nations, like the United States, expand it virtually beyond reason. As an example of what he meant, Tocqueville cited an incident in which he asked a sailor why American ships were built to last only a short time. "The art of navigation," replied the sailor, "is every day making such rapid progress that the finest vessel would become almost useless if it lasted beyond a few years."

Improvement! Human perfectability! Americans worked constantly toward improving ships, tools, machines, institutions, whatever, in order to bring about "the indefinite perfectability of man." In social terms that meant reform. And reform meant the need to revitalize and humanize social institutions, to improve the conditions in which men and women work and live, and to seek the good of one's fellow man—these were some of the important objectives of these extraordinary Americans of the Jacksonian age. Reformers were intent on raising "the life of man by putting it in harmony with his idea of the Beautiful and the Just."

By the 1820s this romantic impulse had begun to sweep across the United States. Although the old commitment to the ideas of the Enlightenment, such as the efficacy of reason and order, continued to persist, the new age emphasized the sensate in man. Reason alone no longer ruled as the sole perceiver of truth and beauty. Now the emotions were granted a prominent role. Human feelings were no longer suspect; they could now be enjoyed and appreciated. Man's intuitive powers were reckoned a mighty instrument in the search for knowledge and truth and self-improvement. "One day," wrote Emerson, "all men will be lovers; and every calamity will be dissolved in the universal sunshine."

THE TRANSCENDENTAL MOVEMENT

The most obvious expression of the romantic age was the Transcendental movement. This was a New England creation that went beyond a belief in man's goodness by proclaiming man's divinity. Transcendentalists—and they included such men and women as George Ripley, Bronson Alcott, Orestes Brownson, Margaret Fuller, Ralph Waldo Emerson, Henry Thoreau, and many others—believed that the world comprised an infinite variety of different beings, all united in the spiritual power of God which Emerson, the greatest exemplar of Transcendentalism, called the over-soul. The over-soul was diffused in man and nature, and man through intuitive contemplation could hear the voice of the Almighty. Actually, Transcendentalists were mystics in their approach to knowledge, for they believed that man could "transcend" experience and reason to discover through his intuitive powers the mysteries of the universe. "Pantheism is said to sink man and nature in God," wrote one Transcendentalist; "Materialism to sink God and man in nature; and Transcendentalism to sink God and nature in man."

A number of Transcendentalists met regularly in the home of George Ripley, a Boston minister. Emerson attended after returning from a tour of Europe, where he encountered the influence of such British writers as Coleridge and Wordsworth, as well as the German philosopher Immanuel Kant. He settled in Concord, Massachusetts, where he turned out an endless stream of poems and essays, all espousing the ideas and concepts of the Transcendental movement. Like others in the movement, Emerson reacted strongly against the corrupting influence of the new industrial society of his age. In his famous essay "Man the Reformer" he wrote: "What is man born for but to be a Reformer, a Re-Maker of what man has made, a renouncer of lies; a restorer of truth and good, imitating that great Nature which embosoms us all?" He was widely read in his own day, especially after he took to the lecture circuit, where his discourses profoundly impressed a large mass of people. . . .

Transcendentalists saw beauty in nature but ugliness everywhere else, especially in the nation's social institutions. The materialism of the day was particularly disturbing, and in many ways Transcendentalism can best be understood as essentially a revolt against materialism. Its disciples denounced society's concern for things. Theodore Parker, a New England minister, used his pulpit to scorch the conscience of a genteel society grown preoccupied with money and material gain. Quite obviously, he was a dangerous agitator and troublemaker in the minds of some of his parishioners.

Many of the Transcendentalists had been raised with a strict religious background. They were ministers or the children of ministers. And what is significant is that many of the reforms of the Jacksonian era were led by religious leaders who believed with a holy zeal in the justice and urgency of what they preached. Some of them felt they pursued a divine mission. They had a calling, a mission. But that was a notion that permeated the thinking of many Americans as they banded together in organizations to reform society and ameliorate the human condition. Among any number of important and worthwhile things, they set out to improve penal institutions and insane asylums, end slavery, provide equal rights for women, promote temperance, help the poor and distressed, better working conditions, and foster peace around the world.

THE SECOND GREAT AWAKENING

Religion, then, provided an important source of creative energy for the reform movements that raked the countryside during the Jacksonian age. Where Transcendentalism was confined pretty much to the New England area, the religious impulse of the early nineteenth century, the so-called Second Great Awakening, affected Americans around the country and provided much of the intellectual and spiritual power of many of the reforms that developed during this era.

Muted at first, and then dismissed later on, were the Puritan beliefs in a stern deity, alert to all infractions of divine law. The notion of sin-prone man hounded by a wrathful God was discarded during the Second Great Awakening. "There is an infinite worthiness in man," declared Emerson, that enables him to surmount all obstacles hindering his advance in wisdom and goodness. Man's *likeness* to God—the touch of divinity that separated and distinguished him from the lower orders—was emphasized; he was not so much depraved (as the result of Adam's fall) as deprived. God's love embraced all and forgave all.

In religious terms the Second Great Awakening emphasized the ability of each person to achieve salvation through submission to the lordship of Christ. The freedom of the will and the right intention of the individual were all important in working out one's salvation. The notion of an elect chosen by God had not the same force and urgency in the individualistic age of Jackson as it had during the colonial period. Anyone could obtain salvation and at any time once one heard God's call and responded. The democratic spirit of the age blew powerfully through the Christian churches and brought with it thousands seeking the saving comfort of divine love. The notion of a theocratic aristocracy was swept aside, just as Jackson's political revolution had swept aside the political aristocracy. The faithful crowded to revival meetings to purge their souls of sin and seek the peace and assurance of salvation.

Charles Grandison Finney was the most prominent revivalist of the day and undoubtedly the originator of modern revivalism in America. As a traveling evangelist he journeyed across the "burned-over district" of western New York along the route of the Erie Canal. His meetings were emotional debauches with wild scenes of men and women confessing their sins, weeping, and tearing their hair in a desperate display of repentance, and barking at trees where they presumed they had trapped the devil. Those who had been born again and acknowledged Christ's lordship and sovereignty over them should "aim at being holy," preached Finney, "and not rest satisfied till they are as perfect as god." And they must look beyond themselves. "The evils have been exhibited," he cried, "the call has been made for reform. . . . Away with the idea, that Christians can remain neutral and keep still, and yet enjoy the approbation and blessing of God."

Sometimes the behavior of these evangelicals resembled the antics of the insane. Mrs. Frances Trollope, who lived for several seasons in the United States and wrote a book on *The Domestic Manners of Americans,* attended one of these revival or camp meetings and was so shaken by what she saw and heard that she retreated in panic and disbelief.

Finney attracted many imitators, and their approach to religion blended so perfectly with the spirit of the Jacksonian age that they enjoyed enormous success and ultimately shaped the standard form of evangelical Protestantism as practiced to this day. And they preached not only the possibility of human salvation but also the reform of society by voluntary associations. "It is part of Christian duty," they lectured, to aid the ignorant, the destitute, and the unfortunate. "It becomes Christians to imitate their Master, and to seek the good of those who are careless of their own good."

Small wonder, then, that the "demon of reform" took hold. Americans saw the evils in society and felt they could expel them through concerted, organized action. They understood their duty and acted upon it. The acceptance of the idea of the perfectability of man brought suggestions and schemes to hasten the perfecting process and clear away the obstacles that blocked it. Men and women organized themselves around one or another of these schemes and held meetings, gave speeches, raised money, and issued printed propaganda to advance their cause. Some hyperactive souls joined several different reform movements at once, such as abolition, temperance, and women's rights. They were volunteers in an army to scourge the nation of the social blight that disfigured it.

PUBLIC EDUCATION

Education was a needed target for reform. Between 1810 and 1820 the number of American colleges virtually doubled. At the same time free primary education was winning acceptance in this increasingly democratic society, and in 1821 Boston established the first public secondary school. Not much later Massachusetts required all towns with a population in excess of 500 families to provide free secondary schooling. The rest of the country was not nearly as progressive, but it was a start, and the idea slowly advanced across the country during the next several decades.

In the forefront of those advocating free public education was Horace Mann, the most significant figure in American education during the Jacksonian period. He, along with others, argued that free education meant the eventual elimination of poverty and the general prosperity of the entire nation. He said it would reduce crime, improve social justice, and strengthen the nation's institutions. "Health, freedom, wisdom, virtue, time, eternity," cry out in behalf of education, he said. "Some causes have reference to temporal interests; some to eternal;— education embraces both." As secretary of the Massachusetts Board of Education, he fought for and won higher appropriations from the legislature, with which he built better schools, improved the curriculum, obtained a minimum six-month school year, and won higher salaries for teachers. He also established the first teacher-training (normal) school in Lexington, Massachusetts, to prepare teachers for their vocation. Because of his concern for their future lives, that it have meaning and purpose, Mann shared a truth with a graduating class at Antioch College in Ohio just a few weeks before his death: "Be ashamed to die until you have won some victory for humanity."

Women's colleges did not begin until after the Civil War, but due to the efforts of such women as Emma Willard and Mary Lyon, institutions of learning for women at the secondary level were improved. Willard founded the Female Seminary in Troy, New York, and Lyon opened Mount Holyoke Seminary in South Hadley, Massachusetts. In 1833 Oberlin College in Ohio inaugurated coeducational instruction by admitting women for the first time. . . .

The improvement in public education for all the citizens of the various states and communities around the country also stimulated the improvement of textbooks. The earliest manuals were generally poor in quality, and not until Noah Webster introduced his *Spelling Book* and *Reader* did it materially improve. In 1836 William H. McGuffey's *Eclectic Reader* appeared and had a tremendous impact on elementary school instruction. The *Reader* emphasized cultural and moral standards and preached a patriotism that inculcated a devotion to country that satisfied the growing sense of nationalism that had been building since the War of 1812. Unquestionably, McGuffey had a greater impact on the shaping of American morality than any writer or politician of the period.

Of particular educational significance during the 1830s was the lyceum movement, a program of public lectures on the arts and sciences. The movement began in Great Britain and was introduced into this country by Josiah Holbrook, who founded the first lyceum in Massachusetts in 1826. Soon the system spread across the northern states and several thousand lyceum organizations were in operation by the 1840s. Famous statesmen, scientists, clergymen, and educators spoke to audiences on a wide range of subjects, from religion and science to art, music, and literature. Ralph Waldo Emerson, Oliver Wendell Holmes, and Daniel Webster were a few of the very popular speakers who lectured around the country. . . .

LABOR REFORM

Artisans, mechanics, and workmen . . . were also the objects of reformers, for the improvement of labor and working conditions in the cities had long been advocated by social critics. "No man can be a Christian," wrote the Transcendentalist Orestes Brownson, "who does not refrain from practices by which the rich grow richer and the poor poorer, and who does not do all in his power to elevate the laboring classes . . . so that each man shall be free and independent." By the late 1820s there appeared a Workingmen's party and the beginning of a trade union movement. Abolition of imprisonment for debt, free public education, mechanics lien laws, higher wages, and a ten hour workday were some of labor's demands. Such labor leaders as George Henry Evans, Thomas Skidmore, Seth Luther, and Ely Moore tried to stir the conscience of the nation about the problems of urban workers, and many of their demands were subsequently met. Some of these leaders gave the union movement a genuine radical cast because of their attacks upon private property, one unique in the history of the American labor movement. Crime exists in society, wrote one labor leader, not because of the "natural depravity of man" but because of the "unequal distribution of wealth." "Give to every man a competency," he declared, "and nine-tenths of the poverty and crime now existing would disappear."

One criticism often heard against the formation of unions was the fear that they would set a "dangerous precedent." Ely Moore, a printer and first president of the General Trades' Union of New York, agreed. "It may, indeed, be dangerous to aristocracy, dangerous to monopoly, dangerous to oppression, but not to the general good or the public tranquility."

Through the use of strikes and political agitation the unions made notable progress in the 1830s, but they sustained a near-fatal blow when the Panic of 1837 plunged the nation into a long and harrowing depression. In a notable ruling in the case *Commonwealth v. Hunt* in 1842, Justice Lemuel Shaw of the Massachusetts high court declared that trade unions and strikes were legal. Also significant in labor history was President Van Buren's order that no one was to work more than ten hours a day on federal public works, an order that was written into the laws of a half dozen states over the following fifteen years.

REFORMING ASYLUMS AND PRISONS

One of the most remarkable and most successful reformers of the Jacksonian period was Dorothea L. Dix, who spent the greater portion of her life working to win improvements in

mental institutions, called insane asylums at the time. She tried
to help the unfortunate souls inhabiting the asylums by reading portions of the Bible to them each week. But the conditions
she observed shocked and angered her. After investigating conditions in Massachusetts she gathered an impressive array of
facts and presented them in 1843 in a *Memorial to the Legislature
of Massachusetts*. "I proceed, gentlemen," she wrote, "briefly to
call your attention to the *present* state of insane persons confined
within this Commonwealth, in *cages, closets, cellars, stalls, pens!
Chained, naked, beaten with rods*, and *lashed* into obedience." Her
documentation embarrassed Massachusetts into building a new
institution. For the next fifteen years she extended her work into
other sections of the country, winning reform and correction in
numerous states and contributing to the building of nearly two
dozen new mental hospitals.

A similar movement produced a demand for the reform of
prisons. Alexis de Tocqueville, who toured the United States in
the 1830s to study American prisons for the French government,
commented on this movement. "A few years ago some pious
people undertook to make the state of the prisons better. The
public was roused by their exhortations, and the reform of criminals became a popular cause. New prisons were then built. For
the first time the idea of reforming offenders as well as punish-
ing them penetrated into the prisons." Although the old prisons remained as monuments to the barbarities of the Middle
Ages, he noted, the new ones were durable tributes to the gen-
tleness and enlightenment of the modern age. They reflected the
Jacksonian belief that man was perfectible, that he could be re-
formed, and that to a very considerable degree he could control
himself and the world around him. . . .

It was a remarkable and life-enhancing age, this Jacksonian
era. The reach for perfection by Americans, the attempt to adopt
new patterns of life, join voluntary associations to eliminate
crippling social disabilities, and restructure their society un-
derscored their vitality and "go ahead" mentality. Their preoc-
cupation with money and material goods was offset to a considerable extent by their concern and regard for the less
fortunate in society. Their moral values were rooted in their religious beliefs and their recognition of the worth of each individual. Their optimism was unbounded and infectious. They
were a new breed. Their colonial and European past was gone.
Their hope rested with the future.

TALL TALES AND THE RISE OF THE AMERICAN POPULAR HERO

DANIEL BOORSTIN

Daniel Boorstin, librarian of Congress from 1975 to 1987, is a noted historian. The following passage is an excerpt from *The Americans: The National Experience*, the middle volume of his prize-winning trilogy on American history. In it, he examines the rise of folk heroes in American popular culture in the early nineteenth century. Among the figures he examines are Tennessee frontiersman Davy Crockett and keelboat pilot Mike Fink—both real people who became legendary heroes and subjects of a "subliterature" of tall tales and vulgar humor. He argues that American folk heroes differed from those of the Old World (such as King Arthur) in that they were often portrayed as comic as well as heroic figures.

E arly 19th-century America offered many obvious features of a Heroic Age—a half-known wilderness where men were threatened by untamed animals and hostile tribes—and it is not surprising that there soon appeared American counterparts of the ancient heroes. But the uncertainties of national boundaries and aspirations and language, and the unsure line between fact and hope, had their counterparts in uncertain boundaries between the heroic and the comic. Our first popular

Daniel Boorstin, *The Americans: The National Experience*, New York: Random House, 1965. Copyright © 1965 by Random House. Reproduced by permission.

heroes came on the scene to a chorus of horse-laughs. The vehicles of national ideals were the butts of national laughter. This unfamiliar combination was a product of American peculiarities.

Precisely how European heroes of the Heroic Age—Achilles, Beowulf, Siegfried, Roland, King Arthur, and others—arose, is of course shrouded in mist. It seems likely that they first appeared in oral legend, only gradually finding their way into formal written literature. From oral legend or minstrelsy to literary epic was a long journey. The passage of centuries distilled and elevated and "purified" the heroic characters, and self-conscious chroniclers gave their subjects grandeur and dignity.

All this was different in the United States. David Crockett (1786–1836) was still alive when oral legends about him began to circulate. He was not yet dead when his exploits, real or supposed, were already embalmed in print. Through his "autobiographical" writings (probably written mostly by others) and other episodic accounts, he became widely known over the continent within a decade of his death.

Two Distinctions of American Heroes

At least two crucial distinctions, then, mark the American making of a popular legendary hero. First, there was a fantastic chronological abridgment: from elusive oral legend to printed form required here a few years rather than centuries. Legends hastened into print before they could be purified of vulgarities and localisms. Second, the earliest printed versions were in a distinctively American form; they were not in literature but in "subliterature"—writings on popular or vulgar subjects, belly-laugh humor, slapstick and tall tales, adventures for the simple-minded. Crockett was not written down in any American counterpart of the *Historia Regum Britanniae* nor in any *Morte d'Arthur*: the Crockett anecdotes plunged headlong, in a decade, from the small world of fireside anecdote and barroom wheeze into the great democratic world of print. Widely circulating, inexpensive publications dispersed the Crockett legends as they fell from the lips of raconteurs. They entered at once into a thriving subliterature.

In Western Europe, too, there was, of course, a subliterature of ballads, broadsides, parodies, almanacs, and other ephemeras of popular entertainment and instruction even as early as the 17th century. But literacy there was long confined to a small fraction of the upper classes. Extensive, dignified works—the

Bible, prayerbooks, sermons, epics, treatises—were being printed long before literacy was widespread. Not until the 19th century had the English working classes generally learned to read. By the time there was a considerable reading audience reaching down into the populace, a vast literature of great dignity, of Shakespearean drama and Miltonic epic, had grown and taken the center of the national stage.

Not so in the United States. Here, from colonial times, literacy had been more widespread than in the mother country. The reading audience for a subliterature already existed at the nation's birth. Thus, in the first century of national life a subliterature grew and flourished at the same time that American writers were trying to give the nation its own dignified and elevated literature. In America, again, the familiar European calendar of cultural development was abridged and confused. A subliterature, which in other countries was made possible by a seeping down of literacy after the nation had established its literature, was to develop in America almost before the nation produced a literature.

DAVY CROCKETT

Davy Crockett was the most important and, for some time, the most widely known popular candidate for national hero-worship. The vehicles which spread his fame, like everything else about him, beautifully illustrate the peculiar American situation. Crockett, the son of a Revolutionary soldier who became a tavern-keeper, was born in northeastern Tennessee in 1786. He ran away from home at the age of 13 to escape a beating, wandered about for several years, and married at the age of 18. Failing to make a go as a farmer, he joined Andrew Jackson in the Creek War of 1813–14 and served for a while as a scout. He later hired a substitute to complete his term of enlistment and moved to southern Tennessee, where he began his career of public service, first as an appointed justice of the peace, then as a colonel of militia. In 1821, Crockett was elected to the state legislature. Moving again, he settled at the extreme western edge of the state (where his nearest neighbor was seven miles away) and was quickly elected to the state legislature again from his new constituency. Then, on a dare, he ran for Congress, and, much to his own surprise, was elected. He served for three terms. When not at the state capital or in Washington, he lived the perilous life of the backwoodsman: during one nine-months period he killed 105 bears; he nearly died while floating a load of barrel-staves down the Mississippi in 1826.

He had little education and little respect for book-learning; the rules of spelling, he said, were "contrary to nature." As a judge (when he did not know the meaning of the word "judiciary") he "relied on natural-born-sense instead of law-learning." In the Tennessee legislature, Crockett had voted against Jackson for senator, and very early he began voting against Jackson's policies in Congress. This made him a welcome backwoods symbol for the anti-Jackson Whig party just being organized, but it angered his Tennessee constituents who finally refused to send him back to Congress. Crockett then left Tennessee, partly in pique and partly moved by enthusiasm for the war for Texas independence. Arriving at the Alamo in February, 1836, he died a martyr's death a few weeks later in its final defense.

The exploits, real or imaginary, of Davy Crockett were quickly circulated in print: in newspapers, in almanacs, and in books. Shrouded—or rather, haloed—in a multiplex ambiguity, even their authorship is uncertain. Crockett himself may have had some hand in books about him published before 1836, and Whig journalists and others also did their own embellishing. Most of the later almanac stories are anonymous. But there is no uncertainty about the popularity and wide circulation of the printed legends of Davy Crockett. *Sketches and Eccentricities of Col. David Crockett* (1833), *An Account of Col. Crockett's Tour to the North and Down East* (1835), and Crockett's *Life of Martin Van Buren* (1835) reached a large audience. *A Narrative of the Life of David Crockett, of the State of Tennessee* (1834), which came to be called his autobiography, reached best-seller proportions. A posthumous literature, including works like *Col. Crockett's Exploits and Adventures in Texas* (1836), grew and whetted the appetite for still more legend. Then came the so-called "Crockett almanacs." The earliest, printed in Nashville in 1835, bore the title, *Davy Crockett's Almanack, of Wild Sports of the West, and Life in the Backwoods. Calculated for all the States in the Union.* In its first issues it drew on the "autobiography" but later offered items (with the ostensible authority of the "heirs of Col. Crockett") which Crockett himself was supposed to have prepared before his death. Nashville imprints were issued until 1841, when other Crockett almanacs began to appear in New York, Philadelphia, Boston, Albany, Baltimore, Louisville, and elsewhere. At least fifty appeared before 1856. These almanacs, embellished by rough woodcuts and as crude in typography as in content, were destined to become expensive collector's items in the mid-20th century.

AMERICAN SUBLITERATURE

The Crockett almanacs, like their predecessors, contained much information and misinformation besides the "true adventures" of Davy Crockett. They included adventures of Mike Fink, Daniel Boone, Kit Carson, and of the more obscure backwoods supermen, and miscellaneous stories of plants and animals, as well as the pithy sayings, medical hints, and helpful facts of weather, astronomy, and astrology, which had long been the staples of the almanacs.

This proliferating subliterature—lowbrow printed matter, fertilized by vulgar humor and the popular imagination—was one of the first characteristically American genres. It is not surprising that the new nation should have expressed itself in a subliterature. For a turbulent, mobile, self-conscious, sanguine, and literate people, it took the place of belles-lettres. In the colonial period, the characteristic American printed matter had been not the book or the treatise but the newspaper, the pamphlet, the how-to-do-it manual, the sermon, and the letter. This new literature was designed for people who did not read books. Intended for a predominantly masculine public, it was self-consciously unliterary and ungenteel, belligerently formless and unashamedly crude. . . .

COMIC HEROES

American humor and American popular heroes were born together. The first popular heroes of the new nation were comic heroes and the first popular humor of the new nation was the antics of its heroic clowns. The comic and the heroic were mixed and combined in novel American proportions. What were the dominant themes of these mock-heroics? What made them comic, and what made them heroic?

The heroic themes are obvious enough and not much different from those of other times and places. . . .

Far more distinctive was the comic quality. All heroes are heroic; few are also clowns. What made the American popular hero heroic also made him comic. The pervasive ambiguity of American life, the vagueness which laid the continent open to adventure, which made the land a rich storehouse of the unexpected, which kept vocabulary ungoverned and the language fluid—this same vagueness suffused both the comic and the heroic. Both depended on incongruity: the incongruity of the laughable and the incongruity of the admirable. In a world full of the unexpected, where norms were vaguely or extravagantly defined, readers of the Crockett legends were never quite certain whether to laugh or to applaud, whether what they saw and heard was wonderful, awful, or ridiculous. . . .

HUMOR AND DETACHMENT

Some of our shrewdest students of comedy agree that detachment, a certain ability to look at oneself from the outside, is essential to the comic spirit. According to Constance Rourke, this explains why the American comic spirit did not begin to flourish until after the War of 1812 had more firmly established the American nation. Americans, feeling themselves more secure, could then look on themselves with a new detachment. A similar sense of detachment, of distance from oneself, is also required for the heroic. Distance makes both heroes and clowns. Great heroes are men from whom one feels at a great distance. Of course, this distance can be provided by the centuries. "Distance lends enchantment," if a cliché, is also an ancient and familiar theme. "Glories," said John Webster, "like glow-worms, afar off shine bright, but look'd too near have neither heat nor light."

SEPARATED BY DISTANCE

Yet there is more than one kind of distance. In America, in this as in many other ways, space played the role of time. If Americans, in their new country, could not be separated from their national popular heroes by hundreds of years, they were in any case separated by hundreds of miles. This sense of distance was possible as it had not been in smaller, more homogeneous nations. The great and varied space provided distance for both heroic and comic perspective.

In 1840 the cultural distance between Boston, New York, or Philadelphia and the Tennessee or farther-western backwoods was probably as great as that between the England of the 12th and the England of the 6th century. And the geographic distance from Boston to the western boundary of Tennessee was greater than that between London and Algiers. The printed matter in which the legends of Crockett and other heroes of the backwoods were most widely circulated came from the remote eastern capitals.

The vastness and variety and freshness of the American landscape, of its flora and fauna, of custom and costume, nourished American subliterature and gave American subjects great promise for the comic and the heroic. This comic-heroic subliterature drew on the whole half-known, unpredictable continent. It garnered oral tales from far-away comers of the nation and retailed them to the amusement, wonder, and delight of fellow Americans who had never seen such places and could not be sure whether what they read was ridiculous or wonderful. It is only a half-truth, therefore, to speak of American humor and American heroics in this period as "regional." Individual stories were regional only in the sense that they were set among the conspicuous peculiarities of some particular region. Many of the best works of the subliterature appeared first in the New Orleans *Picayune,* the St. Louis *Reveille,* the Cincinnati *News,* or the Louisville *Courier.* Then gradually, by compilation and republication, they reached the nation. Their wider comic and heroic appeal, and their place as national legend, finally came from the fact that there was a large audience of fellow Americans remote from these scenes that was eager for entertainment and for sagas to dramatize the distinctive appeal and grandeur of their whole country. Regional distinctions themselves thus made possible a flourishing national subliterature. . . .

MIKE FINK

On the national scene, Crockett's only serious competitor was Mike Fink. Last of the keelboatmen, Fink (1770–1823) had three careers—first fighting the British and the Indians, then fighting the Ohio and the Mississippi in the days before the steamboat, and finally as a Rocky Mountain fur trapper. The Fink stories were most popular between 1830 and 1860 when the Crockett almanacs themselves celebrated Fink's varied exploits. Perhaps it was nostalgia that made the new age of the noisy steamboat romanticize the heroes of an era when men pulled against the river. Fink, like Crockett, was both hero and clown, adept at the marvelous and the ridiculous—"a helliferocious fellow and an almighty fine shot."

On at least one occasion, Fink bested Crockett himself at a famous shooting match. "I've got the handsomest wife, and the fastest horse, and the sharpest shooting iron in all Kentuck," Fink taunted Crockett, "and if any man dare doubt it, I'll be in his hair quicker than hell could scorch a feather." "I've nothing to say against your wife, Mike," answered Davy, "for it cant be denied she's a shocking handsome woman, and Mrs. Crockett's in Tennessee, and I've got no horses. Mike, I dont exactly like to tell you you lie about what you say about your rifle, but I'm d——d if you speak the truth and I'll prove it. Do you see that are cat sitting on the top rail of your potato patch, about a hundred and fifty yards off? If she ever hears agin, I'll be shot if it shant be without ears." And so their shooting match began. It ended when Mike became "sorter wrothy, and he sends a ball after his wife as she was going to the spring after a gourd full of water, and nocked half her coom out of her head, without stirring a hair, and calls out to her to stop for me to take a blizzard at what was left on it. The angeliferous critter stood still as a scarecrow in a cornfield, for she'd got used to Mike's tricks by long practiss. 'No, No, Mike,' sez I, Davy Crockett's hand would be sure to shake, if his iron war pointed within a hundred miles of a she-male, and I give up beat. . . ."

There were other, lesser heroes. Some were city types like Sam Patch, the Rhode Island cotton spinner who survived a jump over Niagara Falls (1827) but died in the Genesee Falls (1829). "There's no mistake in Sam Patch," was his battlecry. He was constantly proving his favorite motto: "Some things can be done as well as others."

All these figures were dramatized by traveling companies which reached into the remote villages, where they acted on improvised stages or in the open air. The stage along with the press . . . helped make these legends national by carrying native folk humor to urban audiences. . . .

The American clownish heroes were supermen. They did not transcend man but exaggerated him. They were flamboyant, gargantuan, and wonderfully efficient, but they lacked grandeur. It was no accident that Americans sought heroes in a subliterature, and never found them there. The American subliterature was a natural birthplace and natural habitat not for heroes but for supermen. The American supermen, the Davy Crocketts of the subliterature, showed Americans strenuously trying to idealize themselves, to make an ideal simply by exaggerating the commonplace. It is not surprising that they did not succeed. The effort was amusing; its result was comic rather than epic.

Rise of the Abolitionist Movement

William L. Barney

The abolitionist movement was one of the largest and most influential of the social reform movements of the Jacksonian era. Historian William L. Barney describes the rise of the abolitionists in the 1830s, comparing the movement with the concurrent rise of national political parties. He argues that a fundamental insight of the abolitionists was how the development of a market society in the United States made slavery more vulnerable to criticism and eradication. Barney also describes the violent resistance the movement inspired in the South, and how the movement benefited from the improvements in the printing press and the work of activist women. The splintering of the abolitionist movement into several rival organizations did not necessarily impair its effectiveness, he asserts. Barney is professor of history at the University of North Carolina at Chapel Hill. His books include *The Passage of the Republic: An Interdisciplinary History of Nineteenth-Century America*, from which the following selection is taken.

In the 1830s, the same decade in which a mass-based party system was built, the abolitionists became an organized reform movement. The simultaneous appearance of the abolitionists and this party system was not coincidental. Both, though in radically different ways, were responding to the new

William L. Barney, *The Passage of the Republic: An Interdisciplinary History of Nineteenth-Century America*, Lexington, MA: D.C. Heath and Company, 1987. Copyright © 1987 by D.C. Heath and Company. Reproduced by permission.

egalitarian ethos in American public life, and both achieved organizational success by innovatively responding to the same breakthroughs in transportation and communication that were instrumental in the emergence of that egalitarian ethos. Thirdly, and most ironically, given their diametrically opposite solutions for preserving the Union, both were a response to the growing fears of disunion in the 1820s.

SLAVERY AND THE MARKET SOCIETY

Whereas the Jacksonians adroitly rode egalitarian currents into political office, the abolitionists followed those currents to their logical end. By viewing society in egalitarian terms along a horizontal axis of freely competing individuals, the abolitionists argued that slavery stood out as a glaring and hideous barrier to economic progress and moral justice. In this way, the abolitionists grasped that the advent of a competitive market society destroyed what had traditionally sanctioned slavery. As long as society was seen as an organic hierarchy structured around natural social dependencies, and as long as work was conceived as something to be extracted and coerced from a naturally idle, lazy population, then slavery was buffered from direct attack. In such a premarket society, slavery, however personally objectionable to some individuals, did not contradict the ethical and ideological basis of social order. Quite the contrary: slavery could be accepted and defended as part of the natural order. Slaves were simply the most dependent of entire classes of social dependents, and slavery represented an unfortunate, but understandable, extreme use of external coercion to extract productive work. Thus in seventeenth- and eighteenth-century England, slavery could be proposed as a permanent cure for the idleness of those poor who failed to respond to treatment in a public poorhouse. The market revolution, as manifested in a bourgeois ideology that redefined work as the self-motivated virtue of economically rational individuals striving to improve themselves in open competition, gradually exposed slavery as an unnatural, and unnecessary, system of unfree labor. The bourgeois definition of itself and its society was based on the internalized controls of individuals who literally possessed themselves free from external restraints. In direct opposition to that bourgeois worldview was slavery, the extreme example of individuals who had lost self-possession.

Slavery was vulnerable in a market society in a way in which it had not been previously. This was the first fundamental insight of the abolitionists. In acting upon that insight, the abolitionists defined an ideological position that set them apart from earlier antislavery movements. Central to that ideology was the doctrine of immediatism. By this the abolitionists meant an immediate, moral commitment by individuals to work toward the end of slavery. Immediate emancipation, though it would have been welcomed with joy, was not necessarily the goal. Instead, what was essential was that the work of emancipation should immediately *begin.* Immediatism did not imply a rejection of gradual programs of emancipation. Indeed, as the abolitionists emphasized, such programs had already been rejected by the South in the 1820s. However, the abolitionists were astute enough to realize that gradualism could not serve as an effective organizing philosophy for the movement. As a practical alternative, it had failed; as an ideological goal, it reinforced preexisting prejudice and complacency and made it all too easy to postpone any action; and, as a moral statement, it was flawed by its suggestion that the establishment of Christian freedom for all could be delayed. Gradualism also contradicted the logic of evangelical ideology. Although there was no one-to-one relationship between evangelicalism and abolitionism, both movements in the North shared a common concern with the unfettered right of the individual to work for self-achievement. In either religious or secular terms, slavery directly violated that right. As Charles Finney put it: "To enslave a man is to treat a man as a thing—to set aside moral agency; and to treat a moral agent as a mere piece of property." Consequently, for Finney and many other evangelicals, abolitionism and revivalism were part of the same holy process of achieving human redemption. The abolitionists, like the revival ministers, insisted that sin could be vanquished only through a total and immediate commitment to its eradication.

WORKING FOR RACIAL EQUALITY

The other defining characteristic of abolitionist ideology was its stand on racial equality. If slavery were ever to be ended without massive violence, then slaveholders had to see that freeing their slaves was a Christian duty they owed to those equal to whites in the sight of God. If this freedom were to be meaningful, and not the mockery imposed on free blacks by white prejudice, then all whites had to accept black equality before the law as a goal that would hasten the end of slavery. By working for racial justice in the free states, Northern whites would undermine the racial defense of slavery by showing Southerners that an egalitarian, biracial society was a living reality.

In their second critical insight, the abolitionists realized that their success was dependent on their skill in performing their self-appointed role as social agitators. Unlike the politician, whose task was to *reflect* public opinion, the reformer in an unpopular moral cause had to *change* public opinion. The core problem was public apathy, the moral numbness by which most whites isolated themselves from the plight of the slave. To break through that apathy, to reach individual consciences and make whites identify with the horrors of bondage, the abolitionists used blunt, uncompromising language. As William Lloyd Garrison, the firebrand who provided the early, driving leadership for the abolitionists, said of his moral indignation, "I have need to be *all on fire*, for I have mountains of ice about me to melt." Wendell Phillips, a Boston lawyer who became the best-known abolitionist orator, articulated a brilliant defense of agitation, which he anchored in classic republican ideology:

> Each man . . . holds his property and his life dependent on the constant presence of an agitation like this of antislavery. Eternal vigilance is the price of liberty: power is ever stealing from the many to the few. . . . Only by continual oversight can the democrat in office be prevented from hardening into a despot: only by unintermitted agitation can a people be kept sufficiently awake to principle not to let liberty be smothered in material prosperity.

Much to the dismay of his critics, Garrison proved correct when he proclaimed in the first issue of the *Liberator* in January 1831 that "I WILL BE HEARD." In making sure that they were heard, the abolitionists were as adept as the party professionals in developing techniques to reach the people. Public rallies, revivalistic exhortations, speakers' series, bureaucratic agencies, and, above all, the printing press were all exploited by the abolitionists in spreading their message. The application of steam power to the printing press in the early 1830s dramatically lowered the cost and raised the output of printed material. The abolitionists could now reach a huge audience for a relatively small capital investment. In 1835 they flooded the nation with over a million pieces of literature, a ten-fold increase over 1834.

The voluntary work of women supplemented this reliance on printing technology. First drawn to abolitionism as just one of many reforms, women soon identified particularly strongly with the movement. In the slaves they came to see fellow victims of social injustice. The slave, like the wife, was legally dependent upon the will of another and was discriminated against on grounds of inherent, biological inferiority. "In striving to strike his irons off," Abby Kelley wrote in 1838, "we found most surely that *we* were manacled *ourselves.*" Often operating out of local church societies, these women were the grassroots organizers of the massive effort in the mid-1830s to inundate Congress with antislavery petitions. By 1838 Congress had received petitions with over 400,000 signatures.

REACTIONS TO THE ABOLITIONISTS

The abolitionists were so loud and so persistent that they provoked a concerted effort to silence them. In the North they were met with mob violence. There were four times as many riots resulting in significant property losses in the 1830s as there had been in the preceding two decades combined. Many of them were triggered by hatred of the abolitionists, a hatred that often spilled over into antiblack violence. In the South, abolitionist literature was burned, and local postmasters, in direct defiance of federal authority, censured the mails to keep out antislavery materials. Slave codes were tightened, and a series of state laws abridging the freedom of speech and the press were speedily passed. In 1836, Congress adopted the so-called Gag Rule, by which antislavery petitions were automatically tabled without a reading.

The intensity of the reactions to the abolitionists was the best indication of how contemporaries perceived them as dangerous radicals. The abolitionists attacked as unsound and impure the critical public institutions that bound together the nation—the churches, political parties, and the Union. All sanctioned slavery, either through their active support or their silence. They were radical in reminding white Americans of what they did not want to hear—that slavery was a national institution and its guilt was shared by all whites. In demanding an end to slavery, they were calling for the destruction of the cornerstone of the American economy in the 1830s. Without slavery and what it produced in export earnings, the national growth of the economy would have been far slower. They bypassed local elites in molding public opinion and heightened lower-class anxieties over black competition for jobs. And, in pushing for racial equality, the abolitionists rejected the almost universal racist assumptions of white Americans. It was no wonder that they aroused such intense fears.

In the South the abolitionists struck at the very roots of the social order. The issue here was as basic as it could be. It was not so much a question of what the abolitionists actually said, which usually consisted of appeals to the Christian consciences of slaveholders, but whether any opponent of slavery should say anything at all. Slaveholders were easily outnumbered by the nonslaveholding Southern majority. They had far too much at stake to permit any public debate on slavery. In admitting this in 1835 Governor Wilson Lumpkin of Georgia argued:

> Should, however, the abolitionists be permitted to proceed without molestation or only have to encounter the weapons of reason and argument, have we not reason to fear, that their untiring efforts may succeed in misleading the majority of a people who have no direct interest in the great question at issue, and finally produce interference with the constitutional rights of the slaveholders.

THE MOVEMENT SPLITS

Partly as a result of the sheer violence and anger directed against them, the abolitionists divided internally. In the 1830s the abolitionists were at least formally united under the leadership of the American Anti-Slavery Society, founded in Philadelphia in 1833. A rival organization, the American and Foreign Anti-Slavery Society, was established in 1840. The Garrisonians, those who remained in control of the AAAS, interpreted the violence to mean that American institutions and values were fundamentally impure and immoral. A complete regeneration, one based on the renunciation of force in all human relationships, be it in the patriarchal family, black slavery, the churches, or government, was necessary if America were ever to return to its revolutionary ideals. Expressed in an ideology of nonresistance, pacifism, and Christian anarchism, the Garrisonian position provoked opposition from more moderate abolitionists. They felt that the Garrisonians, by rashly identifying the movement with radical attacks on all traditional centers of authority, had helped isolate abolitionism from the public at large. The last straw for the moderates was the election of a woman, Abby Kelley, to the Executive Committee of the AAAS in 1840. American institutions were certainly flawed, said the anti-Garrisonians, but the best way to redeem them would be through the political pressure of a third political party devoted exclusively to the single issue of emancipation. Out of this conviction was born the Liberty party.

Entrenched external opposition, combined with the internal split of 1840, did not, however, significantly weaken abolitionism. The fervor of individual members remained high. To many, perhaps most, of the original converts, abolitionism was a commitment to a lifelong career that was only intensified by the repression of the 1830s. Although we are far from having an adequate explanation or theory for what motivated individual abolitionists, their commitment does seem to have represented in an intensified form a generational revolt of the sons and daughters of New England against the crumbling patriarchal authority of their elders. Abolitionism was especially appealing to young Yankee evangelicals struggling with difficult career choices in a commercializing society of dislocating mobility and seemingly unchristian materialism. Set adrift in an America in which the family farm and God-fearing village community, the world of the fathers, could no longer be taken for granted, and alienated from that America by the righteous standards of their parental upbringing, these evangelicals resolved their conflicts of career and conscience in the holy vocation of abolitionism. The struggle against slavery, the institution that personified in a horrifying, magnified form all the greed, lust, and unchecked power that they saw as rampant in America, established their worth in the eyes of God. "Never were men called on to die in a holier cause," wrote the abolitionist Amos Phillips in 1835. As Christians and as Unionists, the abolitionists strode into battle. If the Union were ever to be saved from the bloodbath portended by Nat Turner's rebellion or the breakup portended by the Nullification movement, then no less was demanded than the immediatist solutions of God's secular missionaries to a fallen people.

Despite, and in many cases because of, the opposition, the original core kept the faith in the 1830s. Meanwhile, the abolitionists could point to impressive growth. At the end of the decade some 2,000 local societies claimed a membership of up to 250,000. The nucleus of a popular constituency had been built. In the cities it was organized around artisans, shopkeepers, and manufacturers; the greatest support came from artisans. Heirs to the radical republicanism of Thomas Paine, skilled craftsmen, much more so than the preindustrial elites, were prone to see slavery as a threat to economic independence and political equality. The abolitionists appealed to this antislavery antipathy; James G. Birney of the Liberty party wrote, "The large slaveholder wants no free mechanics about him: he has mechanics among his own slaves: nor does he need the shopkeeper; because he can go to the place where the shop-keeper now purchases, and buy for himself." In rural areas, pockets of abolitionist strength overlapped prosperous, evangelicalized settlements of Yankee farmers. Here, slavery was vulnerable for its denial of the right to self-improvement and its degradation of the moral benefits of labor.

The split of 1840 did not lead to a fragmentation of this constituency. If anything, by fostering a variety of immediatist positions consistent with the makeup of local societies, the split promoted a healthy, democratic pluralism. By the same token, the decision by more conservative abolitionists to engage in direct political action through the Liberty party widened the appeal of the movement. Scattered evidence from western New York suggests that the Liberty party began mobilizing for antislavery a new constituency, mostly journeymen mechanics and laborers. Men without land who never quite established themselves in their new communities, they were responsive to the warnings of the Liberty party that Northern aristocrats, in alliance with slaveholders, were conspiring to reduce all white workers "to the condition of serfs." To be sure, and as predicted by Garrison, the political abolitionists diluted moral suasion in an effort to attract followers. Voting for the Liberty party, a political act, did not require the revolution in moral values that was at the core of the original conversion to abolitionism. Nonetheless, in several Congressional districts Whig politicians, who no longer had a monopoly on the Yankee evangelical vote, were forced into stronger antislavery positions. And simply by being in the political arena with a stand on slavery deemed extremist by the public, the Liberty party made any antislavery stance in the major parties appear more moderate and respectable in comparison.

LIFE ON A SOUTHERN PLANTATION

EMILY P. BURKE

Cotton was the main economic export of the antebellum South, and most cotton was produced on large and self-contained plantations. About three-quarters of America's slave population lived on such large farms. The following descriptions of plantation life are taken from the letters of Emily P. Burke, a Northern schoolteacher who taught and resided in Georgia during the 1830s and 1840s. Burke describes plantation buildings and some aspects of the daily lives of slaves who worked in the homes and on the fields.

A greeable to my promise in my last letter, I will now go on with my description of the buildings belonging to a Southern plantation.

In the first place there was a paling enclosing all the buildings belonging to the family and all the house servants. In the centre of this enclosure stood the principal house, the same I have already in a previous letter described. In this the father of the family and all the females lodged. The next house of importance was the one occupied by the steward of the plantation, and where all the white boys belonging to the family had their sleeping apartments. The next after this was a school house consisting of two rooms, one for a study, the other the master's dormitory. Then the cook, the washer-woman, and the milkmaid, had each their several houses, the children's nurses always sleeping upon the floor of their mistress' apartment. Then again there was the kitchen, the store-house, corn-house, stable, hen-

Emily P. Burke, *Reminiscences of Georgia*, James M. Fitch, 1850.

coop, the hound's kennel, the shed for the corn mill, all these were separate little buildings within the same enclosure. Even the milk-safe stood out under one great tree, while under another the old washer woman had all her apparatus arranged; even her kettle was there suspended from a cross-pole. Then to increase the beauty of the scene, the whole establishment was completely shaded by ornamental trees, which grew at convenient distances among the buildings, and towering far above them all. The huts of the field servants formed another little cluster of dwellings at considerable distance from the master's residence, yet not beyond the sight of his watchful and jealous eye. These latter huts were arranged with a good deal of order and here each slave had his small patch of ground adjacent to his own dwelling, which he assiduously cultivated after completing his daily task. I have known the poor creatures, notwithstanding "tired nature" longed for repose, to spend the greater part of a moonlight night on these grounds. In this way they often raise considerable crops of corn, tobacco, and potatoes, besides various kinds of garden vegetables. Their object in doing this is to have something with which to purchase tea, coffee, sugar, flour, and all such articles of diet as are not provided by their masters, also such clothing as is necessary to make them appear decent in church, but which they can not have unless they procure it by extra efforts.

From this you see the slave is obliged to work the greater part of his time, for one coarse torn garment a year, and hardly food enough of the coarsest kind to support nature, without the least luxury that can be named. Neither can they after the fatigues of the day repose their toil worn bodies upon a comfortable bed unless they have earned it by laboring many a long, weary hour after even the beasts and the birds have retired to rest. It is a common rule to furnish every slave with one coarse blanket each, and these they always carry with them, so when night overtakes them, let it be where it may, they are not obliged to hasten home to go to rest. Poor creatures! all the home they have is where their blanket is, and this is all the slave pretends to call his own besides his dog. . . .

PICKING COTTON

I found after I had been in the country a few months that the season when I first went there was the most gloomy part of the year. At this time there were but few slaves upon the plantation, many of them being let out to boatmen who at this season of the year are busily engaged in the transportation of goods and produce of all kinds up and down the rivers. The sweet singing birds, too, were all gone to their winter quarters still farther South, but when they had all returned, and the trees began to assume the freshness of summer, and the plants to put forth their blossoms, I found it was far from being a dull and gloomy place. During the greater part of the winter season the negro women are busy in picking, ginning, and packing the cotton for market.

In packing the cotton, the sack is suspended from strong spikes, and while one colored person stands in it to tread the cotton down, others throw it into the sack. I have often wondered how the cotton could be sold so cheap when it required so much labor to get it ready for the market, and certainly it could not be if all their help was hired at the rate of northern labor.

The last of January the servants began to return to the plantation to repair the fences and make ready for planting and sowing. The fences are built of poles arranged in a zigzag manner, so that the ends of one tier of poles rests upon the ends of another. In this work the women are engaged as well as the men. They all go into the woods and each woman as well as man cuts down her own pine sapling, and brings it upon her head. It certainly was a most revolting sight to see the female form scarcely covered with one old miserable garment, with no covering for the head, arms, or neck, nor shoes to protect her feet from briers and thorns, employed in conveying trees upon her head from one place to another to build fences. When I beheld such scenes I felt culpable in living in ease and enjoying the luxuries of life, while so many of my own sex were obliged to drag out such miserable existences merely to procure these luxuries enjoyed by their masters. When the fences were completed, they proceeded to prepare the ground for planting. This is done by throwing the earth up in ridges from one side of the field to the other. This work is usually executed by hand labor, the soil is so light, though sometimes to facilitate the process a light plough, drawn by a mule, is used. The ground there is reckoned by tasks instead of acres. If a person is asked the extent of a certain piece of land, he is told it contains so many tasks, accordingly so many tasks are assigned for a day's work. In hoeing corn, three tasks are considered a good day's work for a man, two for a woman and one and a half for a boy or girl fourteen or fifteen years old. . . .

SUMMER GATHERINGS

About seven o'clock, in the summer season, the colored people would generally begin to assemble in the yard belonging to the planter's residence. Here they would kindle little bonfires, not only to ward off the musquitoes, but because they are considered essential in the hot season to purify the air when it is filled with feverish vapors that arise from decayed vegetable matter. Then while two of their number are engaged at the mill, all the rest join in a dance around the burning fagots. In this manner were spent the greater part of the summer evenings, and it was usual for the white members of the family to assemble on the piazza to witness their pastimes, and sometimes at the request of a favorite slave, I have seen the white children engage in the waltz, or take their places in the quadrille. Slaves from adjoining plantations would often come to spend an evening with their acquaintances, and bring their corn with them to grind. The grinding generally commences at about six in the evening, and the hoarse sound of the mill seldom ceased much before midnight.

Though the slaves in general, notwithstanding all their hard toils and sorrows, had their happy hours, there was one old woman on the plantation who always looked cast down and sorrowful, and never appeared to take any interest in what caused the joy and mirth of those around her. She was one of Afric's own home born daughters, and she had never forgotten those who nursed her in infancy, nor the playmates of her childhood's happy hours. She told me she was stolen one day while gathering shells into a little basket on the sea shore, when she was about ten years old, and crowded into a vessel with a good many of her own race, who had also been stolen and sold for slaves, and from that hour when she left her mother's hut to go out to play she had never seen one of her own kindred, though she had always hoped that Providence might bring some of them in her way; "but now," she replied, "I begin to despair of ever seeing those faces which are still fresh in my memory, for now I am an old woman, and shall soon get through all my troubles and sorrows, and I only think now of meeting them in heaven." When requested she would favor us with a song in her own language, learned before she was stolen, but when she came to sing of her native hills and sparkling streams, the tears would trickle down her sun burnt and furrowed cheeks, and my heart could but ache for this poor creature, stolen away in the innocence of youth, from parents, kindred, home, and country, which were as dear to her as mine to me.

LIFE OF A COOK

Of all the house-servants, I thought the task of the cook was the most laborious. Though she did no other housework she was obliged to do every thing belonging to the kitchen department, and that, too, with none of those conveniences without which a Northern woman would think it was impossible for her to prepare a meal of victuals. After having cooked the supper and washed the dishes she goes about making preparations for the next morning's meal. In the first place she goes into the woods to gather sticks and dried limbs of trees, which she ties in bundles and brings to the kitchen on her head, with which to kindle the morning fire; to get as much fuel as she will want to use in preparing the breakfast she is often obliged to go into the woods several times. When this is done she has all the corn to grind for the hommony and bread, then the evening's preparations are completed. In the morning she is obliged to rise very early, for she has every article of food that comes on to the table to cook, nothing ever being prepared till the hour it is needed. When she has gone through with all the duties connected with the morning's repast, then she goes about the dinner, bringing fuel from the woods, grinding corn, etc. In this manner the cook spends her days, for in whatever department the slaves are educated, they are generally obliged to wear out their lives.

AN ACCOUNT OF NAT TURNER'S REBELLION

Thomas Wentworth Higginson

The 1831 slave rebellion in Virginia led by Nat Turner was one of the deadliest outbreaks of slave violence in the antebellum era. In August 1831, Turner led a small group of followers in a killing spree that killed dozens of whites before being suppressed. Turner remained at large for several weeks as fears spread throughout the South of a widespread slave rebellion before he was captured and executed. The state legislature of Virginia debated whether to gradually abolish slavery in the wake of the rebellion, but instead tightened its slave codes.

The following account of Nat Turner's rebellion is taken from an 1861 *Atlantic Monthly* article by Thomas Wentworth Higginson, a clergyman and abolitionist. A graduate of Harvard Divinity School and a prolific writer, Higginson relied on newspaper accounts and slave recollections in recounting the events that shook Virginia in 1831.

N ear the south-eastern border of Virginia, in Southampton County, there is a neighborhood known as "The Cross Keys." It lies fifteen miles from Jerusalem, the county-town, or court-house," seventy miles from Norfolk, and about as far from Richmond. It is some ten or fifteen miles from Murfreesborough in North Carolina, and about twenty-five from the Great Dismal Swamp. Up to Sunday, the 21st of August, 1831, there was nothing to distinguish it from any other rural, lethargic, slipshod Virginia neighborhood, with the due allotment of mansion-houses and log huts, tobacco-fields and

Thomas Wentworth Higginson, "Nat Turner Insurrection," *The Atlantic Monthly*, vol. 8, August 1861.

"old-fields," horses, dogs, negroes, "poor white folks," so called, and other white folks, poor without being called so. One of these last was Joseph Travis, who had recently married the widow of one Putnam Moore, and had unfortunately wedded to himself her negroes also.

In the woods on the plantation of Joseph Travis, upon the Sunday just named, six slaves met at noon for what is called in the Northern States a picnic, and in the Southern a barbecue. The bill of fare was to be simple: one brought a pig, and another some brandy, giving to the meeting an aspect so cheaply convivial that no one would have imagined it to be the final consummation of a conspiracy which had been for six months in preparation. In this plot four of the men had been already initiated,—Henry, Hark or Hercules, Nelson, and Sam. Two others were novices, Will and Jack by name. The party had remained together from twelve to three o'clock, when a seventh man joined them,—a short, stout, powerfully built person, of dark mulatto complexion, and strongly marked African features, but with a face full of expression and resolution. This was Nat Turner.

AN UNUSUAL SLAVE

He was at this time nearly thirty-one years old, having been born on the 2d of October, 1800. He had belonged originally to Benjamin Turner,—from whom he took his last name, slaves having usually no patronymic;—had then been transferred to Putnam Moore, and then to his present owner. He had, by his own account, felt himself singled out from childhood for some great work; and he had some peculiar marks on his person, which, joined to his mental precocity, were enough to occasion, among his youthful companions, a superstitious faith in his gifts and destiny. He had some mechanical ingenuity also; experimentalized very early in making paper, gunpowder, pottery, and in other arts, which, in later life, he was found thoroughly to understand. His moral faculties appeared strong, so that white witnesses admitted that he had never been known to swear an oath, to drink a drop of spirits, or to commit a theft. And, in general, so marked were his early peculiarities that people said "he had too much sense to be raised; and, if he was, he would never be of any use as a slave." This impression of personal destiny grew with his growth: he fasted, prayed, preached, read the Bible, heard voices when he walked behind his plough, and communicated his revelations to the awe-struck slaves. They told him, in return, that, "if they had his sense, they would not serve any master in the world."

The biographies of slaves can hardly be individualized; they belong to the class. We know bare facts; it is only the general experience of human beings in like condition which can clothe them with life. The outlines are certain, the details are inferential. Thus, for instance, we know that Nat Turner's young wife was a slave; we know that she belonged to a different master from himself; we know little more than this, but this is much. For this is equivalent to saying, that, by day or by night, her husband had no more power to protect her than the man who lies bound upon a plundered vessel's deck has power to protect his wife on board the pirate schooner disappearing in the horizon. She may be well treated, she may be outraged; it is in the powerlessness that the agony lies. There is, indeed, one thing more which we do know of this young woman: the Virginia newspapers state that she was tortured under the lash, after her husband's execution, to make her produce his papers: this is all.

What his private experiences and special privileges or wrongs may have been, it is therefore now impossible to say. Travis was declared to be "more humane and fatherly to his slaves than any man in the county;" but it is astonishing how often this phenomenon occurs in the contemporary annals of slave insurrections. The chairman of the county court also stated, in pronouncing sentence, that Nat Turner had spoken of his master as "only too indulgent;" but this, for some reason, does not appear in his printed Confession, which only says, "He was a kind master, and placed the greatest confidence in me.". . .

Whatever Nat Turner's experiences of slavery might have been, it is certain that his plans were not suddenly adopted, but that he had brooded over them for years. . . .

When he came, therefore, to the barbecue on the appointed Sunday, and found not these four only, but two others, his first question to the intruders was, how they came thither. To this Will answered manfully, that his life was worth no more than the others, and "his liberty was as dear to him." This admitted him to confidence; and as Jack was known to be entirely under Hark's influence, the strangers were no bar to their discussion. Eleven hours they remained there, in anxious consultation: one can imagine those dusky faces, beneath the funereal woods, and amid the flickering of pine-knot torches, preparing that stern revenge whose shuddering echoes should ring through the land so long. Two things were at last decided: to begin their work that night; and to begin it with a massacre so swift and irresistible as to create in a few days more terror than many battles, and so spare the need of future bloodshed. "It was agreed that we should commence at home on that night, and, until we had armed and equipped ourselves and gained sufficient force, neither age nor sex was to be spared: which was invariably adhered to.". . .

THE KILLING BEGINS

We must pass over the details of horror, as they occurred during the next twenty-four hours. Swift and stealthy as Indians, the black men passed from house to house,—not pausing, not hesitating, as their terrible work went on. In one thing they were humaner than Indians, or than white men fighting against Indians: there was no gratuitous outrage beyond the death-blow itself, no insult, no mutilation; but in every house they entered, that blow fell on man, woman, and child,—nothing that had a white skin was spared. From every house they took arms and ammunition, and from a few money. On every plantation they found recruits: those dusky slaves, so obsequious to their master the day before, so prompt to sing and dance before his Northern visitors, were all swift to transform themselves into fiends of retribution now; show them sword or musket, and they grasped it, though it were an heirloom from Washington himself. The troop increased from house to house,—first to fifteen, then to forty, then to sixty. Some were armed with muskets, some with axes, some with scythes, some came on their masters' horses. As the numbers increased, they could be divided, and the awful work was carried on more rapidly still. The plan then was for an advanced guard of horsemen to approach each house at a gallop, and surround it till the others came up. Meanwhile, what agonies of terror must have taken place within, shared alike by innocent and by guilty! what memories of wrongs inflicted on those dusky creatures, by some,—what innocent participation, by others, in the penance! The outbreak lasted for but forty-eight hours; but, during that period, fifty-five whites were slain, without the loss of a single slave. . . .

A COSTLY DELAY

When the number of adherents had increased to fifty or sixty, Nat Turner judged it time to strike at the county-seat, Jerusalem.

Thither a few white fugitives had already fled, and couriers might thence be despatched for aid to Richmond and Petersburg, unless promptly intercepted. Besides, he could there find arms, ammunition, and money; though they had already obtained, it is dubiously reported, from eight hundred to one thousand dollars. On the way it was necessary to pass the plantation of Mr. Parker, three miles from Jerusalem. Some of the men wished to stop here and enlist some of their friends. Nat Turner objected, as the delay might prove dangerous; he yielded at last, and it proved fatal.

He remained at the gate with six or eight men; thirty or forty went to the house, half a mile distant. They remained too long, and he went alone to hasten them. During his absence a party of eighteen white men came up suddenly, dispersing the small guard left at the gate; and when the main body of slaves emerged from the house, they encountered, for the first time, their armed

In 1831 Nat Turner led a violent slave rebellion. He was captured after eluding authorities for weeks.

masters. The blacks halted; the whites advanced cautiously within a hundred yards, and fired a volley; on its being returned, they broke into disorder, and hurriedly retreated, leaving some wounded on the ground. The retreating whites were pursued, and were saved only by falling in with another band of fresh men from Jerusalem, with whose aid they turned upon the slaves, who in their turn fell into confusion. Turner, Hark, and about twenty men on horseback retreated in some order; the rest were scattered. The leader still planned to reach Jerusalem by a private way, thus evading pursuit; but at last decided to stop for the night, in the hope of enlisting additional recruits.

During the night the number increased again to forty, and they encamped on Major Ridley's plantation. An alarm took place during the darkness,—whether real or imaginary, does not appear,—and the men became scattered again. Proceeding to make fresh enlistments with the daylight, they were resisted at Dr. Blunt's house, where his slaves, under his orders, fired upon them; and this, with a later attack from a party of white men near Capt. Harris's, so broke up the whole force that they never re-united. The few who remained together agreed to separate for a few hours to see if any thing could be done to revive the insurrection, and meet again that evening at their original rendezvous. But they never reached it.

IN HIDING

Gloomily came Nat Turner at nightfall into those gloomy woods where forty-eight hours before he had revealed the details of his terrible plot to his companions. At the outset all his plans had succeeded; every thing was as he predicted: the slaves had come readily at his call; the masters had proved perfectly defenceless. Had he not been persuaded to pause at Parker's plantation, he would have been master before now of the arms and ammunition at Jerusalem; and with these to aid, and the Dismal Swamp for a refuge, he might have sustained himself indefinitely against his pursuers.

Now the blood was shed, the risk was incurred, his friends were killed or captured, and all for what? Lasting memories of terror, to be sure, for his oppressors; but, on the other hand, hopeless failure for the insurrection, and certain death for him. What a watch he must have kept that night! To that excited imagination, which had always seen spirits in the sky and blood-drops on the corn and hieroglyphic marks on the dry leaves, how full the lonely forest must have been of signs and solemn warnings! Alone with the fox's bark, the rabbit's rustle, and the screech-owl's scream, the self-appointed prophet brooded over his despair. . . .

There he waited two days and two nights,—long enough to satisfy himself that no one would rejoin him, and that the insurrection had hopelessly failed. The determined, desperate spirits who had shared his plans were scattered forever, and longer delay would be destruction for him also. He found a spot which he judged safe, dug a hole under a pile of fence-rails in a field, and lay there for six weeks, only leaving it for a few moments at midnight to obtain water from a neighboring spring. Food he had previously provided, without discovery, from a house near by.

RUMORS OF REBELLION

Meanwhile an unbounded variety of rumors went flying through the State. The express which first reached the governor announced that the militia were retreating before the slaves. An express to Petersburg further fixed the number of militia at three hundred, and of blacks at eight hundred, and invented a convenient shower of rain to explain the dampened ardor of the whites. Later reports described the slaves as making three desperate attempts to cross the bridge over the Nottoway between Cross Keys and Jerusalem, and stated that the leader had been shot in the attempt. Other accounts put the number of negroes at three hundred, all well mounted and armed, with two or three white men as leaders. Their intention was supposed to be to reach the Dismal Swamp, and they must be hemmed in from that side.

Indeed, the most formidable weapon in the hands of slave insurgents is always this blind panic they create, and the wild exaggerations which follow. The worst being possible, every one takes the worst for granted. Undoubtedly a dozen armed men could have stifled this insurrection, even after it had commenced operations; but it is the fatal weakness of a rural slaveholding community, that it can never furnish men promptly for such a purpose. "My first intention was," says one of the most intelligent newspaper narrators of the affair, "to have attacked them with thirty or forty men; but those who had families here were strongly opposed to it."

As usual, each man was pinioned to his own hearth-stone. As

usual, aid had to be summoned from a distance; and, as usual, the United States troops were the chief reliance. Col. House, commanding at Fort Monroe, sent at once three companies of artillery under Liet.-Col. Worth, and embarked them on board the steamer "Hampton" for Suffolk. These were joined by detachments from the United States ships "Warren" and "Natchez," the whole amounting to nearly eight hundred men. Two volunteer companies went from Richmond, four from Petersburg, one from Norfolk, one from Portsmouth, and several from North Carolina. The militia of Norfolk, Nansemond, and Princess Anne Counties, and the United States troops at Old Point Comfort, were ordered to scour the Dismal Swamp, where it was believed that two or three thousand fugitives were preparing to join the insurgents. It was even proposed to send two companies from New York and one from New London to the same point.

When these various forces reached Southampton County, they found all labor paralyzed and whole plantations abandoned. A letter from Jerusalem, dated Aug. 24, says, "The oldest inhabitant of our county has never experienced such a distressing time as we have had since Sunday night last. . . . Every house, room, and corner in this place is full of women and children, driven from home, who had to take the woods until they could get to this place." "For many miles around their track," says another "the county is deserted by women and children." Still another writes, "Jerusalem is full of women, most of them from the other side of the river,—about two hundred at Vix's." Then follow descriptions of the sufferings of these persons, many of whom had lain night after night in the woods. But the immediate danger was at an end, the short-lived insurrection was finished, and now the work of vengeance was to begin. In the frank phrase of a North-Carolina correspondent, "The massacre of the whites was over, and the white people had commenced the destruction of the negroes, which was continued after our men got there, from time to time, as they could fall in with them, all day yesterday." A postscript adds, that "passengers by the Fayetteville stage say, that, by the latest accounts, one hundred and twenty negroes had been killed,"—this being little more than one day's work.

THE HORRORS OF SUPPRESSION

These murders were defended as Nat Turner defended his: a fearful blow must be struck. In shuddering at the horrors of the insurrection, we have forgotten the far greater horrors of its suppression.

The newspapers of the day contain many indignant protests against the cruelties which took place. "It is with pain," says a correspondent of the *National Intelligencer*, Sept. 7, 1831, "that we speak of another feature of the Southampton Rebellion; for we have been most unwilling to have our sympathies for the sufferers diminished or affected by their misconduct. We allude to the slaughter of many blacks without trial and under circumstances of great barbarity. . . . We met with an individual of intelligence who told us that he himself had killed between ten and fifteen. . . . We [the Richmond troop] witnessed with surprise the sanguinary temper of the population, who evinced a strong disposition to inflict immediate death on every prisoner.". . .

Men were tortured to death, burned, maimed, and subjected to nameless atrocities. The overseers were called on to point out any slaves whom they distrusted, and if any tried to escape they were shot down. Nay, worse than this. "A party of horsemen started from Richmond with the intention of killing every colored person they saw in Southampton County. They stopped opposite the cabin of a free colored man, who was hoeing in his little field. They called out, 'Is this Southampton County?' He replied, 'Yes, sir, you have just crossed the line, by yonder tree.' They shot him dead, and rode on." This is from the narrative of the editor of the Richmond *Whig*, who was then on duty in the militia, and protested manfully against these outrages. "Some of these scenes," he adds, "are hardly inferior in barbarity to the atrocities of the insurgents."

SLAVE RECOLLECTIONS

These were the masters' stories. If even these conceded so much, it would be interesting to hear what the slaves had to report. I am indebted to my honored friend, Lydia Maria Child, for some vivid recollections of this terrible period, as noted down from the lips of an old colored woman, once well known in New York, Charity Bowery. "At the time of the old Prophet Nat," she said, "the colored folks was afraid to pray loud; for the whites threatened to punish 'em dreadfully, if the least noise was heard. The patrols was low drunken whites; and in Nat's time, if they heard any of the colored folks praying, or singing a hymn, they would fall upon 'em and abuse 'em, and sometimes kill 'em, afore master or missis could get to 'em. The brightest and best was killed in Nat's time. The whites always suspect such ones. They killed a great many at a place called Duplon. They killed Antonio, a slave of Mr. J. Stanley, whom they shot; then they pointed their guns at him, and told him to confess about the insurrection. He told 'em he didn't know any thing about any insurrection. They shot several balls through him, quartered him, and put his head on a pole at the fork of the road leading to the court." (This is no, exaggeration, if the Virginia newspapers may be taken as evidence.) "It was there but a short time. He had no trial. They never do. In Nat's time, the patrols would tie up the free colored people, flog 'em, and try to make 'em lie against one another, and often killed them before anybody could interfere. Mr. James Cole, high sheriff, said, if any of the patrols came on his plantation, he would lose his life in defence of his people. One day he heard a patroller boasting how many niggers he had killed. Mr. Cole said, 'If you don't pack up, as quick as God Almighty will let you, and get out of this town, and never be seen in it again, I'll put you where dogs won't bark at you.' He went off, and wasn't seen in them parts again."...

Of the capture or escape of most of that small band who met with Nat Turner in the woods upon the Travis plantation, little can now be known. All appear among the list of convicted, except Henry and Will. ...

The number shot down at random must, by all accounts, have amounted to many hundreds, but it is past all human registration now. The number who had a formal trial, such as it was, is officially stated at fifty-five; of these, seventeen were convicted and hanged, twelve convicted and transported, twenty acquitted, and four free colored men sent on for further trial and finally acquitted. "Not one of those known to be concerned escaped." Of those executed, one only was a woman, "Lucy, slave of John T. Barrow."...

WHITE PANIC

Meanwhile the panic of the whites continued; for, though all others might be disposed of, Nat Turner was still at large. We have positive evidence of the extent of the alarm, although great efforts were afterwards made to represent it as a trifling affair. A distinguished citizen of Virginia wrote, three months later, to the Hon. W.B. Seabrook of South Carolina, "From all that has come to my knowledge during and since that affair, I am convinced most fully that every black preacher in the country east of the Blue Ridge was in the secret." "There is much reason to believe," says the Governor's Message on Dec. 6, "that the spirit of insurrection was not confined to Southampton. Many convictions have taken place elsewhere, and some few in distant counties." The withdrawal of the United States troops, after some ten days' service, was a signal for fresh excitement; and an address, numerously signed, was presented to the United States Government, imploring their continued stay. . . .

It is astonishing to discover, by laborious comparison of newspaper files, how vast was the immediate range of these insurrectionary alarms. Every Southern State seems to have borne its harvest of terror. On the eastern shore of Maryland, great alarm was at once manifested, especially in the neighborhood of Easton and Snowhill; and the houses of colored men were searched for arms even in Baltimore. In Delaware, there were similar rumors. . . .

In North Carolina, Raleigh and Fayetteville were put under military defence, and women and children concealed themselves in the swamps for many days. The rebel organization was supposed to include two thousand. . . .

In Macon, Ga., the whole population were roused from their beds at midnight by a report of a large force of armed negroes five miles off. In an hour, every woman and child was deposited in the largest building of the town, and a military force hastily collected in front. . . .

In Alabama, at Columbus and Fort Mitchell, a rumor was spread of a joint conspiracy of Indians and negroes. At Claiborne the panic was still greater: the slaves were said to be thoroughly organized through that part of the State, and multitudes were imprisoned; the whole alarm being apparently founded on one stray copy of the Boston *Liberator*. . . .

FINALLY CAPTURED

Meanwhile the cause of all this terror was made the object of desperate search. On Sept. 17 the governor offered a reward of five hundred dollars for his capture; and there were other rewards, swelling the amount to eleven hundred dollars,—but in vain. No one could track or trap him. On Sept. 30 a minute account of his capture appeared in the newspapers, but it was wholly false. On Oct. 7 there was another, and on Oct. 18 another; yet all without foundation. Worn out by confinement in his little cave, Nat Turner grew more adventurous, and began to move about stealthily by night, afraid to speak to any human being, but hoping to obtain some information that might aid his escape. Returning regularly to his retreat before daybreak, he might possibly have continued this mode of life until pursuit had ceased, had not a dog succeeded where men had failed. The creature accidentally smelt out the provisions hid in the cave, and finally led thither his masters, two negroes, one of whom was named Nelson. On discovering the formidable fugitive, they fled precipitately, when he hastened to retreat in an opposite direction. This was on Oct. 15; and from this moment the neighborhood was all alive with excitement, and five or six hundred men undertook the pursuit.

It shows a more than Indian adroitness in Nat Turner to have escaped capture any longer. The cave, the arms, the provisions, were found; and, lying among them, the notched stick of this miserable Robinson Crusoe, marked with five weary weeks and six days. But the man was gone. For ten days more he concealed himself among the wheat-stacks on Mr. Francis's plantation, and during this time was reduced almost to despair. . . . On the 25th of October, he was at last discovered by Mr. Francis as he was emerging from a stack. A load of buckshot was instantly discharged at him, twelve of which passed through his hat as he fell to the ground. He escaped even then; but his pursuers were rapidly concentrating upon him, and it is perfectly astonishing that he could have eluded them for five days more.

On Sunday, Oct. 30, a man named Benjamin Phipps, going out for the first time on patrol duty, was passing at noon a clearing in the woods where a number of pine-trees had long since been felled. There was a motion among their boughs; he stopped to watch it; and through a gap in the branches he saw, emerging from a hole in the earth beneath, the face of Nat Turner. Aiming his gun instantly, Phipps called on him to surrender. The fugitive, exhausted with watching and privation, entangled in the branches, armed only with a sword, had nothing to do but to yield,—sagaciously reflecting, also, it's he afterwards explained, that the woods were full of armed men, and that he had better trust fortune for some later chance of escape, instead of desperately attempting it then. He was correct in the first impression, since there were fifty armed scouts within a circuit of two miles. His insurrection ended where it began; for this spot was only a mile and a half from the house of Joseph Travis. . . .

TRIAL AND EXECUTION

When Nat Turner was asked by Mr. T.R. Gray, the counsel assigned him, whether, although defeated, he still believed in his own Providential mission, he answered, as simply as one who came thirty years after him, "Was not Christ crucified?" In the same spirit, when arraigned before the court, "he answered, 'Not guilty,' saying to his counsel that he did not feel so." But apparently no argument was made in his favor by his counsel, nor were any witnesses called,—he being convicted on the testimony of Levi Waller, and upon his own confession, which was put in by Mr. Gray, and acknowledged by the prisoner before the six justices composing the court, as being "full, free, and voluntary." He was therefore placed in the paradoxical position of conviction by his own confession, under a plea of "Not guilty." The arrest took place on the 30th of October, 1831, the confession on the 1st of November, the trial and conviction on the 5th, and the execution on the following Friday, the 11th of November, precisely at noon. He met his death with perfect composure, declined addressing the multitude assembled, and told the sheriff in a firm voice that he was ready. Another account says that he "betrayed no emotion, and even hurried the executioner in the performance of his duty." "Not a limb nor a muscle was observed to move. His body, after his death, was given over to the surgeons for dissection."

The confession of the captive was published under authority of Mr. Gray, in a pamphlet, at Baltimore. Fifty thousand copies of it are said to have been printed; and it was "embellished with an accurate likeness of the brigand, taken by Mr. John Crawley, portrait-painter, and lithographed by Endicott & Swett, at Baltimore." The newly established *Liberator* said of it, at the time, that it would "only serve to rouse up other leaders, and hasten other insurrections," and advised grand juries to indict Mr. Gray. I have never seen a copy of the original pamphlet; it is not easily to be found in any of our public libraries; and I have heard of but one as still existing, although the Confession itself has been repeatedly reprinted. Another small pamphlet, containing the main features of the outbreak, was published at New York during the same year, and this is in my possession. But the greater part of the facts which I have given were gleaned from the contemporary newspapers.

AFRICAN AMERICAN SLAVE CULTURE AND THE ABSENCE OF LARGE-SCALE SLAVE REVOLTS

JOHN B. BOLES

The 1831 Nat Turner rebellion described in the previous selection was in many ways an anomaly. Whites of the American South lived in constant fear of a large-scale slave rebellion such as those that occurred in Latin America and the Caribbean, but such rebellions never materialized. Historian John B. Boles examines reasons for the absence of large-scale slave revolts. He notes that, unlike other slave societies in the Americas, whites outnumbered blacks in the South. The United States also lacked hinterlands where escaped slaves could survive and avoid capture. Also, slaves in America, in contrast to those elsewhere, often lived in family groups. All of these factors served as restraining influences against violent rebellion, according to Boles. African American slaves created their own culture that fostered different forms of rebellion, such as running away or resisting overwork. Boles teaches history at Rice University and edits *The Journal of Southern History*.

John B. Boles, *Black Southerners, 1619–1869*, Lexington: The University Press of Kentucky, 1983. Copyright © 1983 by the University Press of Kentucky. Reproduced by permission.

T he one overriding fact about slave rebellion in the Old
      South was the almost complete absence of large-scale
      armed insurrection such as occurred in Latin America and
the Caribbean and lay like a horrible specter in the back of the
minds of countless southern planters. Explaining nonoccur-
rences is always difficult, and this case is no exception. But even
a partial explanation does shed light on two important components of any historical analysis, the comparative and the temporal. The situation in the South after about 1800 was significantly different from that elsewhere in the Americas. Moreover,
one must remember the wide variety of rebellious acts that
stopped short of insurrection, rebellious acts as diverse and individualized as the planter-slave confrontations themselves. Yet
during the heyday of the Old South, in the final decades before
the Civil War when cotton was king and the slave population
was at its highest, the broad surface of the plantation society was
remarkably smooth and stable despite the many small eddies of
unrest and the strong, deep current of slaves' cultural and psychological rejection of enslavement. That apparent calm, experienced even by those acute observers who suspected the
swirling torrents underneath, has helped perpetuate many
myths about the Old South and its two peoples, black and white.

FACTORS PREVENTING INSURRECTION

Many factors mitigated against successful armed insurrection
by slaves in the Old South. Unlike the situation in Latin America, in the Old South as a whole whites far outnumbered slaves,
and of course totally controlled the police power of the states.
. . . In certain regions like the sea islands of South Carolina and
Georgia and the sugar districts of Louisiana, blacks were in a
significant majority, yet even there the distance between individual plantations and the maze of unbridged estuaries, rivers,
bayous, sloughs, and swamps made communication and travel
between plantations difficult. The geography of the Old South
conspired with demography to complicate still further slave attempts at rebellion and escape. Slaves in Brazil and in the
Guiana region of northeastern South America, for example, had
the huge, unexplored jungle fastness of the Amazon River basin
in which to escape; similarly, plantations were located on the
perimeters of the West Indian islands, whose interiors offered
sure havens for runaways. In both regions slaves escaped to the
interior and in maroon settlements often managed to survive

for years, occasionally fighting white authorities to a standstill and achieving treaty recognition of their status (often in exchange for returning newly escaped slaves).

This kind of escape from slavery was never possible for the overwhelming majority of bondsmen in the Old South. Except for those few who lived near the Dismal Swamp on the eastern Virginia–North Carolina boundary, and some in Florida and Georgia near the Okefenokee Swamp and the trackless Everglades, there was no safe hinterland where maroons could survive. Moreover, cold winters, particularly in the Upper South, made the prospect of hiding out in the woods uninviting. In the early decades of plantation development, the Indians in the backcountry quickly learned they would be rewarded for capturing and returning slave runaways. The Indians were replaced in later decades by yeoman farmers who either returned the runaways for the reward or kept them. For most slaves the freedom territory north of the Mason-Dixon line or the Ohio River was simply too far away, and while several thousand bondsmen in the last half-century of slavery did escape by way of the Underground Railroad, most of them came from the border states of Maryland and Kentucky.

In Latin America and the Caribbean Islands, where hundreds of slaves lived on huge plantations, the owners were absent, and the working conditions were far more harsh than those typical in the South, desperate slaves, often plagued with famine as well as overwork, occasionally struck out against their brutal oppression and escaped to preexisting maroon communities. The working conditions on the tropical sugar plantations drove slaves to rebellion, and the example of successful escape offered by the maroon settlements in the backcountry emboldened otherwise hesitant bondsmen to act. There was, in other words, a heritage of insurrection in the Caribbean and Latin America that offered slaves not only incentive to rebel but the expectation of success. No such vital spark of hope was possible in the Old South. The few insurrections were small, localized, and quickly and brutally suppressed, with many innocent slaves usually punished and the general restrictions against all slaves made temporarily more harsh.

After 1808 the foreign slave trade to the United States ended, but in the slave societies to the south the transatlantic trade in humans continued. As always, the African imports were disproportionately young males, maintaining the highly unequal slave sex ratios in Latin America and the Caribbean. This, combined with the rigorous work routines, the cruelty of managers on absentee plantations, and the disease-induced high death rates produced a degree of despair that seldom obtained in the Old South. A work force of mostly young males, with neither wives nor families to be concerned about, with expectations of a life that could only be "nasty, brutal, and short," with an almost impenetrable backcountry beckoning them and the ever-present example of successful maroons suggesting that escape was possible, and with the number of superintending whites tiny in proportion to the black population—there is no wonder that out of this unstable situation slave resistance and insurrection were constant realities. Yet by the time there were significant numbers of blacks in the antebellum South, the demographic situation was so different as to provide in effect a check on potential slave unrest.

During the era of the cotton kingdom most slaves were American born, the sex ratio was practically equal (more so than the white ratio), and slaves typically lived in family groupings. As a result the slave family became the single most important bond holding members together, and as we have seen, naming practices and kinship systems evolved to cement relationships made fragile by the possibility of sale or removal. This demographic development also prevented slave insurrection.

While a population composed mostly of unattached young males can be very explosive (especially when faced with harsh conditions and the possibility of escape), a population where males and females are equally present, family relationships have been formed and there are small children to love and care for, is far more conservative. The possibility of an entire family escaping was practically nil, and parents were loath to forsake their children to save themselves. Likewise few men would leave their loved ones for an escape attempt with little chance of success. If family attachments lessened runaway efforts, so much more did the ties of family affection reduce the possibilities of insurrection. Few male slaves would risk almost sure death when to do so would leave their families fatherless. Moreover, the knowledge that family members and innocent bystanders would be pitilessly punished and their rights severely circumscribed in the aftermath of a rebellion attempt must have restrained many discontented slaves.

In the Old South, where family structures, leisure time, and fairly good living conditions prevented most slaves from being driven into utter desperation, slaves usually found less risky avenues of countering the dehumanization of chattel bondage. Because hunger and abject hopelessness were less common in the Old South, slaves calculated their options more carefully, waiting—sometimes all their lives—for good chances for successful rebellion. Thousands did not find the right moment to strike until the Civil War and the presence of Union troops profoundly changed the balance. Then no one was more shocked than complacent planters when droves of their seemingly most devoted, most responsible slaves "deserted" and chose freedom.

DIFFERENT KINDS OF RESISTANCE

The realities of power and geography in the Old South also minimized the kind of slave rebellion that often occurred in the other New World plantation societies. In the antebellum South, slaves were very seldom driven to mindless, suicidal acts of outrage and rebellion. Fully aware of their situation, they learned, socialized, and passed on to their children a wide range of behavior—voice intonations, facial expressions, feigned illness, purposeful laziness and slowness of motion, dumb-like-a-fox incomprehension—that combined equal portions of insubordination and minor rebellion to produce a constant undercurrent of resistance to psychological bondage. Although never completely giving in to authority, most slaves were able, at least in the eyes of their master, to acquiesce in their state of servitude and thus survive with their essential humanity intact. In the most fundamental sense, racial slavery as it existed in the Old South was premised on the assumption by whites that blacks were inferior, either a subhuman or a permanently childlike race. Planters' everyday experience, of course, gave the lie to this assumption, and therein may have been the cause of the guilt that some historians believe troubled many whites, particularly those who constructed elaborate proslavery defenses. Had slaves in general accepted this racial subordination and aspired to be only what the white man prescribed, then blacks would have been total slaves, and all resistance—except occasional outbursts of violence—would have disappeared. But the rich panoply of Afro-American culture, their tales, music, art, and religion protected bondsmen from complete capitulation. Out of the inner reserves of their humanity slaves in measured ways resisted servitude and defended the limited rights that had become, through mutual accommodation, accepted by whites. The black community evolved a culture from which proceeded all forms of slave resistance other than rebellion.

Owners were most concerned with their slaves' labor output, and for that reason bondsmen developed a repertoire of techniques to gain a modicum of control over the amount of work required of them. While some slaves were downright lazy, a low-incentive labor system like slavery obviously gave them few reasons to overexert themselves. Even the application of force soon became counterproductive. Slaves realized they had to work at a moderate pace, for their physical well-being and the stability of their family relationships depended on the success of the plantation. While there was never enough incentive or mobility to turn bondsmen into competitive men-on-the-make, they did accept a responsibility to work at a productivity level that eventually came to be accepted by master and slave alike. Often there was a perpetual low-grade war of wills between the two, with masters cajoling, threatening, and occasionally whipping and slaves complaining, moving at a deliberate pace (though the nature of the crop culture required careful labor that outside observers apparently misunderstood at times for indolence), and even practicing minor agricultural sabotage like breaking tools, "accidentally" plowing up crops, "carelessly" letting the teams get out of the barn-lot, and so on. To what extent owners realized what was going on is problematical; usually they ascribed such behavior to the accepted irresponsibility and childishness of slaves, but surely they at times must have comprehended the guerilla resistance under way. (It should be said that such sabotage had a negligible effect on the total agricultural system.) Slaves frequently acted dumb, carefully "misunderstood," and—in earlier days—confessed ignorance of English as effective ways to minimize the demands placed on them.

When a master or overseer tried to force slaves to work harder, or longer hours, than convention had come to establish as the norm, slaves were quick to protest. Not only did the war of the wills heat up, but slaves were sometimes quite bold in their insistence against being pushed beyond endurance or general practice. Particularly if an overseer was the offending taskmaster, slaves did not hesitate to take their case to their masters. Whether the overseer was the culprit or not, aggrieved and protesting slaves complained and shuffled along, slowed their pace, and feigned illness. On any plantation at any given moment there were always several laid up for sickness, real and pretended, a tactic planters were ultimately helpless to counteract. If conditions persisted, or when personal relations between a slave and his owner or overseer became extremely strained—as when a slave felt himself unjustly punished—bondsmen often ran away.

SLAVE RUNAWAYS

Slave runaways were a perennial problem for southern planters. Over the course of the slave-plantation system in the South the nature of runaways and their destinations changed, but in the antebellum period, after the spread of cotton and sugar cultivation, bondsmen ran away for three general reasons. Probably most common and of least worry to owners were those who in response to a real or felt injustice ran away for a short period simply to deprive the owner of a portion of the slave's labor. After all, here was a way for a slave to exert himself, to thwart his owner's intentions, to make a statement about his rights even if it came at some eventual cost to himself. Periodically when an owner or overseer forced slaves to work too hard or on the accepted weekend off (usually Saturday afternoon and Sunday), punished one unjustly, blamed one unfairly, or insulted a specially favored or skilled slave, the offended bondsman would disappear for several days or for three or four weeks.

Masters sometimes came to accept with a shrug this type of protest, knowing the absent slave would soon reappear, having in the meantime been living probably on the fringes of the plantation, maybe even slipping back to the quarters at night for food. Usually when the runaway did return he would receive a whipping or some other punishment, but occasionally owners disregarded the infraction of their rules and welcomed the runaway's return without disciplinary measures. This kind of commonplace running away was not a threat to the institution of slavery. The runaways themselves were protesting less the institution itself than invasions of their perceived rights as slaves. Owners seldom hunted for, probably never advertised for, such absent—not escaped—slaves. Because such limited running away was an accepted if unconscious method for aggrieved or angered slaves to work out their feelings in a bold but, from the owner's view, safe and harmless form, it no doubt relieved tensions, allowed resentments on both sides to cool, and incidentally reduced the possibility that hidden or suppressed rage might build to explosive levels.

While temporary running away was in effect a safety valve, a second common reason for running away represented a longer-term threat to slavery. The separation of slave families caused many bondsmen to leave their plantations in an effort to reunite with loved ones. Even if runaways of this kind eventually returned to their owners, the absence was often long enough to persuade the owner to place advertisements for their return in local newspapers. These advertisements, written as accurately as possible in hopes that the described slave would be located, frequently included hints that the runaway had joined his spouse or children at a certain location. Perhaps there is no stronger indication of the strength and resiliency of family ties among bondsmen than these efforts against all obstacles to see once again kin separated by distance. Even when runaways like these were recaptured and returned to their owners, the more realistic owners frequently would sell them to someone living in the vicinity of the loved one, knowing full well that the bonds of affection were stronger than discipline. Certainly many callous sellers and buyers of men disdained any human sympathies, but just as many—for reasons of practicality if not humanity—tried not to separate families unless in their view economic necessity required them to do so. Slavery's defenders as well as its critics recognized that the separation of families was a moral sore spot in the theoretical justification of bondage, and for that reason very seldom were small children parted from their mothers. Nevertheless, the trauma associated with sales of whatever nature forced many slaves to risk great danger and even greater hardships to see once more the faces of dear ones stolen away from them.

Despite the various factors that minimized slave rebellion and running away, there were nonetheless always situations, personality clashes, misunderstandings that drove slaves to cast aside their doubts and fears and escape to freedom. Often slaves who could not endure their bondage any longer but recognized the futility of individual violence or the inhospitableness of the countryside simply ran away to southern cities where they blended into the sizable free black population and disappeared. Skilled, articulate slaves, well-versed in the ways and expectations of their masters, were at the same time those most able to direct a potential slave insurrection and those most able, and likely, to succeed and even prosper as free blacks in Richmond,

Charleston, or New Orleans. In yet another way southern cities, by offering a refuge to highly skilled slave runaways, helped defuse the potential for rebellion that might destroy the institution of bondage. Permanent slave escapees, then, whether they fled north or to southern cities to gain their freedom, had the ironic effect of making the existing system of slavery more stable by depriving the larger population of bondsmen of their most vocal, most able leaders.

While slave owners often convinced themselves that the possibilities of large-scale slave insurrection were remote and failed to recognize the intent of resistance present in malingering and short-term running away, they realized that there were lethal individualistic ways of rebelling. Slaves were often suspected of arson and poisoning, in part because the causes of destructive fires and fatal diseases were so often mysterious. There are of course recorded instances of bondsmen using either of these to strike back at their owners, and surely both were successfully employed occasionally without raising undue suspicions. Contemporaries seem sometimes to have become almost hysterical over the imagined presence of vindictive slaves behind every unexplained fire or death. It would be a mistake, however, to follow the lead of overwrought, guilt-ridden slave owners. Sparks from fireplaces, poorly constructed chimneys, accidents associated with the smoking of meat or drying of tobacco, spontaneous combustion, and a lengthy list of barely understood and misdiagnosed diseases were probably more often at the bottom of sudden fires and unexplained illnesses.

THE SAMBO MYTH

The absence of a tradition of armed slave uprisings in the Old South in no way supports the old myth of Sambo, the contented slave. Certainly there were passive, fawning, irresponsible, childlike Sambos, but they must have been but a fraction of the slave population. Far more common were the realistic slaves, men and women who knew they had to accept at least the physical constraints of bondage, who had a healthy sense of the possible and for whom family concerns were restraints against self-destructive rage. Whether it was understood or not, the vital Afro-American culture protected realistic slaves from being dehumanized; their culture provided them alternative ways of viewing life and did not allow the white man to control their inner world of values and dreams. By having something of their own to hold to, most bondsmen survived slavery, bending when survival dictated but not letting their spirit be broken.

They learned by necessity to cope with their existence, being by turns passive and assertive; knowing when to fawn and dissemble and when to protest; knowing how to get by guile what they had to have and how to avoid punishment. This indispensable know-how was transmitted from parents to children in a variety of ways. Whites, who seldom could see beyond their slaves' black faces, comprehended them all as Sambos, but again and again, when pushed too far, slaves resisted with a firmness and forthrightness that surprised their masters. To suppress their guilt over slaveholding, most southern whites tried desperately to convince themselves that blacks were a permanent child-race who needed and preferred slavery. When time after time slaves reacted with a maturity and boldness that should have called the racial stereotype into question, whites instead suspected outside forces—abolitionists, the example of free blacks, emancipationist literature—at work.

These realistic slaves represented the huge middle range of character types; at the opposite end of the spectrum from true Sambos were an equally small number of true rebels who with every fiber of their being rejected enslavement. Slave parents, knowing the consequence of attitudes of this kind, would try to dissuade their children from conspicuous rebellion. If the warnings were of no avail, sooner or later rebels were usually killed or suffered such brutality that their spirit was permanently broken, with suicide or self-mutilation sometimes the ultimate result. Too much attention has been focused on Sambos and rebels; most slaves were neither, though they could be a little of both as the occasion required.

With the invention of the cotton gin in 1793, the closing of the foreign slave trade in 1808, and the opening of the Old Southwest to the expansion of slavery after 1815, the political and economic foundations of the cotton kingdom were laid. The Revolutionary era imperceptibly merged into the Old South, with the institution of slavery like a giant black glacier inexorably spreading across the land, grinding down the rocks of resistance along the way and changing the entire social and cultural landscape in its wake. Nothing and no one remained untouched across the face of the South. Only a cataclysmic civil war could wrench blacks out of bondage and transform even incompletely a land so marked by natural beauty and human tragedy.

Manifest Destiny, 1840–1850

CHAPTER 4

COMMERCIAL CULTURE AND DOMESTIC LIFE

MRS. A.J. GRAVES

Mrs. A.J. Graves wrote a number of popular advice books and treatises on femininity that were published in the 1840s. Her writings are an example of what historians have labeled the "cult of domesticity"—the idea that women should confine their activities to the home. The following excerpts from her 1843 treatise *Woman in America: Being an Examination into the Moral and Intellectual Condition of American Female Society* illustrate some themes of this particular vein of social thought.

One is the social ramifications of the urbanization and industrialization of American society. Prior to the nineteenth century, most American women lived on farms in which the home and workplace were the same, and where both the husband and wife contributed to the economic fortunes of the family. In the nineteenth century, however, growing numbers of women occupied homes in which the men's workplace was at a separate office or factory. Women—at least middle and upper class "respectable" women—no longer worked for money, but were expected to keep house and raise the children. Many social commentators of this time regarded this economic division of labor a preordained and important mandate for women to be the moral guardians of home and family—to be active in improving their "domestic sphere" while men fulfilled their duty of providing for them. In the following excerpts Graves decries the tendency of men to become overly involved in outside eco-

Mrs. A.J. Graves, *Woman in America: Being an Examination into the Moral and Intellectual Condition of American Female Society*, New York: Harper and Brothers, 1843.

nomic and political pursuits to the extent that men and women live lives of virtual separation. Her solution is not that men and women give up their separate spheres, but should make more effort to engage with each other (with women having the special domestic duty to "entice" their husbands to spend a few more hours at home). Graves urges women to seek knowledge and cultivate their intellect, as long as they do not abandon their "true and allotted sphere—domestic life."

T he great principles of liberty and equal rights, which are about to overthrow the long-existing institutions of despotism, and are stirring the hearts of men of every station, in every clime, have penetrated even into the quiet havens of domestic life. While men are fiercely contending for their prerogatives upon the world's arena, without seeming yet to have settled what should be their relative position in regard to each other, women have come forward to claim immunities which ancient usage has long denied them. "The Rights of Woman" are almost as warmly and wildly contested as "The Rights of Man"; and there is a revolution going on in the female mind at the present day, out of which glorious results may arise; though in this, as in all other revolutions, ultraism, and fanaticism may retard the development of good by their excesses, and their disregard of the dictates of sound wisdom and sober discretion. We lament the erratic course of many of our female reformers, believing that they have inflicted deep injury where they intended good, by drawing woman away from her true and allotted sphere—domestic life. . . .

NARROWING OF INTERESTS

To woman it belongs . . . to elevate the intellectual character of her household, to kindle the fires of mental activity in childhood, and to keep these steadily burning with advancing years . . . The men of our country, as things are constituted among us, find but little time for the cultivation of science and general literature—studies so eminently calculated to refine the mind and purify the taste, and which furnish so exhaustless a fund of elevated enjoyment to the heart. And this is the case even with those who have acquired a fondness for intellectual pursuits in early life. The absorbing passion for gain, and the pressing demands of business, engross their whole attention. Thus the merchant becomes a merchant, and nothing more; and the mind of the lawyer is little else than a library of cases and precedents, of legal records and commentaries. The physician loses sight of the scientific studies to which his profession so naturally directs him, contents himself with the same beaten track, and becomes a mere practitioner or operator. And the mechanic and agriculturist too often settle down into mere manual laborers, by suffering practical details wholly to occupy their minds as well as their bodies. The only relief to this absorbing devotion to "material interests" is found in the excitement of party politics.

These two engross the whole moral, intellectual, and physical man; and, to be convinced of this, we need not follow the American to his place of business or to political meetings—we have only to listen to his fireside conversation. It might be supposed that the few waking hours he spends at home in the bosom of his family, he would delight to employ upon such subjects as would interest and improve his wife and children, and that he would avail himself of these opportunities to refresh his wearied mind with new matters of thought. But in place of this, what is the perpetual theme of his conversation? Business and politics, six per cent, bank discounts, stockjobbing, insolvencies, assets, liabilities—cases at court, legal opinions and decisions—neuralgia, gastric irritation, fevers, etc.—Clay, Webster, the Bank bill, and other political topics of the day: these are the subjects incessantly talked about by the male members of the family when at home, and which the females, of course, are neither expected to take any special interest in nor to understand. Or perhaps the wife may take her turn in relating the history of the daily vexations she experiences in her household arrangements, while the husband's eye is gazing on vacancy, or his mind is occupied by his business cares. Woman should be made to take an intelligent interest in her husband's affairs, and may be benefited by a knowledge of the value of money, its best mode of investment; or by being instructed in the laws of physiology and of hygiene; but she can receive neither pleasure nor profit from hearing the cabalistic terms familiar only to the initiated in the mysteries of financiering, or the occult words and phrases which the professional man employs to communicate his knowledge or the results of his observations. The husband should doubtless sympathize with the wife in her domestic trials; but he cannot, nor ought he to, become interested in every trivial vexation she may meet with. There should, then, be some common ground on which both may meet with equal pleasure and advantage to themselves and to their offspring; and what is there so appropriate to this end as *intellectual pursuits?*

A Mother's Duties

What a certain writer has said of sons, may also be said, with equal truth, of many husbands: "they seem to consider their homes as mere places of boarding and lodging"; and, we may add, forget that it is the dwelling-place of their wives and children. So long as they provide for the physical wants of their families, they think their duty is fulfilled; as though shelter, food, and clothing could satisfy the necessities of immortal minds. They are liberal, perhaps, even to profusion, in surrounding their families with all that can minister to physical comfort, and the indulgence of vanity and pride, but they neglect to excite or to satisfy the more exalted desire for intellectual adorning and spiritual improvement. It is here our men are wanting; and female influence must supply the defect. A mother should sedulously cultivate the intellectual tastes of her children, and surround them with objects calculated to stimulate and gratify their ambition for knowledge. Her own mind should not only be richly stored with the wisdom of the past, but she should keep herself familiar with the current literature of the day, with the progress of science, and the new and useful truths it is constantly bringing to light. Out of all this fullness of knowledge she should communicate freely to her children, and labor by her conversation gently to draw her husband away from his contracted sphere of thought, to enter with her upon a more extended field of observation and reflection. She should entice him to forget his business and his politics, and to devote the few hours he spends at home to those higher pleasures of the mind, which will not only yield a delightful refreshment at the time, but enable him to return with renewed vigor to the routine of his daily labors.

THE REVOLUTIONARY SHOWMANSHIP OF PHINEAS T. BARNUM

ROBERT E. GARD AND DAVID H. SEMMES

Phineas T. Barnum was one of the most successful popular entertainers of the antebellum era. A pioneer in promotion and advertising, Barnum's museums and traveling show business attractions amused thousands of Americans, many of whom had moral qualms about attending plays but happily enjoyed performances in his American Museum's "lecture room." The following excerpts from *America's Players*, a history of American theater by Robert E. Gard and David H. Semmes, explores highlights of Barnum's career and his influence on American popular culture. Robert E. Gard was for many years a professor of theater at the University of Wisconsin at Madison. A folklorist and playwright, he also wrote novels and works of nonfiction. Coauthor David H. Semmes was a high school teacher and drama coach who later became a professor of communication arts at the University of Wisconsin.

S howmanship is an elusive quality. Dictionaries could devote paragraphs to the attempt to define it. But perhaps just one word, one name, is sufficient definition: Barnum. Phineas Taylor Barnum was probably America's greatest exponent of showmanship. He was the father of high pressure salesmanship, developing methods which virtually compelled the American public to buy his special brand of entertainment.

Robert E. Gard and David H. Semmes, *America's Players*, New York: Seabury Press, 1967. Copyright © 1967 by Robert E. Gard and David H. Semmes. Reproduced by permission.

FAMILIAR NAMES

His most famous attractions are still well known to the American public one hundred years after they were introduced. For example, today the words "Tom Thumb" immediately evoke an image of a midget, but that wasn't always the case. Barnum, with a nose for the strange, learned how to exploit for mutual profit the unusual people he found. When Barnum discovered Charles Stratton, a tiny five-year-old just twenty-four inches high and weighing only fifteen pounds, he renamed him Tom Thumb. Barnum then built Tom's image through publicity and advertising until the entire world recognized his name and talents.

In the same way "Siamese twins" came to be the term used to refer to all humans who are joined biologically. The original "Siamese Twins," Chang and Eng, were Chinese. It was Barnum, too, who first called a large elephant Jumbo and again gave our language a new term, now used to connote unusual size whether in elephants or detergent bottles.

Before Barnum, the circus was strictly a one-ring affair and circus parades unheard of. He made "three-ring circus," "circus parade," and "Barnum" practically synonymous terms.

How did this unusual man build his career and powerful influence? A native of Bethel, Connecticut, Phineas Taylor Barnum started as a clerk, and then in quick succession became a storekeeper, a lottery agent, an auctioneer, a newspaper editor, and a boardinghouse keeper. Although none of these occupations proved to be successful, Barnum learned about people in each of them and unwittingly started preparing himself for his future career of manipulating the public's tastes.

GEORGE WASHINGTON'S MAID

Barnum's name first appeared before the public as the promoter of one Joice Heth. It was in 1835, when New York was jolted into a clamor over this crippled, blind little colored woman who, it was claimed, was not only one hundred sixty-one years old, but had been George Washington's first nursemaid. Barnum purchased the ancient slave from another showman, R.W. Lindsay, who had exhibited her for a while in Philadelphia and then grown tired of the whole enterprise. Barnum sold his interest in his grocery store, borrowed everything he could, used all his savings, and paid $1000 for Joice.

From William Niblo, Barnum leased a large apartment next door to Niblo Gardens, the famous open air music hall in New

York. From Niblo, also, Barnum received money to pay for all of Barnum's promotion ideas. In return, Barnum agreed to pay Niblo half of the net profit. Barnum made the rounds of the newspaper offices for a week before he introduced Joice to the public. He not only purchased advertising space in the newspapers, he also convinced the various editors of the veracity of his exhibition. He claimed that Joice was a very religious woman and would like to converse with the local clergy, as well as anyone else who would care to visit.

Along with Joice Heth, Barnum had purchased what seemed to be certain proof of her remarkable claims, a bill of sale from George Washington's father to his sister-in-law for Joice Heth. It was yellowed and torn, but readable, and it, too, was exhibited to the doubting public. Customers flocked into the apartment when Barnum finally allowed them to "visit." For months he netted over a thousand dollars a week and when New Yorkers had seen their fill of Joice, he toured her to Boston, exhibiting her at Concert Hall. Again the crowds were huge and when they started to wane after a few weeks, Barnum decided to try a hoax on the Boston public. He planted a story in a newspaper which claimed that Joice wasn't real, but an elaborate doll made of rubber and that her exhibitor was a ventriloquist. No matter whether they had seen her or not, or believed the story, curious Bostonians again flocked to see the old slave. And Barnum's pockets bulged with a bankroll larger than he had ever known in his life.

Barnum exhibited Joice Heth in one city after another until she died in 1836. Her remains were turned over to a prominent physician, Dr. David L. Rogers, who had requested an autopsy. Barnum saw a chance for still more publicity, and he invited a number of other doctors and editors to be present. Then, of course, it was discovered that while Joice had undoubtedly been an old woman, she couldn't possibly have been one hundred sixty-one. The story, labeling Barnum a charlatan and the whole exhibit a hoax, was widely repeated. Barnum claimed to be just as surprised as everyone else.

Only twenty-six years old then, Barnum had learned that the American public wanted to believe the impossible. He had also learned that he had the talent to give that public what it wanted.

THE AMERICAN MUSEUM

In 1841, Barnum bought Scudder's Museum in New York. Scudder had founded his museum in 1810, filled it with stuffed animals, models, and dusty relics, and gradually developed it into a profitable venture. However, when Scudder died in 1840, leaving a large fortune and the museum to his daughters, they were unable to continue his successful management. Within a year, business had fallen off to the point where Barnum could make a deal, paying only $15,000 for the entire collection.

In a few years, Barnum's American Museum and Gallery of Fine Arts in New York City was a landmark. For just twenty-five cents a person could roam through five stories of rooms filled with relics, paintings, stuffed animals, waxworks of famous heroes and villains, a menagerie of live animals, automatons, variety performers such as acrobats and jugglers, Indians, gypsies, and strange people of every description and size known (and unknown) to man.

Phineas T. Barnum

On that same twenty-five cent admission the visitor to the American Museum could spend a few hours in Barnum's "lecture hall," a full-sized theatre seating three thousand patrons. Barnum understood the moral pressures and prejudices prevalent among many groups against the theatre. But while other producers tended to abandon the hope of gaining these groups as patrons, Barnum's shrewd knowledge of his fellow man found a way to lure even the most pious puritan into his audiences. The "lecture room" in the "museum" led everyone to believe that a play performed there must be strictly moral and edifying.

Barnum's lecture room became one of the most profitable theatres in New York. After opening with the most famous temperance play of the age, *The Drunkard,* he went on to produce nearly everything from farces to melodramas, and created programs that appealed not only to regular theatregoers, but also to family groups and to declared moral opponents of the theatre. Barnum's foresight and understanding proved that the right approach could move his fellow man to accept nearly anything.

Late in the 1840's, Barnum took Tom Thumb to Europe and while presenting his tiny prodigy to the various crowned heads as well as capacity crowds, he heard of Jenny Lind. His promotion of the little Swedish soprano was probably the greatest single job of publicity in his long career.

Jenny Lind had toured Europe and England receiving critical accolades wherever she appeared. Barnum became fascinated with her and offered to sponsor her American debut. Miss Lind, however, refused. It was guessed she was either afraid to leave Europe or wished to make a better financial deal. Barnum persisted and finally won her contract signature by depositing $187,000 in her London bank as security. The contract called for Miss Lind to sing 150 concerts in the United States for which she would receive a basic $1000 per concert plus fifty per cent of the profits over $5500. These terms were unheard of at that time, but Barnum was confident.

Back in the United States, Barnum went to work exciting New York (and the rest of the nation) to a feverish pitch of expectancy before the arrival of "The Swedish Nightingale." He agitated for the erection of a new concert hall in which to present her New York debut. Construction of Tripler Hall was started for just this purpose. Barnum then announced that the tickets for the initial concert would be sold not at the box office, but at a special auction on the grounds of Castle Garden theatre. Nearly 3000 people paid a small admission fee to witness the auction. On just the first day of the auction over a thousand tickets were sold for a gross of more than ten thousand dollars!

Through Barnum's manipulations, Miss Lind's arrival on board a steamship was greeted with more pomp than was usually accorded royalty. Tens of thousands of people lined the streets of New York to see her carriage pass and a huge mass cheered her entrance into the hotel. Tripler Hall wasn't yet completed so Jenny Lind's first few concerts were at Castle Garden. Her debut on September 11, 1850, was greeted by the press with a few critical reservations regarding Miss Lind's musical greatness, but the public was enthralled and eventually even the newspapers were admitting that Barnum's "Nightingale" was a "musical phenomenon," with "astonishing virtuosity" in her "execution of . . . chromatic passages."

Jenny Lind toured to 137 American cities, meeting capacity crowds everywhere. She dominated the American entertainment scene so strongly that other performers, competing at the same time for the public's attention, had a difficult struggle. Miss Lind's tour was planned to take her as far west as San Francisco, but she never got there. She had fallen in love with a

Boston pianist, Otto Goldschmidt, and in May, 1852, she decided to marry him and return to New York. San Francisco, in anticipation of her visit, had built a new theatre and even though she didn't get there they named the theatre for her.

The Swedish Nightingale's farewell concerts in New York were again sold out, and she returned to Europe in the summer of 1852 a wealthy and adored star. P.T. Barnum, who had maneuvered the whole adventure, was a wealthy man even before Mrs. Goldschmidt returned his London security deposit. . . .

Professor William Lyon Phelps of Yale University called Barnum, "the greatest psychologist who ever lived . . . the Shakespeare of advertising." Barnum himself said that the one indispensable qualification of a good showman is "a thorough knowledge of human nature, which of course included the faculty of judiciously applying soft soap. . . . the faculty to please and flatter the public so judiciously as not to have them suspect your intention." In more negative terms, he is reputed to have said, "There's a sucker born every minute."

THE ANNEXATION OF TEXAS IS PART OF AMERICA'S MANIFEST DESTINY

JOHN L. O'SULLIVAN

The use of the term "manifest destiny" to promote and justify the spread of American rule and democracy over the North American continent is believed to date from the following essay, published in July 1845. Its author is John L. O'Sullivan, editor of the *New York Morning News* and founder and editor of *United States Magazine and Democratic Review*. O'Sullivan had been a vociferous advocate of the U.S. annexation of Texas—a former province of Mexico that had declared itself independent in 1836 when Anglo-American settlers rebelled against Mexican rule. Texas annexation was opposed by Mexico, by Great Britain and France who wanted to prevent U.S. expansion, and by Americans who objected to a new slave state entering the Union. In February 1845, however, Congress passed a joint resolution favoring annexation, and Texas became the nation's 28th state on December 29, 1845.

O'Sullivan argues that the annexation of Texas is but part of what he envisions for America. He predicts that California (then a Mexican province) and even Canada will eventually become part of the United States as well—a development he welcomes as ongoing proof of America's greatness.

John L. O'Sullivan, "Annexation," *United States Magazine and Democratic Review*, July 1845.

I t is time now for opposition to the Annexation of Texas to cease, all further agitation of the waters of bitterness and strife, at least in connection with this question, even though it may perhaps be required of us as a necessary condition of the freedom of our institutions, that we must live on forever in a state of unpausing struggle and excitement upon some subject of party division or other. But, in regard to Texas, enough has now been given to party. It is time for the common duty of patriotism to the country to succeed; or if this claim will not be recognized, it is at least time for common sense to acquiesce with decent grace in the inevitable and the irrevocable.

Texas is now ours. Already, before these words are written, her convention has undoubtedly ratified the acceptance, by her congress, of our proffered invitation into the Union; and made the requisite changes in her already republican form of constitution to adapt it to its future federal relations. Her star and her stripe may already be said to have taken their place in the glorious blazon of our common nationality; and the sweep of our eagle's wing already includes within its circuit the wide extent of her fair and fertile land. She is no longer to us a mere geographical space—a certain combination of coast, plain, mountain, valley, forest, and stream. She is no longer to us a mere country on the map. She comes within the dear and sacred designation of our country; no longer a *pays* [country], she is a part of *la patrie* [homeland]; and that which is at once a sentiment and a virtue, patriotism, already begins to thrill for her too within the national heart.

It is time then that all should cease to treat her as alien, and even adverse—cease to denounce and vilify all and everything connected with her accession—cease to thwart and oppose the remaining steps for its consummation; or where such efforts are felt to be unavailing, at least to embitter the hour of reception by all the most ungracious frowns of aversion and words of unwelcome. There has been enough of all this. It has had its fitting day during the period when, in common with every other possible question of practical policy that can arise, it unfortunately became one of the leading topics of party division, of presidential electioneering. But that period has passed, and with it let its prejudices and its passions, its discords and its denunciations, pass away too. The next session of Congress will see the representatives of the new young state in their places in both our halls of national legislation, side by side with those of the old

Thirteen. Let their reception into "the family" be frank, kindly, and cheerful, as befits such an occasion, as comports not less with our own self-respect than patriotic duty towards them. Ill betide those foul birds that delight to file their own nest, and disgust the ear with perpetual discord of ill-omened croak.

FOREIGN INTERFERENCE

Why, were other reasoning wanting, in favor of now elevating this question of the reception of Texas into the Union, out of the lower region of our past party dissensions, up to its proper level of a high and broad nationality, it surely is to be found, found abundantly, in the manner in which other nations have undertaken to intrude themselves into it, between us and the proper parties to the case, in a spirit of hostile interference against us, for the avowed object of thwarting our policy and hampering our power, limiting our greatness and checking the fulfillment of our manifest destiny to overspread the continent allotted by Providence for the free development of our yearly multiplying millions. This we have seen done by England, our old rival and enemy; and by France, strangely coupled with her against us, under the influence of the Anglicism strongly tinging the policy of her present prime minister, [Francois-Pierre-Guillaume] Guizot.

The zealous activity with which this effort to defeat us was pushed by the representatives of those governments, together with the character of intrigue accompanying it, fully constituted that case of foreign interference, which Mr. [Henry] Clay himself declared should, and would unite us all in maintaining the common cause of our country against the foreigner and the foe. We are only astonished that this effect has not been more fully and strongly produced, and that the burst of indignation against this unauthorized, insolent, and hostile interference against us, has not been more general even among the party before opposed to annexation, and has not rallied the national spirit and national pride unanimously upon that policy. We are very sure that if Mr. Clay himself were now to add another letter to his former Texas correspondence, he would express this sentiment, and carry out the idea already strongly stated in one of them, in a manner which would tax all the powers of blushing belonging to some of his party adherents.

It is wholly untrue, and unjust to ourselves, the pretense that the Annexation has been a measure of spoliation, unrightful and unrighteous—of military conquest under forms of peace and law—of territorial aggrandizement at the expense of justice, and justice due by a double sanctity to the weak. This view of the question is wholly unfounded, and has been before so amply refuted in these pages, as well as in a thousand other modes, that we shall not again dwell upon it.

The independence of Texas was complete and absolute. It was an independence, not only in fact, but of right. No obligation of duty toward Mexico tended in the least degree to restrain our right to effect the desired recovery of the fair province once our own—whatever motives of policy might have prompted a more deferential consideration of her feelings and her pride, as involved in the question. If Texas became peopled with an American population, it was by no contrivance of our government, but on the express invitation of that of Mexico herself; accompanied with such guaranties of state independence, and the maintenance of a federal system analogous to our own, as constituted a compact fully justifying the strongest measures of redress on the part of those afterward deceived in this guaranty, and sought to be enslaved under the yoke imposed by its violation.

She was released, rightfully and absolutely released, from all Mexican allegiance, or duty of cohesion to the Mexican political body, by the acts and fault of Mexico herself, and Mexico alone. There never was a clearer case. It was not revolution; it was resistance to revolution: and resistance under such circumstances as left independence the necessary resulting state, caused by the abandonment of those with whom her former federal association had existed. What then can be more preposterous than all this clamor by Mexico and the Mexican interest, against Annexation, as a violation of any rights of hers, any duties of ours? . . .

TEXAS AND SLAVERY

Nor is there any just foundation for the charge that Annexation is a great pro-slavery measure—calculated to increase and perpetuate that institution. Slavery had nothing to do with it. Opinions were and are greatly divided, both at the North and South, as to the influence to be exerted by it on slavery and the slave states. That it will tend to facilitate and hasten the disappearance of slavery from all the northern tier of the present slave states, cannot surely admit of serious question. The greater value in Texas of the slave labor now employed in those states,

must soon produce the effect of draining off that labor south-
wardly, by the same unvarying law that bids water descend the
slope that invites it.

Every new slave state in Texas will make at least one free state
from among those in which that institution now exists—to say
nothing of those portions of Texas on which slavery cannot
spring and grow—to say nothing of the far more rapid growth
of new states in the free West and Northwest, as these fine regions are overspread by the emigration fast flowing over them
from Europe, as well as from the Northern and Eastern states of
the Union as it exists. On the other hand, it is undeniably much
gained for the cause of the eventual voluntary abolition of slavery, that it should have been thus drained off toward the only
outlet which appeared to furnish much probability of the ultimate disappearance of the Negro race from our borders.

The Spanish-Indian-American populations of Mexico, Central America, and South America, afford the only receptacle capable of absorbing that race whenever we shall be prepared to
slough it off—to emancipate it from slavery, and (simultaneously necessary) to remove it from the midst of our own. Themselves already of mixed and confused blood, and free from the
"prejudices" which among us so insuperably forbid the social
amalgamation which can alone elevate the Negro race out of a
virtually servile degradation; even though legally free the regions occupied by those populations must strongly attract the
black race in that direction; and as soon as the destined hour of
emancipation shall arrive, will relieve the question of one of its
worst difficulties, if not absolutely the greatest. . . .

The country which was the subject of Annexation in this case,
from its geographical position and relations, happens to be—or
rather the portion of it now actually settled, happens to be—a
slave country. But a similar process might have taken place in
proximity to a different section of our Union; and indeed there
is a great deal of Annexation yet to take place, within the life of
the present generation, along the whole line of our northern
border. Texas has been absorbed into the Union in the inevitable
fulfilment of the general law which is rolling our population
westward; the connexion of which with that ratio of growth in
population which is destined within a hundred years to swell
our numbers to the enormous population of *two hundred and
fifty millions* (if not more), is too evident to leave us in doubt of
the manifest design of Providence in regard to the occupation

of this continent. It was disintegrated from Mexico in the natural course of events, by a process perfectly legitimate on its own part, blameless on ours; and in which all the censures due to wrong, perfidy and folly, rest on Mexico alone. And possessed as it was by a population which was in truth but a colonial detachment from our own, and which was still bound by myriad ties of the very heartstrings to its old relations, domestic and political, their incorporation into the Union was not only inevitable, but the most natural, right and proper thing in the world—and it is only astonishing that there should be any among ourselves to say it nay. . . .

CALIFORNIA IS NEXT

California will, probably, next fall away from the loose adhesion which, in such a country as Mexico, holds a remote province in a slight equivocal kind of dependence on the metropolis. Imbecile and distracted, Mexico never can exert any real government authority over such a country. The impotence of the one and the distance of the other, must make the relation one of virtual independence; unless, by stunting the province of all natural growth, and forbidding that immigration which can alone develope its capabilities and fulfill the purposes of its creation, tyranny may retain a military dominion, which is no government in the legitimate sense of the term. In the case of California this is now impossible. The Anglo-Saxon foot is already on its borders. Already the advance guard of the irresistible army of Anglo-Saxon emigration has begun to pour down upon it, armed with the plough and the rifle, and marking its trail with schools and colleges, courts and representative halls, mills and meetinghouses. A population will soon be in actual occupation of California, over which it will be idle for Mexico to dream of dominion. They will necessarily become independent. All this without agency of our government, without responsibility of our people—in the natural flow of events, the spontaneous working of principles, and the adaptation of the tendencies and wants of the human race to the elemental circumstances in the midst of which they find themselves placed.

And they will have a right to independence—to self-government—to the possession of the homes conquered from the wilderness by their own labors and dangers, sufferings and sacrifices—a better and a truer right than the artificial title of sovereignty in Mexico, a thousand miles distant, inheriting from Spain a title good only against those who have none better. Their right to independence will be the natural right of self-government belonging to any community strong enough to maintain it—distinct in position, origin and character, and free from any mutual obligations of membership of a common political body, binding it to others by the duty of loyalty and compact of public faith. This will be their title to independence; and by this title, there can be no doubt that the population now fast streaming down upon California will both assert and maintain that independence.

A Transcontinental Railroad

Whether they will then attach themselves to our Union or not, is not to be predicted with any certainty. Unless the projected railroad across the continent to the Pacific be carried into effect, perhaps they may not; though even in that case, the day is not distant when the empires of the Atlantic and Pacific would again flow together into one, as soon as their inland borders should approach each other. But that great work, colossal as appears the plan on its first suggestion, cannot remain long unbuilt. Its necessity for this very purpose of binding and holding together in its iron clasp our fast-settling Pacific region with that of the Mississippi Valley—the natural facility of the route—the ease with which any amount of labor for the construction can be drawn in from the overcrowded populations of Europe, to be paid in the lands made valuable by the progress of the work itself—and its immense utility to the commerce of the world with the whole eastern coast of Asia, alone almost sufficient for the support of such a road—these considerations give assurance that the day cannot be distant which shall witness the conveyance of the representatives from Oregon and California to Washington within less time than a few years ago was devoted to a similar journey by those from Ohio; while the magnetic telegraph will enable the editors of the *San Francisco Union*, the *Astoria Evening Post*, or the *Nootka Morning News*, to set up in type the first half of the President's inaugural before the echoes of the latter half shall have died away beneath the lofty porch of the Capitol, as spoken from his lips.

A Look to the Future

Away, then, with all idle French talk of balances of power on the American Continent. There is no growth in Spanish America! Whatever progress of population there may be in the British

Canadas, is only for their own early severance of their present colonial relation to the little island 3,000 miles across the Atlantic; soon to be followed by annexation, and destined to swell the still accumulating momentum of our progress.

And whosoever may hold the balance, though they should cast into the opposite scale all the bayonets and cannon, not only of France and England, but of Europe entire, how would it kick the beam against the simple, solid weight of the 250, or 300 millions—and American millions—destined to gather beneath the flutter of the stripes and stars, in the fast hastening year of the Lord 1945!

AMERICA IN 1846

TIMOTHY FOOTE

Timothy Foote provides a multifaceted overview of the year 1846—a pivotal moment in American history, he argues. President James K. Polk waged aggressive diplomacy to secure from Great Britain the land that now consists of the states of Oregon and Washington in an 1846 treaty. Similar diplomatic ventures against Mexico, however, resulted in war between the two countries—a war out of which America eventually acquired California, Arizona, and New Mexico. Foote also describes other important and interesting happenings of 1846, including the struggles of pioneers traveling from Missouri to Oregon and California, the publication of Herman Melville's novel *Typee*, and the growing influence of the abolitionist movement. Foote is an editor of *Smithsonian* magazine and a former editor at *Time* magazine.

It was a year when people were reading "The Raven" by a neurotic genius who had flunked out of West Point. It was the year when Melville scored a hit with *Typee*, his first South Seas adventure; five years later *Moby-Dick* stirred hardly a ripple. The first game of baseball (*not* invented by Abner Doubleday) was played with present-day rules. Walt Whitman, age 26, landed a job as editor of the *Brooklyn Eagle*. In Manhattan P.T. Barnum, already rich and famous for "exhibiting all that is monstrous, scaley, strange and queer," was pleasing crowds with the latest of his Fat Boys.

It was a year when, at a great industrial fair in the nation's capital, inventor Elias Howe showed off his amazing new sewing machine. The first telegraph lines had been strung between Baltimore and Washington. During an operation at Massachusetts General Hospital in Boston a dentist named William

Timothy Foote, "America in 1846: A Country on the Move," *Smithsonian*, vol. 27, April 1996, pp. 39–50. Copyright © 1996 by *Smithsonian*. Reproduced by permission.

Morton administered ether in the first public demonstration of its use as an anesthetic. Thereafter the help of three or four men need no longer be required to amputate a leg or pull a tooth. . . .

In Independence, Missouri, several thousand emigrants, westward bound out of the United States for the Oregon territory and for California, then part of Mexico, were about to set off toward Fort Laramie and the Platte River, an early stop on what was to become famous as the Oregon Trail. . . .

1846

The year, of course, was 1846. . . .1846 was an astonishing year. It was the year the Mexican War began. The year when the country, taking a quantum leap forward, suddenly completed the westward course of empire that Jefferson had dreamed of when he sent Lewis and Clark out exploring 40 years before. As 1846 began, the Union occupied less than half of what is the continental United States today; when it was over we possessed, or were soon to possess, all of it.

This was accomplished by means that are controversial to this day—the canny use of cash, diplomatic deal-making, the threat of war and, finally, when the others failed, war itself. The war left us with 13,000 American dead—only 1,721 died in battle, most of the rest from disease. President James Polk's policies changed the contour of the country by adding more than a million square miles of territory. Some claimed they changed the content of our national character—and for the worse. . . .

Alexis de Tocqueville regarded America as one of the hopes of the world but nevertheless noted that Americans were "slaves of slogans." The slogan of choice in 1846 was "Manifest Destiny." The term had been coined in 1845 by a New York publisher named John O'Sullivan, eager to encourage, or get out ahead of, the curve of national expansion. It has drawn much scorn of late. In the 19th century, belief in Manifest Destiny would lead to some deplorable policies and even more deplorable rhetoric. But at first it simply meant that Providence had a universal design for Americans to carry their democratic machinery and customs across the continent.

POLK'S PROMISES

In 1846, the man who more than any other set all this in motion was James K. Polk. A Scotch-Irish lawyer from Tennessee, Polk was a dyed-in-the-wool Democrat, a Presbyterian and a compulsive political micromanager. Though he had served five years as Speaker of the House (then made up of only 228 Congressmen) he was so little known to the voting public that when the Democratic convention at Baltimore finally chose him on the ninth ballot in 1844, the rival Whig Party jeered happily, "Who is James K. Polk?"

When the jeering stopped, he was the 11th President of the United States, with 170 electoral votes to famous Henry Clay's 105, though there was only a 38,000-popular-vote difference between them. Polk worked a 10- to 12-hour day, kept a diary of everything that he did or said (it ran to 25 handwritten volumes), complained bitterly about how hard the job was, but quickly set about becoming the first President to keep all his promises. He said he would serve only one term. He said he would fix up the federal treasury. He said he would adjust customs duties—in an era when Southern states sometimes threatened secession over tariffs. He said he would acquire Oregon ("54–40 or fight!"), a huge, disputed territory claimed by both Great Britain and the United States since the joint-occupancy treaty of 1827. He said he would annex the Republic of Texas. He said he would acquire California. He did all that and more.

Oregon was simple. All he had to do was to make it seem as if Americans were willing to risk war over it, discover that the British weren't, outbluff the British a time or two, and get a touchy Congress to pass an aggressive bill abrogating the 1827 treaty. In the end Polk had to settle for everything south of the 49th parallel—which meant that he got part of Idaho and all of what are now the states of Washington and Oregon.

Texas and California launched him into . . . high-stakes, peace-or-war diplomatic maneuvering. . . . California still belonged to Mexico; only ten years earlier Texas had won its independence by defeating strongman Santa Anna's forces at San Jacinto. Sporadically raided and threatened with war by Mexico, the breakaway Texas Republic was kept out of the Union because adding a slave state would disturb the uneasy political balance in the U.S. Senate. But before Polk's Inauguration, through an initiative taken by Polk's predecessor, John Tyler, Congress admitted Texas as the 28th state—with Wisconsin shortly added to balance. Overnight, the border dispute between Texas and Mexico became a problem for the United States.

Polk opened talks with Mexico to clear things up—as well as settle long-outstanding money claims on Mexico by U.S. citizens. He named John Slidell, a Louisiana trader, as special minister plenipotentiary authorized to offer Mexico $25 million for California and $5 million for New Mexico. Both Texas and the U.S. Government now claimed the Rio Grande as the western Texas-Mexico border. Mexico bitterly insisted the border was the Nueces River, 120 miles to the east. Polk quietly moved 2,000 men under veteran Indian fighter Zachary Taylor toward the Nueces. The Mexican government kept Slidell (and Polk) waiting for weeks, then refused to receive Slidell, at least as minister plenipotentiary. By April, Taylor's army, considerably reinforced, had been moved on down to the mouth of the Rio Grande—either the southern tip of Texas or well inside Mexican territory—whichever way you saw it, a provocative move. Mexico saw it as invasion and again threatened war, this time with the United States.

Not only threatened. On April 25 a Mexican army crossed the Rio Grande with a view to cutting off Taylor's forces. It met with a startled American patrol, killed 11 troops, wounded 5 and took 47 prisoner. Stirred to action and outnumbered nearly two to one, Taylor's little army won two quick battles, then crossed the river, took the Mexican town of Matamoros and set up headquarters there. Taylor's dispatches did not reach Polk until May 8. On May 13, the President, declaring that Mexico had "shed American blood upon the American soil," signed a joint resolution stating that war had begun.

Polk was not a man to leave things to chance. When the unstable Mexican government was slow to come to terms, he got involved in a secret plot to bring the exiled leader Santa Anna to power—in return for a quick peace. Santa Anna double-crossed him. But Polk's aim had always been bloodless conquest. Whatever happened below the Rio Grande, he figured to stir up local revolutions in other restless Mexican territories. Weeks before the war, he had sent representatives to Santa Fe, in the huge Mexican province of New Mexico, to bribe its governor and to promise (correctly) that conditions would dramatically improve should revolution or a U.S. takeover occur. Now he ordered Gen. Stephen Kearny at Fort Leavenworth, Kansas, to take a force of dragoons to Santa Fe. For years, far more American than Mexican goods had been offered for sale in Santa Fe, so Kearny reached New Mexico closely followed by a traders' wagon train. On August 18 he took the capital of New Mexico without spilling any blood.

CALIFORNIA

California was, as it usually is, a whole story in itself. In 1846 it was a sleepy province of Mexico, almost empty and dramatically ill-governed to the extent it was governed at all. The most remote and underpopulated part of the collapsed Spanish empire, it ran itself without much help from distant, usually bankrupt and chaotic Mexico City. From time to time one genial California general would snatch power from a rival in a bloodless coup, which, as an observer reported, mostly meant "that the revenue [had] fallen into other hands." The total California population ran to about 6,000 Mexicans in addition to the local Indians, often reduced to devout near-servitude on behalf of religious missions. The land was controlled by Mexican cattle ranchers. There were some 800 ragtag Americans, most having come by ship around Cape Horn to trade for hides.

Polk being Polk, his cash offer to Mexico for California was not his only ploy. Early on he had sent secret orders to Commodore John Sloat, commander of our Pacific naval squadron, and to Thomas Larkin, a trader who served as U.S. consul in California. If war came, or if the British Navy made any move, Sloat was to occupy all California ports. Larkin was to cultivate his contacts with the lax local authorities and encourage any move on their part to declare independence from Mexico City. Mostly he was to impress on them not to accept the protection of any foreign power except the United States.

Polk's third secret message may have included orders to flamboyant John C. Frémont, at 33 a famous writer-explorer. Frémont always claimed it did, as did his father-in-law, Thomas Hart Benton, a powerful Senator from Missouri, and of course Frémont's wife, Jessie, whose editing of her husband's exploring accounts gave them much of their charm and readability. In any case, on the 9th of May, 1846, a messenger from the nation's capital, Marine Lieut. Archibald Gillespie, caught up with Frémont near Klamath Lake in Oregon. Frémont was bound east from his fourth mountain exploration. Whether from ambition or acting under orders, he abruptly turned back toward California, where he soon was fomenting revolution. He had raised a band of roughnecks. Creating a theatrical distraction, they captured the "microscopic hamlet" of Sonoma (it "could have been captured by Tom Sawyer and Huck Finn," says historian Bernard DeVoto) and, running a flag with a lumpily painted bear on it up the pole there, declared California an independent republic.

Frémont got himself made acting governor. In fairly short order, California was under the control of the United States of America. The fact was confirmed by the Treaty of Guadalupe Hidalgo, under the terms of which America got not only California but the land that today is Arizona, New Mexico, Nevada and Utah, as well as chunks of Colorado and Wyoming. Mexico got $15 million.

It is the custom now for Americans to judge the American past harshly and with a really notable lack of understanding, as if the people who lived then were exactly like us. But even the passionate abolitionists, pure spirits, and New England Whig politicians who bitterly condemned the Mexican War at the time, could not have imagined a country like our own, deeply concerned with the condition of its minorities, a country rich and secure enough even to debate whether wolves should be reintroduced into Yellowstone Park. The America of 1846 was nothing like that.

AMERICA IN 1846

In that year the nation consisted of an uneasy union of 28 still very sovereign states. It had a population, including Indians and slaves, of less than 20 million, about as many people as live in New York State today. Its western border ran roughly on a north-south line from Wisconsin to Louisiana. Beyond that lay what maps referred to as the "Great American Desert."

Americans were not much given to the kind of self-criticism we now practice. Or to criticism of any kind. Chest thumping was more our collective style. We were already noted for being miffed by critiques from Europeans who were always coming over to tell us how rude, violent, greedy and tasteless we were, as well as ragging us for spitting tobacco juice on the carpet, keeping slaves and terminating Indians with extreme prejudice.

All that was more or less true, of course, but, according to the prevailing American view, beside the point. In 1846 Eastern and Midwestern Indians had been crushed or brushed aside with treaties, for the time being. They were treated deceitfully by the government and would be treated worse as the century wore on. But in the struggle, they had done things to settlers that were not forgiven or forgotten. This was especially the case with people who already regarded them as savages and had little reason not to regard them as entirely inimical to the creation of towns, schools, railroads and real estate deals, which then, as now, passed for the spread of civilization. Slavery was seen as a problem and, by some, as a sin, but we had tried to contain its divisive thrust with the Compromise of 1820: no slave states north of 36 degrees 30 minutes north latitude. If we kept expanding westward, we might keep it from splitting the Union for a while, and perhaps it would wither away.

In 1844, the antislavery candidate got just 62,000 votes; it was only in 1845 that Congress lifted a decade-long ban on debating slavery issues in the House. In 1848, the Free-Soil Party polled just 290,000. If women didn't vote, well, they didn't vote anywhere else either, did they? Europe, after all, was a place we'd broken away from by force of arms, a place governed by tyrants and frozen into rigid social classes. Meanwhile, over here, the franchise was steadily expanding. Almost anyone could walk into the White House and see the President. In 1846, America was the only place in the world where the people got to elect their head of state.

The country was not yet embarrassed by patriotism. Settlers rolling west in covered wagons read the Declaration of Independence aloud to each other on the Fourth of July. Americans were deeply religious. They had no trouble believing that God had created the world in all its infinite variety (Charles Darwin's findings on evolution were 13 years away) or that Providence was watching over America, the greatest experiment in freedom and democracy ever. It followed (and was mostly true) that any place annexed by America was likely to be better off than it had been before.

By dog-eared tradition America's remarkable growth and prosperity depended on private liberty, more of it than any stable political system had tried before, and public land, more of it tillable and easily acquired than history had yet seen. Because of it there was no income tax; the federal government and those of many states ran mainly on the sale of public land. (Frugally, of course—Polk had only one private secretary to help him with his paperwork.) Land policy varied. Real estate scams abounded. But generally the old cliché of the American Frontier did apply: a family with grit could move west, carve a life out of the wilderness, squat there and have a good chance of buying the place, sometimes for as little as $1.25 an acre.

Because of land the immigrants came. Starting in 1846 the latest wave, more than a million, were refugees from Ireland's potato blights and killing famine. At first they did not go to the frontier; the only farming they knew was the cultivation of an acre or two of potatoes. Instead, they huddled in the seaboard cities and soon were dying by the thousands of cholera. They displaced free people of color as servants to the rich and slowed incipient attempts to organize labor by their need to work at almost any wage. Most were Catholic and many spoke only Gaelic, and they sometimes found themselves treated as half-human. Thousands volunteered for the war (monthly pay $7). Of these enough deserted to the Mexican side to form the "San Patricio" battalion. The Mexicans promised 320 acres of free land and did not fail to point out that fellow Catholics should not be fighting alongside black-hearted Protestant gringos.

Zachary Taylor's volunteer soldiers struggling into Mexico and the hundreds of wagons creaking and bumping westward in the summer of 1846 were the vanguard and living proof that the idea of Manifest Destiny had taken root. New England Whigs lambasted the Mexican War as a betrayal of American ideals. A fair number of people today can hardly mention it without wincing as if for the transgression of a shady relative. But in the South and West it set off a blaze of patriotic feeling. Though the peace treaty was slow to be signed, we had whipped the Mexican Army. Settlers were about to take on the Great American Desert.

THE JOURNEY WEST

Entering it, you were emigrating outside the United States. Back East, people knew very little about it except that it was forbidding. A vast expanse of plains with Indians. Sometimes mountainous and hard to cross—like the Rockies and the Sierra Nevada. Sometimes flat, baking hot and waterless. Even the tree-less, near-to-hand prairies, which eventually became the bread-basket of the nation, were little known. Westering settlers thus far had been used to cutting farms out of forest, braving Indians, running a few pigs as livestock. They figured that any place where trees did not grow wouldn't be much for growing anything else. Besides, without trees, how could you build a cabin?

It would be two decades before a rush of homesteaders settled these prairies and got used to grim sod huts and great corn crops. But in the early 1840s a few thousand farmers and home-steaders dared to try the grueling five-month trek across the often deadly 2,000 miles or so that lay between Independence,

With the opening of territory in the west, many emigrants began the long and arduous journey across the plains.

Missouri, and the alluring green of Oregon's Willamette Valley. In 1846, of some 2,700 people gathered for westward migration at Independence, more than 1,200 were aiming for California. They were the real start of a rush there that ran wild in 1849 after gold was found. . . .

The trek continued for nearly 20 years. It became one of the set pieces of American history. The routes to Oregon and California were the same at first: up the south fork of the Platte River, over South Pass (at 7,500 feet) in what is now Wyoming, north past Soda Springs in Idaho, then down the Snake River. Those California bound turned south beyond the Great Salt Lake to follow the Humboldt River to the Sierra Nevada and Sacramento. . . .

It took considerable substance to get together the supplies thought necessary for a family of four, including: a covered wagon that could run you $200 even if you bought the cover in Missouri to save money; four yoke of oxen (more durable than horses and less often stolen by Indians) at $20 to $30 per yoke; for each male traveler a rifle, a shotgun and maybe one of Samuel Colt's new single-action revolvers (about $50); 200 lbs. flour; 75 lbs. bacon; 300 lbs. "pilot" bread, or hardtack; 10 lbs.

salt; 20 lbs. sugar; 5 lbs. coffee; 2 lbs. tea; 25 lbs. rice, and a small keg of vinegar. At a rough total, front $700 to $1,500. Many people sold off all their land and livestock to get the cash.

Between 1845 and 1859 some 280,000 souls took the Oregon Trail; an estimated 30,000 died along the way. Many were babies and toddlers who, on the trail or off it, in the America of 1846 often did not live past age 5. Dysentery, fever, almost any sort of infection, swept them away. Cholera became a notable killer; settlers, not expecting to pass that way again, were slapdash about latrines and garbage, and those following them suffered. Women died in childbirth. But generally people were killed by carelessness; children fell out of wagons and were run over; guns went off accidentally, though some wagon trains required that most guns be kept unloaded during the day's run. The dead were carried along till evening, then buried. Next day all the wagons would roll over the grave to obliterate it and pack it down as a protection from marauding varmints. Until the 1860s, contrary to the impression given by the movies, Western Indians rarely killed migrating settlers along the trail, though they stole horses, shot poison arrows at oxen and sometimes fired on passing wagons. . . .

THE PROBLEM OF SLAVERY

Critics of Polk and the Mexican War attacked the President with self-righteous passion and some Whiggish hypocrisy for nudging the country from domestic innocence to incipient imperialism. But it was, and is, hard for most Americans to believe it would have been better for the United States and the world if Mexico or some other country (Britain? Spain?) controlled much of what we now call our own. In 1846 even the most violent abolitionists hadn't a clue about how to free—or later deal with—some three million slaves. War was, in fact, the only way to abolish slavery in the United States. But like most people confronted by an unsolvable and shameful problem—and by such a destructive alternative—Americans generally tried not to face it, hoping it would go away.

The Lasting Significance of America's War with Mexico

Donald A. Rakestraw

Donald A. Rakestraw is a professor of history at Georgia Southern University. In the following selection he analyzes the significant historical consequences of America's 1846–1848 war with Mexico. He argues that many Americans enthusiastically supported the war and celebrated the country's victory as a vindication of American ideals and its "manifest destiny" of expansion. The war provided a proving ground for the U.S. Army and placed the United States on the path to becoming a global power. However, Rakestraw also notes that the Mexican War brought out sectional divisions within American society regarding slavery and its spread—divisions that the existing national political parties (the Democrats and Whigs) could not eliminate, and which eventually threatened the dissolution of the United States.

F ew other events in U.S. history have produced greater effect—both immediate and over the long term—than the war with Mexico in the 1840s. Coming as the climax to an expansionist quest, the war was the product and the reflection of a unique and critical stage in the development of the nation. Woven within the pull and tug of a people whose diverse and

Donald A. Rakestraw, "Interpretive Essay on the War with Mexico," *Events That Changed America in the Nineteenth Century*, edited by John E. Findling and Frank W. Thackeray, Westport, CT: Greenwood Press, 1997. Copyright © 1997 by Greenwood Press. Reproduced by permission.

often incompatible interests defied national identity, the Mexican War's significance rests on its positive contribution to American unity and national growth as well as its ominous portents for national disaster and fragmentation. The war's place in the course of American civilization is located within the mundane calculations of miles and acres and the grand reckoning of consequences and legacies.

GRAPPLING WITH IDENTITY

As America approached midcentury, it continued to grapple with questions of identity, world context, and direction. Societal changes that were the consequence of a young nation in transition to adulthood generated a certain amount of tension and insecurity. Thomas Jefferson's agrarian ideal seemed threatened by a society following in Britain's industrial footsteps. Writer Washington Irving observed that the "march of mechanical inventions is driving everything political before it." Farm was challenged by factory, rural commonwealth by urban oligarchy. A romantic season of nationalist introspection and pride yielded to a shallower and more materialistic age committed to trade and industry. In this atmosphere, Americans strained to find a mooring. The memory of revolutionary progress had faded and with it, some feared, the rationale for the American experiment. The growth of the American population and a series of financial calamities undercut the personal independence and self-sufficiency of the Jacksonian "'common man." His redemption lay in the active pursuit of what Andrew Jackson aptly called the "area of freedom."

At the same time a reactionary Europe seemed determined to contain the liberal principles of republican government and to squelch democracy with monarchical rule. Rumors were rife that France had designs on a throne for Mexico and that abolitionist Europeans were set to pounce at the first sign of weakness to cordon off America's slave system and to lock the United States behind its current restrictive borders. There, they hoped, slavery (dubbed the "peculiar institution") would die and democracy would decay. If, however, Americans could break that containment and revive their fervor for patriotism and republican virtue, a new era would be theirs. Expansionism seemed the perfect vehicle for such a revival. Rooted in the colonial tradition and encouraged by the vision of Thomas Jefferson and the continentalism of John Quincy Adams, territor-

ial expansion could unharness the energy of America's burgeoning population, spark nationalist pride with images of
western vistas, and transform an insulated and parochial people
into a hemispheric power. It was, according to the journalist,
John L. O'Sullivan, their "manifest destiny."

The concept was made a cause célèbre in the 1840s by news-
papermen who found that technology had supplied them with
the ability to broadcast their enthusiasm for expansion throughout the country. Northern editors from east to west tirelessly
heralded America's geographic calling. Many were driven by
the belief that farm surplus and packed warehouses could be
relieved only by the continued cultivation of new markets. To
them, territorial expansion would create the markets and at the
same time temper the ardor for industrialization and urbanization by opening new land for rural living.

Equally essential was another type of cultivation, that of liberty and freedom. The Mexican War affirmed a sense that the
United States was on a divine mission, the course of which
could not be altered even if it meant the forcible appropriation
of another nation's land. The zeal with which America pursued
the accession of the Southwest demonstrated what some students of the period have dubbed exceptionalism—that feeling
that the United States was uniquely positioned to elevate humanity to the next stage of development. What had previously
been scorned as vulgar imperialism when undertaken by other
nations was somehow different when effected by the United
States. Washington's energies were driven, leaders would argue, not by greed or animus but by a noble desire to dissemi-
nate benevolent American institutions.

A WAR OF CONQUEST

There was no better evidence of this thinking than the war of
conquest in the American Southwest. Although an unintended
consequence of U.S. determination to follow the hand of providence to the shores of the Pacific Ocean, alleged Mexican intran-
sigence opened the door for an awesome and glorious means to
the expansionist end. Supplanting the tedious prodding of American settlers along the Oregon Trail, armed conflict offered the expansionist movement intangibles like heroism, patriotism, and
the chance to showcase America's military prowess.

Communities from across the nation dispatched their young
heroes to the battlefields under the banner of God, country, and

retribution for the alleged shedding of the blood of their brothers at the Rio Grande. The war made manifest destiny, previously the preserve of editors and pioneers, real to the entire population. American soldiers would return having experienced more than war and victory: a wide and exotic world where people spoke, ate, worshipped, and generally behaved differently. Never again would Americans be the insular and at times ingenuous citizens that they once were. The war would expand more than the territorial limits of the republic. It would expand America's perspective and, as predicted, awaken the nationalist pride of a unified people. Volunteers from one end of the United States to the other stood together in crisis and in battle for the United States of America. It is small wonder that the July Fourth festivities following the victorious end to the war in 1848 seemed charged with excitement and promise.

In Washington the celebration of American Independence Day seemed to herald the opening of a new and prosperous era in the development of American civilization. As celebrants in the nation's capital commemorated the date by laying the foundation stone for a monument to George Washington, they were captivated by the magnitude of their accomplishment. Before the day ended, Polk received news of the Mexican government's ratification of the Treaty of Guadalupe Hidalgo. Coinciding with word that the French had thrown off the yoke of monarchy and rekindled the spark of liberty in Europe with another revolution, the news of the treaty confirmed for the crowd that their republic had indeed inaugurated a new order: it had secured its manifest destiny to extend liberty across the continent and simultaneously proved the value, ability, and stamina of democracy. To many Americans, the war was a test of their democratic institutions. Not only had the test been passed, but the reputation of republicanism had been elevated even in the eyes of Europeans, who considered no better gauge to success than a victorious war. Even the Whig party leaders in Congress, skeptical of any expansion beyond the limited addition of Pacific harbors, hoisted their own valiant generals in celebration.

A Test for the U.S. Army

The Mexican War provided a proving ground where the U.S. Army could demonstrate its capabilities and where national reputations could be shaped. In fact, the war produced seasoned leaders for the American Civil War, among them future

Confederate commander Robert E. Lee and his Union counterpart, Ulysses S. Grant.

The conflict with Mexico also produced, to the chagrin of
Democrat James K. Polk, the next two Whig presidential candidates. President Polk provoked the war by dispatching American forces to the Rio Grande under the command of Whig general Zachary Taylor. Winning immediate affection at home by
suffering the first casualties of the war—on American soil, according to Polk—Taylor quickly led his outmanned troops into
Mexico. The general shortly reported a series of victories at such
soon-to-be-immortalized places as Monterrey and Buena Vista.
In the process he ensured for himself an esteemed reputation
throughout the country from which he could later transpose
military campaigns into a successful political campaign for the
White House. In tandem with Taylor's successes was a brilliant
move by another Whig General, Winfield Scott. Demonstrating
sagacity and daring, Scott used the first landing craft in U.S.
military history to deploy an amphibious operation at Vera
Cruz. From there, in defiance of the opinions of the best European military strategists, he marched an army overland to Mexico City to press the Mexican government to come to terms.
Even the duke of Wellington, Britain's famed conqueror of
Napoleon, was impressed.

The Mexican War added to the U.S. military's thin resumé an
impressive list of firsts, not the least of which was the successful landing at Vera Cruz. The war experience transformed internal military communications as the army became increasingly dependent on the electric telegraph and effected external
reporting with the introduction of war correspondents to ensure
that the folks back home were appropriately informed of the
heroics of their native sons and the advance of the troops. Field
hospitals in future conflicts would be far more humane thanks
to the army's adoption of ether for anesthesia. Among the other
novel experiences credited to the Mexican War were the military occupation of an enemy's capital, the institution of martial
law on foreign soil, and the U.S. army's first successful offensive war. These firsts combined with the success of a volunteer
army deployed by a true (some would say *the true*) republic
against a professional army fielded by a dictatorship to impress
Europeans. The military performance won new respect for the
United States and the "Napoleon of the backwoods," as the
British press dubbed Polk, among the community of nations.

INTERNATIONAL STATUS SECURED

The successful prosecution of the war had a tremendous impact on U.S. security and international status. Victory in the war with Mexico established the ability of a republic to engage in foreign war without jeopardizing its democratic values, mobilizing both its people and its resources. Although the war did not elevate the United States to great power status in the European sense, it did draw the nation considerably closer to that rank and made it the undisputed bully of the Western Hemisphere. Even Britain would concede America's preeminence in the hemisphere two years after the war in the Clayton-Bulwer agreement that compromised British influence in Central America. After the Mexican War, the great powers would not again seriously challenge the United States by force in the Western Hemisphere. When Spain helped to usher the United States across the divide to major power status in the Spanish-American War at the end of the nineteenth century, it did so not by choice but because Washington's assertion of U.S. interests in the Caribbean left them no alternative.

Polk's revival and expansion of the Monroe Doctrine, which had decreed the hemisphere off-limits to European imperialists, left little doubt that the United States had adopted a sort of paternal obligation to the Americas. Unlike earlier intrusions, such as Britain's appropriation of the Falkland Islands and French bombardment of Mexico in the 1830s, Europeans moved more gingerly in America's neighborhood after Polk's Mexican adventure. The United States, now a continental power, could justifiably claim leadership as the world's most successful and powerful republic, and it could press its economic interests in the Western Hemisphere and perhaps even consider an isthmian canal.

Although a small affair when measured against the yardstick of similar wars of conquest, to the patriotic zealots in the United States, "Mr. Polk's War" was the most laudable event since Jackson's defeat of the British at New Orleans in 1815. At a cost of just over $100 million, including both military expenditures and the treaty award to Mexico, and a loss of about 13,000 American lives, the United States had acquired over 500,000 square miles of territory, including the Rio Grande boundary for Texas and all contiguous land from the river to the Pacific. And if the cost was not adequately balanced by the acquisition of millions of acres, the soon-acknowledged wealth of upper California went far to pacify even the most frugal citizen. In the four years following the war, the value of gold extracted from that newly annexed territory more than doubled the fiscal expense of the war. Augmenting the natural wealth of the territory, the addition of San Francisco and San Diego to the harbors of Puget Sound in the Oregon territory gave the United States control of virtually the entire Pacific coast of North America, allowing Washington to cast more than an avaricious eye on Asia. It could now work to advance America's influence on Pacific commerce. With the capture of the Pacific coast through diplomacy in Oregon and war in the Southwest, Asia had been drawn closer to the United States than ever before. There was little doubt that Americans would pursue its exploitation in their typically dogged fashion. Within a decade, Washington had negotiated treaties in the Far East, and American ships carried approximately one-third of China's trade with the Western world. . . .

Beneath the euphoric surface, however, the war had exposed dangerous fault lines that would ultimately rearrange the political landscape and fracture the republic. . . .

THE WILMOT PROVISO

Underneath the partisan banners of the 1840s were sectional cracks that stood ready to widen into irreparable crevices at the proper time and with the proper issue. Northern politicians had been most apprehensive about the war because they assumed that new territory in the southwest would invite the expansion of the South's slave economy. Although there was adequate evidence that this would not be the case, antislavery Whigs would not run the risk. And considering the later reclamation of land in the southwest through irrigation and the emergence of cotton as a staple, perhaps they were correct to be cautious. Their skepticism at the time prompted the introduction of the topic to the war debate. A freshman Democrat from Pennsylvania who favored expansion, David Wilmot, tried to dissociate slavery from the issue of territorial indemnity. Shortly after the war began, Wilmot attached an addendum to an appropriation request from Polk for $2 million to purchase peace (and California) from Mexico. His so-called Wilmot Proviso amounted to a disclaimer that slavery would be barred from any territory ceded by Mexico to the United States as a result of the conflict. Wilmot unwittingly rerung the "firebell," signaling the awakening of the dormant and potentially disastrous debate over slavery. His ten-minute presentation had won for him instant notoriety and a prominent place in the most onerous legacy of the Mexican War.

The motion exposed the frailty of party cohesion among both Democrats and Whigs. For years, the Democratic party had exhibited surprising homogeneity, but the issues resulting from the war proved that it had been little more than an illusion. Northern Democrats were disenchanted with the Polk administration, believing that he was driven by his southern cousins to pacify their promotion of their economic system. Democrats as well as some Whigs saw Wilmot's proposal as the perfect opportunity to express their discontent and oppose slavery without being classified among the zealot abolitionists. In fact, some had determined that support for the maintenance of Mexican territorial spoils as "free soil" could work to preserve the West for white farmers and restrict blacks to the South.

Although Wilmot's suggestion could never garner enough support to pass both houses, it opened the way for political realignment on the basis of section over party. When a New York congressman revived the notion, it exposed the fracture in the Democratic party as Martin Van Buren's "Barnburners" moved to join with antislavery forces of the North while southern Democrats tagged Wilmot and his associates as traitors. Whigs too broke by section. Mostly northern "Conscience Whigs" heralded the proviso as if sent down from heaven; southern or "Cotton Whigs" condemned Wilmot and their northern Whig associates as troublemakers. Democrats and Whigs both crossed lines and began to vote with one another as sectional division prevailed over party unity. . . .

THE 1848 ELECTION

In the 1848 presidential campaign, both parties, appreciating its disruptive nature, tried to set the slavery issue aside. The Democrats chose [Lewis] Cass, who hoped to remain silent on the subject. The Whigs, to Polk's dismay, chose General Zachary Taylor, a slaveholder who would run on his battlefield laurels and sidestep the controversy. But this was wishful thinking. There was no avoiding the matter. Antislavery Whigs and rebellious northern Democrats joined with Van Burenites to put forward former president Martin Van Buren as the candidate of the Free Soil party in 1848. By splitting the Democratic vote in New York, the free-soilers ensured the Whig victory. More important, they spelled the beginning of the end of political sta-

262 Antebellum America: 1784–1850

bility. The sections were going their separate ways. The shears were at work. National parties that had forged national institutions based on common interests and beliefs that overcame sectional bias were breaking apart. The issues created by the war had produced the ingredients of a new party, one that was almost entirely sectional, the party of Abraham Lincoln.

The generation of the Mexican War would witness Republican victories that so alienated the South and stratified the nation as to make the dissolution of the Union nearly certain. The Mexican War had laid bare the incompatibility of an expansionist policy proclaiming the goal of liberty while insisting on the progress of slavery. The bitter contest over the Wilmot Proviso foreshadowed the tragic course that the nation had unwittingly plotted toward hardening sectional lines and ultimate disintegration. . . .

A FORGOTTEN WAR

Over the decades since the Guadalupe Hidalgo treaty, the war has rarely been exalted by the American public as one of the highlights of its history. The war's omission from such a list seems curious considering its many ramifications for American civilization. The American Revolution, the Constitutional Convention, the Louisiana Purchase, even the War of 1812 customarily arouse more familiarity with the general reader. This is partly due to the Mexican conflict's proximity to the Civil War, which tends to obscure all other topics in its vicinity. But this is only part of the explanation. Although the topic of a plethora of books and articles, the Mexican War fell out of favor because of a certain sense of guilt. Despite the salving of conscience at the time with the acceptance of Polk's rather lame argument that *they* started it, an uncomfortable feeling emerged that the United States had engaged in an old-fashioned war of conquest—a feeling that did not seem compatible with the principles of the republic. This judgment, however, is perhaps too harsh. Assessed within the confines of America's idealist opinion of its model republic, the war earns ignominy. Evaluated within the reality of the nineteenth-century world, however, Polk's accomplishments, despite the dreadful residue, set the United States on track to become first a continental, then a hemispheric, and ultimately a global power.

THE IRISH POTATO FAMINE AND MIGRATION OF THE IRISH TO AMERICA

ROGER DANIELS

The decade from 1840 to 1850 was a time of unprecedented mass emigration from Europe to the United States. Many of these immigrants came from Ireland. In 1846, historian Roger Daniels writes, famine swept through Ireland as disease wiped out its potato crop (Daniels also blames the inaction of the British government for the famine). As a result, more than 1 million Irish emigrated to the United States over the next several years. Daniels examines the difficult experiences of those who made the voyage from Ireland to America and the enduring psychological effects of the famine on the Irish and on Irish Americans. He notes that many of the new Irish immigrants found themselves at the bottom of America's economic structure. He also examines the rise of nativist prejudice against Irish immigrants, which he contends was fueled by anti-Catholicism. Roger Daniels is a professor of history at the University of Cincinnati and the author of numerous books on Asian Americans and other American ethnic groups.

B y 1845 Irish immigration was growing and would un- doubtedly have continued to grow at a quickening pace in normal circumstances. But the great famine which be-

Roger Daniels, *Coming to America: A History of Immigration and Ethnicity in American Life,* New York: HarperPerennial, 1991. Copyright © 1990 by Visual Education Corporation. Reproduced by permission.

gan in that year and its aftermath influenced not only Irish immigration, but also the whole Irish American community, for decades to come.

THE FAMINE YEARS

In Ireland the burgeoning population had the inevitable effect of reducing in size the already small holdings of Irish farmers. Thus economic deterioration was steady, although minor improvements were made in the political situation of Irish Catholics. Those willing to swear fealty to England could buy, bequeath, and inherit property, those with a certain income could vote, and, thanks to the agitation led by Daniel O'Connell, the Emancipation Act of 1829 allowed Irish Catholics to be members of Parliament and to hold any civil office short of becoming lord lieutenant (governor) of Ireland or lord chancellor (chief justice) of England.

As their plots grew smaller and smaller and rents grew higher and higher, more and more Irish farmers sold their grain and came to subsist largely on the potato. The potato, itself a immigrant *from* the New World, part of what Alfred Crosby has called the "Columbian Exchange," was easily cultivated and took little labor and practically no equipment. An acre and a half of potatoes could feed a family of six. It has been estimated that a third of the Irish poor—much of the population—ate almost nothing else, and it formed the bulk of the diet of many more. The greatest drawback of the potato was its susceptibility to disease, particularly the fungus *Phytophthora infestans,* commonly known as the potato blight. Blight was no stranger in Ireland: It had struck at least twenty times in the century and a quarter before 1845. So, when another outbreak began in October 1845, no great hue and cry was raised. It would mean, of course, more hunger and misery, but these were not strangers in Ireland either. Thus began the last great peacetime famine in western European history.

The next year, 1846, saw the worst outbreak of the blight; nearly the entire crop was destroyed, leaving a stinking, rotting mass. The twentieth-century Irish writer Sean O'Faoláin said, "The land blackened as if the frown of God had moved across it." Most Irish cotters (small farmers) were reduced to eating the potatoes they normally would have kept for seed, so that in 1847, a year in which the blight abated, only about a sixth of a normal potato crop was even planted. Concurrently disease, the inevitable partner of famine, began to wreak havoc on the weakened population. Epidemic diseases, chiefly those borne by ticks and lice, such as typhus and relapsing fever, raged.

To say that the reaction of the British government was inadequate is to understate the situation greatly. Although close students of the matter can differentiate between the policies of the two prime ministers, the Tory Robert Peel and the Liberal John Russell, each was utterly incapable of dealing with the situation. Like Herbert Hoover nearly a century later, their ideological predilections kept them from taking the one step that would have relieved, at least in the short run, most of the suffering: feeding the hungry. The potato blight was unavoidable; but the Great Famine, in the words of Professor Kerby Miller, was "largely the result of Ireland's colonial status and grossly inequitable social system." Both British prime ministers honestly believed that the Irish needed to be more enterprising—a classic case of blaming the victim—and that they should go to work to earn money to buy imported food. Some public works jobs were provided, but these were too little and too late. Even worse were the views of Charles Trevelyan, the treasury official in charge of Irish relief. He was largely concerned that too much relief would damage the character of the Irish people, demoralize them, and make them dependent, and he was sure that what he called Ireland's "great veil" was not famine but deficient moral fiber: "the selfish, perverse and turbulent character of the people."

IRISH EMIGRATION

The census of 1851 showed clearly the results of natural disaster and human mismanagement; there were about two and a half million fewer people in Ireland than there would have been under normal conditions, About half, 1,000,000 to 1,500,000 human beings—perhaps a sixth of the population—died from a combination of hunger and disease. An equal number emigrated, most to America. Our concern will be the latter.

Although emigration was viewed as an escape, for many it was no escape at all. Even before the famine years, the number of Irish lost at sea had been quite high. The small timber ships on which so many traveled were not designed for the transportation of people, and many were old and unfit for the heavy seas of the North Atlantic. In the single year 1834—a particularly stormy time—at least 17 immigrant ships sank with the loss of 731 passengers. By midcentury and after, the ships were larger and safer and subject to some regulation by both the British and American governments, but when there was a major accident, as is the case with today's jumbo jets, the carnage was fearful. In 1848 a fire aboard the British sailing ship *Ocean Monarch* took 176 lives; the worst disaster of the immigrant trade was in the age of steam in 1858, when a fire—ironically, caused by a health measure, as hot tar being used to fumigate the steerage—ignited a blaze on the Hamburg-Amerika Line's iron steamship *Austria* that took the lives of 500 emigrant passengers. And, in a final example, four years earlier the iron-hulled steamer *City of Glasgow* sailed from Liverpool with 480 emigrants and was lost without trace. But the great killer of immigrants was disease, and no emigrants were more susceptible than the weakened Irish poor of the famine years.

Typhus, cholera, dysentery, and what was called "ship fever"—in the mistaken belief that shipboard conditions caused the epidemics—were the great killers. We now know—and medical authorities at midcentury were beginning to realize—that these diseases did not originate at sea but were brought aboard by either passengers or crew. Once aboard the conditions on the crowded and unsanitary ships were ideal for the propagation of disease. In the famine year of 1847—the worst year in terms of mortality—perhaps 100,000 men, women, and children embarked for Canada from British ports. Some 17,000 died at sea and another 20,000 died of disease after landing, mostly along the shores of the St. Lawrence. At just one place, the quarantine station at Grosse Isle off Quebec City, between mid-May and early November 1847, 8,691 persons were admitted to a hospital whose normal capacity was 200; 3,228 died. Conditions at Grosse Isle defy description; during the latter half of 1847 "only" 850 of the 7,000 admitted to New York's new quarantine hospital died. Nor did the horrors end in 1847. Kerby Miller estimates that in the cholera year of 1853, 10 percent of the 180,000 Irish emigrants died at sea.

All told, in the famine years something more than two million Irish went overseas. Most of them, nearly a million and a half, came to the United States; a third of a million went to Canada, and many of those came sooner or later to the United States; perhaps a quarter of a million settled in Britain, and thousands of others went to Australia and elsewhere, The total emigration was about a quarter of the prefamine population.

More people left Ireland in the eleven years 1845–55 than in its previous recorded history.

ENDURING SCARS

Almost all historians writing about the American Irish agree that the famine years left enduring scars on the Irish and on Irish American psyches, exacerbating, in many ways, attitudes that were already there. While not all scholars agree with the conclusions of Kerby Miller on this matter, his notions should be taken into account. He argues that:

> First, both collectively and individually the Irish—particularly Irish Catholics—often regarded emigration as involuntary exile, although they expressed that attitude with varying degrees of consistency, intensity, and sincerity. Second, this outlook reflected a distinctive Irish worldview—the impact of a series of interactions among culture, class, and historical circumstance on Irish character. Finally, both the exile motif and its underlying causes led Irish emigrants to interpret experience and adapt to American life in ways which were often alienating and sometimes dysfunctional, albeit traditional, expedient, and conducive to the survival of Irish identity and the success of Irish-American nationalism.

Views of national and ethnic character, even in the hands of a careful scholar like Miller, always run the risk of blending into stereotype. Certainly the cultural baggage that immigrants brought with them can never be ignored and there are observable differences in the collective behavior of American immigrant and ethnic groups. But it seems to many that views like Miller's go too far. Were he correct, it seems to me, the experiences of the Canadian Irish and the Australian Irish would be more similar to those of the American Irish than they are. The view presented here will always stress—perhaps too much—the role of the American environment, the impact of the material and social conditions of American life on the experience of the immigrant and in formation and development of American ethnic groups.

Those circumstances, as indicated, made the Irish highly urban, and their experiences prefigure, in many ways, those of very different immigrant groups who began to come in the late nineteenth century. The Irish were concentrated in cities, but not all cities. . . .

Wherever they lived in urban America in the middle decades of the nineteenth century, large numbers of Irish were at the very bottom of the economic structure, overrepresented as common laborers and domestic servants and as residents in various municipal institutions—poor houses, jails, and charity hospitals. Whenever Irish and blacks were present in significant numbers, significant competition between them developed, sometimes murderously, as in the draft riots in New York City in July 1863. In the antebellum South it was widely believed that Irish should be employed in dangerous, high mortality jobs rather than risking the loss of valuable Negro slaves. New Orleans's New Canal, for example, one of the great Southern public works in the 1830s, was largely dug by immigrant Irish laborers, who died in great numbers during the four years of construction. Whether the traditional figure of 20,000, as expressed in song, is accurate, no one can say:

> Ten thousand Micks, they swung their picks
> To dig the New Canal.
> But the choleray was stronger 'n they,
> An' twice it killed them all.

But the concentration of Irish workers at the bottom of society, though pronounced, can be overemphasized. The most widely read book on urban Irish immigrants, Oscar Handlin's study *Boston's Immigrants*, which set the pattern for urban ethnic group biography, may well have been an examination of the worst case. Boston, as Handlin makes clear, was not a magnet for immigrants: Irish were, in a way, trapped there in large numbers. . . . Yet, even in Boston, at the height of the famine immigration, more than a third of Irish-born workers were not in the lowest occupational ranks and by 1880 a slight majority were not. In 1850 Irish born were represented in every one of the sixty-two occupational categories Handlin uses, although, to be sure, very thinly in some of them. Only one of Boston's thirty-two undertakers was Irish born, but nearly a tenth of its physicians were and, even at that early date, just over a tenth of its police.

In other cities the Irish fared somewhat better, or perhaps *less badly* is the proper term to use. In Philadelphia, for example, as Dennis Clark has written, "there was simply a better chance for Irishmen to compete," largely because of more rapid growth in the City of Brotherly Love. But even in Philadelphia the over-representation of Irish born among laborers was quite high, although lower than in Boston. . . .

In the Far West—which of course, was out of reach for famine immigrants and other poor Europeans—the Irish experience was entirely different, as the English scholar R.A. Birchall has shown. In San Francisco—which in 1870 was almost half foreign born and had the highest percentage of immigrants of any large American city—Irish were more than 15 percent of the population, and they were largely members of what modern sociologists would call the lower middle class. Of course, the presence of a large Chinese population tended to "promote" the status of all whites. . . .

THE ROMAN CATHOLIC CHURCH IN AMERICA

The massive Irish immigration of the 1840s, not surprisingly, utterly transformed the Roman Catholic Church in America. The twenty-five thousand Catholics of 1790 had probably grown to about 100,000 by the end of the War of 1812. By 1860, there were three and a half million, and Catholics were the largest single denomination in the United States, although still a small minority of the population. As late as 1830 the leadership of the American church was largely French or French trained: Of ten bishops in the nation then, six fitted that description. French and French-trained priests, many of them exiles from France, were a bulwark of the church in the early national period. Anti-Irish sentiment was not restricted to natives and Protestants. English-born and French-trained James Whitfield, fourth archbishop of Baltimore, wrote a fellow cleric in 1832 about a vacancy in an American see:

> If possibl[e] . . . let an American born be recommended and (between us in strict confidence) I do really think we should guard against having more Irish bishops. . . .
> This you know is a dangerous secret, but I trust it to one in whom I have full confidence.

In the next twenty years, however, what can be called the Hibernization of the American Roman Catholic Church was well begun: The major struggle was not between Irish (and later Irish Americans) and French, but between them and Germans (and later German Americans).

What was crucial, in the final analysis, was not the appointment of Irish or Irish American bishops, although that did hap-

pen, with Irish-born John Hughes, bishop from 1838 to 1850 and
from 1850 to 1864 archbishop of New York, playing perhaps the
key role. What was crucial was more than a million Catholic immigrants, most of them Irish but with a substantial minority of
Germans, who came between the end of the War of 1812 and
1860. They and their children made up the vast majority of the
church membership, and the Roman Catholic church had become an immigrant church. . . .

NATIVISM AND ANTI-CATHOLICISM

When relatively large numbers of Irish and German Catholic
immigrants, many of them desperately poor, began to arrive in
the late 1820s and early 1830s, what had been a largely rhetorical anti-Catholicism became a major social and political force in
American life. Not surprisingly, it was in eastern cities, particularly Boston, where anti-Catholicism turned violent, and much
of the violence was directed against convents and churches. Beginning with the burning down of the Ursuline Convent just
outside Boston by a mob on August 11, 1834, well into the 1850s
violence against Catholic institutions was so prevalent that in-
surance companies all but refused to insure them. Much of this
violence was stirred up by Protestant divines, ranging from eminent church leaders such as Lyman Beecher (1775–1863) to
anonymous self-appointed street preachers. . . .

It was against this background of religiously inspired anti-
Catholicism, that the political and economic anti-immigrant attitudes of the pre-Civil War decades take on their full meaning.
Many of the immigrants, as we have seen, were poor, others utterly destitute. The costs of maintaining the poor were mounting and were borne solely by the port cities and their states. In
an effort to regain these costs, some eastern states passed modest head taxes—New York charged $1.50 for cabin passengers,
Massachusetts a simple $2.00 a head—to be paid by the owners
of the immigrant vessels. Not in themselves a great deterrent to
immigration, they led the United States Supreme Court to lay
down an important principle. In the *Passenger Cases* (1849) the
court declared these state laws unconstitutional, holding that
the right to regulate immigration under the commerce clause of
the Constitution—Article 1, Section 9, gives Congress the power
"to regulate Commerce with foreign nations, and among the
several states, and with the Indian Tribes"—was prescriptive.
Thus even though Congress had passed no legislation concern-

ing immigration, individual states could not tax it for any purpose, since, as [Supreme Court Justice] John Marshall had put it earlier, the power to tax was the power to destroy. For the time being the court left the police powers of the states unimpaired: A state could, for example, quarantine a ship on which smallpox or cholera was raging.

This ruling only added supporters to an anti-immigrant bloc that was already flourishing in the country. As early as 1837 a nativist-Whig coalition was able to elect a mayor and council in New York City, and in Germantown, Pennsylvania, a Native American Association was formed that opposed foreign-born officeholders and voters. In New Orleans a similarly named organization denounced the immigration to the United States of "the outcast and offal of society, the vagrant and the convict—transported in myriads to our shores, reeking with the accumulated crimes of the whole civilized world." The major strategies of these movements, which coalesced in the 1840s and early 1850s in the American, or Know-Nothing, party, were to call for a change in the naturalization laws. The most common proposal was to require a twenty-one-year period for naturalization and bar the foreign born from holding any but minor local offices. Other measures proposed in Congress including forbidding the immigration into the United States of paupers, criminals, idiots, lunatics, insane persons, and the blind. Although such proposals had much support on both ideological and economic grounds, they never had enough to force a vote on them in either house of Congress.

RELIGIOUS AND UTOPIAN MOVEMENTS OF THE 1840S

PHILIP JENKINS

Historian Philip Jenkins contends that the 1830s and 1840s were a time of new religious movements. Previously established denominations found themselves losing members to upstart religious leaders, movements and sects, many of which preached utopian visions. Among these new religions was the Church of Jesus Christ of Latter Day Saints, or the Mormons, which suffered violent persecution including the death of its founder, Joseph Smith, in 1844. Subsequently Brigham Young led thousands of Mormon settlers west to what would eventually become the state of Utah. Jenkins is a professor of history and religious studies at Penn State University.

During these years American cultural differences with Europe became more marked, as the American people began to explore the implications of their radically democratic society and the weakness of state or ecclesiastical controls on thought and behaviour. As in politics, the spirit of the time was marked by a sense of limitless opportunity and a thoroughgoing challenge to established or traditional elites, a Biblical casting down of the mighty from their seats. Radicalism was often expressed in religious forms, with the years around 1830 and 1848 being especially productive of new sects and enthusiastic movements.

By the middle of the century the older and more staid religious

Philip Jenkins, *A History of the United States*, New York: St. Martin's Press, 1997. Copyright © 1997 by Philip Jenkins. Reproduced by permission.

denominations had been supplanted by democratic and enthusiastic groupings. American Christianity was dominated by three
huge Protestant denominations: Baptist, Methodist and Presbyterian. The Congregationalist and Episcopalian Churches were
firmly relegated to the second rank, where they were already being rivalled by denominations such as Lutheran and Catholic that
had had only a limited presence in 1790. Also at this level was the
Christian Church/Disciples of Christ, a new evangelical body
with entirely American roots that had been forged in the succes-
sive fires of revivalism. By the end of the century the national pre-
dominance of Baptists and Methodists was still more marked. . . .

A PROLIFERATION OF SECTS

However horrifying they might have been to the mainstream
denominations of colonial days, Baptists and Methodists were
both orthodox and acceptable compared with the members of
the countless sects that flourished in the United States after the
removal of official regulation on spiritual experimentation. The
proliferation of heresy and religious innovation proceeded at all
levels, intellectual and popular, elite and plebeian. In the more
intellectual category was the attack on Trinitarian orthodoxy,
and with it many of the once basic Christian doctrines about human sinfulness, the divinity of Christ and his work of atone-
ment. Under the leadership of William Ellery Channing, Uni-
tarianism spread rapidly from about 1820, especially in New
England, where its ideas were summarized as involving 'the fa-
therhood of God, the brotherhood of man, and the neighbour-
hood of Boston'. Universalism asserted a belief that all would
be saved. Both traditions exalted human reason and the potential for social improvement.

By the 1830s the intellectual world of New England was influenced by the new philosophical current known as Transcendentalism, an Americanized version of German Idealism. This
found the only authentic reality in the world of the spirit, a realm
that could be interpreted through reason. One of the most distinguished leaders of the movement in the United States was
Ralph Waldo Emerson, a member of a long-established New England clerical family, who abandoned the Unitarian church in
1831. In 1836 his book *Nature* summarized his new Transcendentalist position, which he continued to expound over the next
four decades, and from 1842 to 1844 he helped edit the magazine
The Dial. Emersonian ideas stressed individual liberation,

autarchy, self-sufficiency and self-government, and strenuously opposed social conformity. In the political sphere, Transcendentalist thought was progressive, leading its followers to support causes such as abolitionism and women's suffrage. Apart from Emerson, the best-known advocates of the position included Margaret Fuller, Henry David Thoreau and Bronson Alcott. Very different in origin but sharing a similar optimism was spiritualism, which in 1848 began an astonishing vogue that penetrated all classes of society. Its great popularity in part stemmed from its claims to provide scientific proof for doctrines about the continuation of human progress through the illusory veil of death.

UTOPIAN COMMUNITIES

Common in the religious thought of the time was a sense of utopianism, the idea that humanity could achieve a kind of perfection in this life, and not have to postpone that prospect until reaching heaven or the day of judgment. Perfectionist ideas were put into practice in a series of utopian communes and social experiments that sought to reform the human condition through new patterns of common property ownership, sexual relationships and (commonly) changes in diet. In the 1820s and 1830s these communities often followed the socialist models advocated by the European reformers Robert Owen and Charles Fourier. From the 1840s American prophets came to the fore. In 1841 a former Unitarian minister named George Ripley began a collective settlement at Brook Farm in Massachusetts, which attracted many Transcendentalists by its emphasis on simple living and a return to the soil. Still more radical was the colony established by John Humphrey Noyes on the principle that the Second Coming had already occurred, so that the saints should live according to new rules of sexual and social conduct. His group practised community of property and experimented with ideas of complex marriage and selective breeding. In 1847 the commune took up residence at Oneida in New York state, where it flourished into the 1880s. There were also several branch communities.

Among the most successful of the communal groups were the Shakers. They were founded in the 1770s but attained their greatest popularity between about 1830 and 1860, when perhaps 6000 members were scattered among 19 settlements. The sect was well known for its elaborate dance rituals, while among other remarkable features were belief in the total equality of the sexes and the observance of strict celibacy, on the ground that sin originated in the sexual act. Shakers adhered to other doctrines that would become the common currency of the radical fringe: they organized séances years before the rise of the spiritualist movement; their belief in spiritual healing foreshadowed the later ideas of Christian Science; and their ideas were based on the principle that the Second Coming was either at hand or had already occurred.

Other religious traditions of the day grew out of the belief that Biblical prophecies would be fulfilled both rapidly and literally, and that the United States would play a special role in God's prophetic plan. A well-known prophet in this respect was William Miller, a veteran of the War of 1812 whose theological studies convinced him that the end of the world was scheduled for 1843 (or possibly 1844). He attracted countless thousands of followers, a core of whom remained undismayed by the 'great disappointment' caused by the continuance of material existence. Apocalyptic notions survived in the new Adventist Churches, which took the lead in social and dietary experimentation. Millenarian ideas reached new intensity nationwide with the great revival of 1857.

The coming millennium and the Second Coming dominated Protestant thought, and often motivated political action. Rebellious slaves such as Nat Turner were fired by millenarian ideas, while in 1861 supporters of the federal union marched to war singing the popular song that linked the martyrdom of John Brown to a package of Biblical images about the end of the world and the coming of Christ. Revivalism promoted wide-ranging reforms in government and social services, instituting at least the goal of humane and reformative treatment in prisons, insane asylums and juvenile institutions, while both the temperance and the abolition movements were similarly inspired by visions of removing those structural injustices that impeded the coming of the earthly millennium and the reign of Christ on earth. The social reformers of this period usually shared a common intellectual baggage drawn from evangelical revivalism, millenarian thought and Temperance.

THE MORMONS

Millenarian enthusiasm was most marked in regions of western New York state that were so frequently licked by the fires of religious revival that they became known as the 'burned over district'. Not coincidentally, this region of religious excess was the primary base of one of the most remarkable religious movements of the age, the Church of Jesus Christ of Latter Day Saints, commonly known as the Mormons. The group was formed in the late 1820s in response to the angelic visions claimed by Joseph Smith, who announced that he had been mystically led to uncover the gold plates upon which were written the records of a Jewish civilization that had flourished in ancient America and had received visits from the risen Christ. The sources of this saga are controversial, but recent writers emphasize the many mystical influences on Smith and his circle, ideas drawn from occult, hermetic, Masonic and alchemical traditions, as well as folk magic and the lore of treasure hunting, curious notions that had survived in the religious underworld of southern New England.

Smith's new dispensation developed under the guidance of new revelations, upon the basis of which he and his followers began a westward migration in order to build a theocracy directed by a restored order of Biblical patriarchs, practicing the polygamy ordained in the Old Testament. Financial and other scandals resulted in several relocations, until the Mormon settlers built what would briefly become the largest city in the new state of Illinois, protected by a paramilitary force known as the 'Nauvoo Legion'. A virtual civil war ensued with local non-Mormons, 'Gentiles', and both Smith and his brother were assassinated in 1844. After a period of discord the sect found a new charismatic leader in Brigham Young, who led the Mormons on a further pilgrimage in quest of the new kingdom. In 1847 they settled in the Valley of the Salt Lake and founded the colony that would eventually become the state of Utah. By 1849 the Mormons were laying claim to a huge western territory of 'Deseret', including most of the southern Rockies. Sixty thousand Mormon converts reached Utah before the coming of the railway.

Though the Mormons undoubtedly attracted false accusations about their moral and sexual misconduct, their rule was indeed accompanied by violence against rivals and dissidents. For example, in 1857 Mormon paramilitaries allied with Indians to massacre over a hundred settlers travelling in a passing wagon train. Apart from this unsavoury quality, their practice of polygamy so appalled orthodox Christians that the Mormons were unable to achieve the legal status of a regular denomination until the end of the century, when a new revelation permitted the ending of the practice. Utah joined the union in 1896, but some polygamist families flourish to the present day.

THE SENECA FALLS CONVENTION ON WOMEN'S RIGHTS

GERDA LERNER

Gerda Lerner is a prominent historian and pioneer in the field of women's studies. In books such as *The Majority Finds Its Past: Placing Women in History*, she has examined the role of women in history and analyzed historical events and trends that had been neglected by previous scholars. One such neglected event, she argues, was the Seneca Falls Women's Rights Convention, held in 1848 in the state of New York. That meeting, in which women gathered together to publicly air their grievances for all women, marked an important development in the nascent women's rights movement, Lerner contends. In the following article she examines the convention's background and achievements. The organizers, including Elizabeth Cady Stanton and Lucretia Mott, and many of the participants were experienced public speakers and activists in both women's rights and abolitionism, Lerner notes. She also examines how the convention's "Declaration of Sentiments" was debated and adopted by the Convention, arguing that by modeling itself after America's Declaration of Independence and listing specific grievances, it provided a model and goals for future women's rights conventions.

In 1848, according to Karl Marx and Frederick Engels, "a specter [was] haunting Europe—the specter of communism." In that same year, the upstate New York village of Seneca Falls hosted a gathering of fewer than three hundred people,

Gerda Lerner, "The Meaning of Seneca Falls: 1848–1998," *Dissent*, Fall 1998, pp. 35–39.
Copyright © 1998 by Gerda Lerner. Reproduced by permission.

earnestly debating a Declaration of Sentiments to be spread by newsprint and oratory. The Seneca Falls Woman's Rights Convention marked the beginning of the woman's rights movement.

The specter that haunted Europe developed into a mighty movement, embracing the globe, causing revolutions, wars, tyrannies and counterrevolutions. Having gained state power in Russia, China and Eastern Europe, twentieth-century communism, in 1948, seemed more threatening a specter than ever before. Yet, after a bitter period of "cold war," which pitted nuclear nations against one another in a futile stalemate, it fell of its own weight in almost all its major centers.

The small spark figuratively ignited at Seneca Falls never produced revolutions, usurpation of power or wars. Yet it led to a transformation of consciousness and a movement of empowerment on behalf of half the human race, which hardly has its equal in human history.

Until very recently, the Seneca Falls convention of 1848 was not recognized as significant by historians, was not included in history textbooks, not celebrated as an important event in public schools, never mentioned in the media or the press. In the 1950s, the building where it was held, formerly the Wesleyan chapel, was used as a filling station. In the 1960s, it housed a laundromat. It was only due to the resurgence of modern feminism and the advances of the field of Women's History that the convention has entered the nation's consciousness. The establishment of Women's History Month as a national event during the Carter administration and its continuance through every administration since then has helped to educate the nation to the significance of women's role in history. Still, it took decades of struggle by women's organizations, feminist historians and preservationists to rescue the building at Seneca Falls and finally to persuade the National Park Service to turn it into a historic site. Today it is a major tourist attraction and has been enhanced by the establishment of a National Women's Hall of Fame on the site. This history of "long forgetting and short remembering" has been an important aspect of women's historic past, the significance of which we only understood as we began to study women's history in depth.

ORIGINS OF THE MEETING

Elizabeth Cady Stanton, the great communicator and propagandist of nineteenth-century feminism, has left a detailed account of the origins of the Seneca Falls convention both in her autobiography and in the monumental *History of Woman Suffrage*. The idea for such a meeting originated with her and with Lucretia Mott, when they both attended the 1840 World Antislavery Convention in London, at which representatives of female antislavery societies were denied seating and voting rights. Outraged by this humiliating experience, Stanton and Mott decided in London that they would convene a meeting of women in the United States to discuss their grievances as soon as possible. But her responsibilities as mother of a growing family intervened, and Stanton could not implement her plan until 1848, when Lucretia Mott visited her sister Martha Wright in Waterloo, a town near Seneca Falls. There, Stanton met with her, her hostess Jane Hunt and their friend Mary Ann McClintock. Stanton wrote: "I poured out that day the torrent of my long accumulating discontent with such vehemence and indignation that I stirred myself, as well as the rest of the party, to do or dare anything." The five drafted an announcement for a "Woman's Rights Convention" to be held at Seneca Falls on the nineteenth and twentieth of July, and placed the notice in the local paper and the abolitionist press.

The five women who issued the call to the Seneca Falls convention were hardly as naive and inexperienced as later, somewhat mythical versions of the events would lead one to believe. Lucretia Mott was an experienced and highly acclaimed public speaker, a Quaker minister and longtime abolitionist. She had attended the founding meeting of the American Antislavery Society in 1833, which admitted women only as observers. She was a founder of the Philadelphia Female Anti-Slavery Society and its long-term president. The fact that she was announced as the principal speaker at the Seneca Falls convention was a distinct drawing card.

Elizabeth Cady Stanton's "long accumulating discontent" had to do with her struggle to raise her three children (she would later have four more) and run a large household in the frequent absences of her husband Henry, a budding lawyer and Free Soil politician. Still, she found time to be involved in the campaign for reform of women's property rights in New York state, where a reform bill was passed just prior to the convention, and she had spoken before the state legislature.

Martha Wright, Jane Hunt and Mary Ann McClintock were all separatist Quakers, long active in working to improve the position of women within their church. All of them were veterans of reform and women's organizations and had worked on antislavery fairs.

An Apt Site

The place where they held their convention was particularly suited for attracting an audience of radical thinkers. The region had for more than two decades been the center of reform and utopian movements, largely due to the economic upheavals brought by the opening of the Erie Canal and the ensuing competition with western agriculture, which brought many farmers to bankruptcy. Economic uncertainty led many to embrace utopian schemes for salvation. The region was known as the "burned-over" district, because so many schemes for reforms had swept over it in rapid succession, from the evangelical revivalism of Charles Grandison Finney, to temperance, abolition, church reform, Mormonism and the chiliastic movement of William Miller, who predicted the second coming of Christ with precision for October 12, 1843 at three A.M. The nearly one million followers of Miller had survived the uneventful passing of that night and the similarly uneventful revised dates of March or October 1844, but their zeal for reform had not lessened.

The men and women who gathered in the Seneca Falls Wesleyan chapel were not a national audience; they all came from upstate New York and represented a relatively narrow spectrum of reform activists. Their local background predisposed them to accept radical pronouncements and challenging proposals. Most of them were abolitionists, the women having been active for nearly ten years in charitable, reform, and antislavery societies. They were experienced in running petition campaigns and many had organized antislavery fund-raising fairs. Historian Nancy Isenberg, who has analyzed the origins and affiliations of those attending the convention, showed that many were religious dissidents, Quakers, who just two months prior had separated from their more traditional church and would shortly form their own group, New York Congregationalist Friends. Another dissident group were Wesleyan Methodists who had been involved in a struggle within their church about the role of women and of the laity in church governance. Yet another group came from the ranks of the temperance movement. Among the men in attendance several were local lawyers with Liberty Party or Free Soil affiliations. Also present and taking a prominent part in the deliberations was Frederick Douglass, the former slave and celebrated abolitionist speaker, now editor of the *North Star.*

Far from representing a group of inexperienced housewives running their first public meeting, the majority of the convention participants were reformers with considerable organizational experience. For example, Amy Post and six other women from Rochester who came to Seneca Falls were able to organize a similar woman's rights convention in Rochester just two weeks later. One of the significant aspects of the Seneca Falls convention is that it was grounded in several organizational networks that had already existed for some time and could mobilize the energies of seasoned reform activists.

Most of the reformers attending had family, church and political affiliations in other areas of the North and Midwest. It was through them that the message of Seneca Falls spread quickly and led to the formation of a national movement. The first truly national convention on Woman's Rights was held in Worcester, Massachusetts in 1850. By 1860 ten national and many local woman's rights conventions had been organized.

THE DECLARATION OF SENTIMENTS

The first day of the Seneca Falls meeting was reserved to women, who occupied themselves with debating, paragraph by paragraph, the Declaration of Sentiments prepared by Elizabeth Cady Stanton. Resolutions were offered, debated and adopted. At the end of the second day, sixty-eight women and thirty-two men signed their names to a Declaration of Sentiments, which embodied the program of the nascent movement and provided a model for future woman's rights conventions. The number of signers represented only one third of those present, which probably was due to the radical nature of the statement.

The inequities cited and the demands raised in this Declaration were not entirely novel. Like all major social and intellectual movements, feminism has many and diverse antecedents.

By selecting the Declaration of Independence for their formal model and following its preamble almost verbatim, except for the insertion of gender-neutral language, the organizers of the convention sought to base their main appeal on the democratic rights embodied in the nation's founding document. They also put the weight and symbolism of this revered text behind what was in their time a radical assertion: "We hold these truths to be self-evident: that all men and women are created equal."

The feminist appeal to natural rights and the social contract had long antecedents on the European continent, the most important advocate of it being Mary Wollstonecraft. Her work was well known in the United States, where the same argument had been well made by Judith Sargent Murray, Frances Wright, Emma Willard, Sarah Grimké and Margaret Fuller.

The second fundamental argument for the equality of woman was religious. As stated in the Declaration:

> Resolved, That woman is man's equal—was intended to be so by the Creator, and the highest good of the race demands that she should be recognized as such.

And one of the "grievances" is:

> He [man] has usurped the prerogative of Jehovah himself, claiming it as his right to assign to her a sphere of action, when that belongs to her conscience and her God.

The feminist argument based on biblical grounds can be traced back for seven hundred years prior to 1848, but the women assembled at Seneca Falls were unaware of that fact, because of the nonexistence of anything like Women's History. They did know the Quaker argument, especially as made in her public lectures by Lucretia Mott. They had read Sarah Grimké's *Letters on the Equality of the Sexes,* and several of the resolutions in fact followed her text. They knew the biblical argument by Ann Lee of the Shakers and they echoed the antislavery biblical argument, applying it to women.

The Declaration departed from precedent in its most radical statement:

> The history of mankind is a history of repeated injuries and usurpations on the part of man toward woman, having in direct object the establishment of an absolute tyranny over her.

The naming of "man" as the culprit, thereby identifying patriarchy as a system of "tyranny," was highly original, but it may have been dictated more by the rhetorical flourishes of the Declaration of Independence than by an actual analysis of woman's situation. When it came to the list of grievances, the authors departed from the text and became quite specific.

Woman had been denied "her inalienable right to the elective franchise"; she had no voice in the making of laws; she was deprived of other rights of citizenship; she was declared civilly dead upon marriage; deprived of her property and wages; discriminated against in case of divorce, and in payment for work. Women were denied equal access to education and were kept out of the professions, held in a subordinate position in Church and State and assigned by man to the domestic sphere. Man has endeavored to destroy woman's self-respect and keep her dependent.

They concluded that in view of the disfranchisement of one-half the people of this country

> ... we insist that [women] have immediate admission to all the rights and privileges which belong to them as citizens of these United States.

It has been claimed by historians, and by herself, that Stanton's controversial resolution advocating voting rights for women—the only resolution not approved unanimously at the convention—was her most important original contribution. In fact, Sarah and Angelina Grimké had advocated woman's right to vote and hold office in 1838, and Frances Wright had done so in the 1830s. It was not so much the originality, as the inclusiveness of the listed grievances that was important.

The Declaration claimed universality, even though it never mentioned differences among women. Future woman's rights conferences before the Civil War would rectify this omission and pay particular attention to the needs of lower class and slave women.

While grievances pertaining to woman's sexual oppression were not explicitly included in the Declaration of Sentiments, they were very much alive in the consciousness of the leading participants. Elizabeth Cady Stanton had already in 1848 begun to include allusions to what we now call "marital rape" in her letters and soon after the Seneca Falls convention made such references explicit, calling on legislatures to forbid marriage to "drunkards." She soon became an open advocate of divorce and of the right of women to leave abusive marriages. Later woman's rights conventions would include some of these issues among their demands, although they used carefully guarded language and focused on abuses by "drunkards." This was a hidden feminist theme of the mainstream woman's temperance movement in the 1880s and caused many temperance women to embrace woman suffrage. What we now call "a woman's right to her body" was already on the agenda of the nineteenth-century woman's rights movement.

It was the confluence of a broad-ranging programmatic declaration with a format familiar and accessible to reformers that gave the event its historical significance. The Seneca Falls convention was the first forum in which women gathered together to *publicly* air their own grievances, not those of the needy, the enslaved, orphans or widows. The achievement of a public voice for women and the recognition that women could not win their rights unless they organized, made Seneca Falls a major event in history.

LOOKING FOR GOLD IN CALIFORNIA

E. GOULD BUFFUM

The discovery of gold in California in 1848 brought a rush of fortune hunters to the region—one hundred thousand in 1849 alone. One of the first books to be published about this interesting episode in American history was *Six Months in the Gold Mines*, written by E. Gould Buffum, a military officer. After completing his military term of service in Los Angeles, California, in 1848, Buffum immediately set off with a group of fellow Mexican-American war veterans to try his luck at prospecting. The following excerpts from his book tells of his experiences in California and descriptions of the "wet" and "dry" techniques of gold mining. The book was published in 1850, the year California was admitted to the United States, and probably played a small part in attracting even more Americans to venture to the new state.

Next morning early, in better spirits than we had enjoyed for a week previously, we started for Yuba River. About a mile from the camping-place we struck into the mountains, the same range at whose base we had been before travelling, and which are a portion of the Sierra Nevada. The hills here were steep and rugged, but covered with a magnificent growth of oak and red-wood. As we reached the summit of a lofty hill, the Yuba River broke upon our view, winding like a silver thread beneath us, its banks dotted with white tents, and fringed with trees and shrubbery.

We had at last reached the "mines," although a very different portion of them than that for which we started. We turned out

E. Gould Buffum, *Six Months in the Gold Mines*, Philadelphia: Lea and Blanchard, 1850.

our tired horses, and immediately set forth on an exploring expedition. As my clothing was all dirty and wet, I concluded to indulge in the luxury of a new shirt, and going down to the river found a shrewd Yankee in a tent surrounded by a party of naked Indians, and exposing for sale jerked beef at a dollar a pound, flour at a dollar and a half do., and for a coarse striped shirt which I picked up with the intention of purchasing, he coolly asked me the moderate price of sixteen dollars! I looked at my dirty shirt, then at the clean new one I held in my hand, and finally at my little gold bag, not yet replenished by digging, and concluded to postpone my purchase until I had struck my pick and crowbar into the bowels of the earth, and extracted therefrom at least a sufficiency to purchase a shirt. The diggings on Yuba River had at that time been discovered only about three months, and were confined entirely to the "bars," as they are called, extending nearly a mile each way from where the road strikes the river, on both its banks. The principal diggings were then called the "upper" and the "lower diggings" each about half a mile above and below the road. We started for the upper diggings to "see the elephant," and winding through the hills, for it was impossible to travel all the way on the river's bank, struck the principal bar then wrought on the river. This has since been called Foster's Bar, after an American who was then keeping a store there, and who had a claim on a large portion of the bar. Upon reaching the bar, a curious scene presented itself. About one hundred men, in miner's costume, were at work, performing the various portions of the labour necessary in digging the earth and working a rocking machine. The apparatus then used upon the Yuba River, and which has always been the favourite assistant of the gold-digger, was the common rocker or cradle, constructed in the simplest manner. It consists of nothing more than a wooden box or hollowed log, two sides and one end of which are closed, while the other end is left open. At the end which is closed and called the "mouth" of the machine, a sieve, usually made of a plate of sheet iron, or a piece of raw hide, perforated with holes about half an inch in diameter, is rested upon the sides. A number of "bars" or "rifflers," which are little pieces of board from one to two inches in height, are nailed to the bottom, and extend laterally across it. Of these, there are three or four in the machine, and one at the "tail" as it is called, i.e. the end where the dirt is washed out. This, with a pair of rockers like those of a child's cradle, and a handle to rock it with, complete the description of the machine, which being placed with the rockers upon two logs, and the "mouth" elevated at a slight angle above the tail, is ready for operation. Modified and improved as this may be, and as in fact it already has been, so long as manual labour is employed for washing gold, the "cradle" is the best agent to use for that purpose. The manner of procuring and washing the golden earth was this. The loose stones and surface earth being removed from any portion of the bar, a hole from four to six feet square was opened, and the dirt extracted therefrom was thrown upon a raw hide placed at the side of the machine. One man shovelled the dirt into the sieve, another dipped up water and threw it on, and a third rocked the "cradle." The earth, thrown upon the sieve, is washed through with the water, while the stones and gravel are retained and thrown off. The continued motion of the machine, and the constant stream of water pouring through it, washes the earth over the various bars or rifflers to the "tail," where it runs out, while the gold, being of greater specific gravity, sinks to the bottom, and is prevented from escaping by the rifflers. When a certain amount of earth has been thus washed (usually about sixty pans full are called "a washing"), the gold, mixed with a heavy black sand, which is always found mingled with gold in California, is taken out and washed in a tin pan, until nearly all the sand is washed away. It is then put into a cup or pan, and when the day's labour is over is dried before the fire, and the sand remaining carefully blown out. This is a simple explanation of the process of gold-washing in the placers of California. At present, however, instead of dipping and pouring on water by hand, it is usually led on by a hose or forced by a pump, thereby giving a better and more constant stream, and saving the labour of one man. The excavation is continued until the solid rock is struck, or the water rushing in renders it impossible to obtain any more earth, when a new place is opened. We found the gold on the Yuba in exceedingly fine particles, and it has always been considered of a very superior quality. We inquired of the washers as to their success, and they, seeing we were "green horns" and thinking we might possibly interfere with them, gave us either evasive answers, or in some cases told us direct lies. We understood from them that they were making about twenty dollars per day, while I afterwards learned, from the most positive testimony of two men who were at work there at the time, that one hundred dollars a

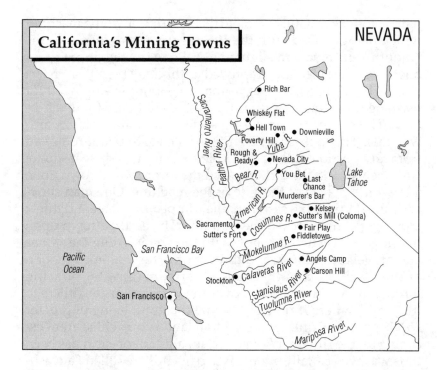

man was not below the average estimate of a day's labour.

On this visit to Foster's Bar I made my first essay in gold-digging. I scraped up with my hand my tin cup full of earth, and washed it in the river. How eagerly I strained my eyes as the earth was washing out, and the bottom of the cup was coming in view! and how delighted, when, on reaching the bottom, I discerned about twenty little golden particles sparkling in the sun's rays, and worth probably about fifty cents. I wrapped them carefully in a piece of paper, and preserved them for a long time,—but, like much more gold in larger quantities, which it has since been my lot to possess, it has escaped my grasp, and where it now is Heaven only knows.

The labour on Yuba River appeared very severe, the excavations being sometimes made to a depth of twelve feet before the soil containing the gold, which was a gravelly clay, was reached. We had not brought our tools with us, intending, if our expedition in the mountains had succeeded, that one of our party should return for our remaining stock of provisions and tools. We had no facilities for constructing a machine, and no money to buy one (two hundred dollars being the price for which a mere hollowed pine log was offered us), and besides, all the bars upon which men were then engaged in labour were "claimed" a claim at that time being considered good when the claimant had cleared off the top soil from any portion of the bar. We returned to our camp, and talked over our prospects, in a quandary what to do. Little did we then dream that, in less than six months, the Yuba River, then only explored some three miles above where we were, would be successfully wrought for forty miles above us, and that thousands would find their fortunes upon it.

We concluded to return to the *Embarcadero* [Sacramento], and take a new start. Accordingly, next morning we packed up and set off, leaving at work upon the river about two hundred men. . . .

As the ox-team was a slow traveller, and quarters were to be looked for in our new winter home . . . Higgins and myself were appointed a deputation to mount two horses we had brought with us and proceed post-haste to the "dry diggings." We started at 10 A.M., and travelled through some beautiful valleys and over lofty hills. As we reached the summit of a high ridge, we paused by common consent to gaze upon the landscape and breathe the delicious air. The broad and fertile valleys of the Sacramento and San Joaquin lay stretched at our feet like a highly coloured map. The noble rivers which lend their names to these rich valleys were plainly visible, winding like silver threads through dark lines of timber fringing their banks; now plunging amid dense forests, and now coming in view sparkling and bright as the riches they contain; the intermediate plains, here parched and browned with the sun's fierce rays; there brilliant with all the hues of the rainbow, and dotted with the autumnal flowers and open groves of evergreen oak. Herds of elk, black-tailed deer, and antelope browsed near the mountain sides, on the summit of which the eagle builds his eyry. The surrounding atmosphere, fragrant with delightful odours, was so pure and transparent as to render objects visible at a great distance, and so elastic and bracing as to create a perceptible effect on our feelings. Far in the distance the massive peak of Shaste reared its snow-capped head, from amid a dense forest, fourteen thousand feet into the sky. We arrived at what was then called Weaver's Creek, about dusk. . . .

The day after our arrival, in anticipation of the immediate commencement of the rainy season (a time dreaded by strangers in all California, and particularly in the northern region), we determined to build a log house, and were about to commence operations, when we received an offer for the sale of one. We examined it, and found a little box of unhewn logs, about twenty feet long by ten wide, which was offered us at the moderate price of five hundred dollars. The terms, however, were accommodating, being ten days' credit for the whole amount. With the reasonable expectation that we could pay for our house by gold-digging in a less time than it would require to build one, we purchased it, and ere nightfall were duly installed in the premises. . . .

DRY DIGGINGS

The "dry diggings" of Weaver's Creek being a fair specimen of dry diggings in all parts of the mining region, a description of them will give the reader a general idea of the various diggings of the same kind in California. They are called "dry" in contradistinction to the "wet" diggings, or those lying directly on the banks of streams, and where all the gold is procured by washing. As I before said, the stream coursed between lofty tree-clad hills, broken on both sides of the river into little ravines or gorges. In these ravines most of the gold was found. The loose stones and top earth being thrown off, the gravelly clay that followed it was usually laid aside for washing, and the digging continued until the bottom rock of the ravine was reached, commonly at a depth of from one to six feet. The surface of this rock was carefully cleared off, and usually found to contain little crevices and holes, the latter in miner's parlance called "pockets," and in which the gold was found concealed, sparkling like the treasures in the cave of Monte Cristo. A careful examination of the rock being made, and every little crevice and pocket being searched with a sharp pointed-knife, gold in greater or less quantities invariably made its appearance. I shall never forget the delight with which I first struck and worked out a crevice. It was the second day after our installation in our little log hut; the first having been employed in what is called "prospecting," or searching for the most favourable place at which to commence operations. I had slung pick, shovel, and bar upon my shoulder, and trudged merrily away to a ravine about a mile from our house. Pick, shovel, and bar did their duty, and I soon had a large rock in view. Getting down into the excavation I had made, and seating myself upon the rock, I commenced a careful search for a crevice, and at last found one extending longitudinally along the rock. It appeared to be filled with a hard, bluish clay and gravel, which I took out with my knife, and there at the bottom, strewn along the whole length of the rock, was bright, yellow gold, in little pieces about the size and shape of a grain of barley. Eureka! Oh how my heart beat! I sat still and looked at it some minutes before I touched it, greedily drinking in the pleasure of gazing upon gold that was in my very grasp, and feeling a sort of independent bravado in allowing it to remain there. When my eyes were sufficiently feasted, I scooped it out with the point of my knife and an iron spoon, and placing it in my pan, ran home with it very much delighted. I weighed it, and found that my first day's labour in the mines had made me thirty-one dollars richer than I was in the morning. . . .

Our party's first day's labour produced one hundred and fifty dollars, I having been the most successful of all. But we were satisfied, although our experience had not fulfilled the golden stories we had heard previous to our reaching the *placers*. Finding the average amount of gold dug on Weaver's Creek at that time to be about an ounce per day to a man, we were content so long as we could keep pace with our neighbours. There is a spirit of emulation among miners which prevents them from being ever satisfied with success whilst others around them are more successful. We continued our labours for a week, and found, at the end of that time, our whole party had dug out more than a thousand dollars; and after paying for our house, and settling between ourselves our little private expenses, we were again on a clear track, unencumbered by debt, and in the heart of a region where treasures of unknown wealth were lying hidden in the earth on which we daily trod.

About this time, the most extravagant reports reached us from the Middle Fork, distant in a northerly direction about thirty miles from Weaver's Creek. Parties who had been there described the river as being lined with gold of the finest quality. One and two hundred dollars was not considered a great day's labour, and now was the time to take advantage of it, while in its pristine richness. The news was too blooming for me to withstand. I threw down my pickaxe, and leaving a half-wrought crevice for some other digger to work out, I packed up and held myself in readiness to proceed by the earliest opportunity, and with the first party ready to go for the Middle Fork. . . .

ADVICE FOR PROSPECTIVE MINERS

It is proper, before closing this work, and it will probably be expected, that I should make a sort of recapitulation, and give some advice in regard to prospects and plans of proceeding in the gold mines of California. To advise is always a difficult task, and in this instance it is peculiarly so; but I will endeavour to give a fair statement of facts, and the best advice I can. The number of persons at present labouring in the various portions of the mining region is about one hundred thousand. Of these, at least one-third are Mexicans, Chilenos, Pacific Islanders, and Chinese, and the remainder Americans, English, French, and Germans; and I should divide their locations as follows: on the North, Middle, and South Forks, say twenty thousand; on the Stanislaus, Mokelumne, Tuolumne, Merced, Mariposa, and other tributaries of the San Joaquin, forty thousand; on Yuba and Feather Rivers, twenty thousand; and, scattered over the various dry diggings, twenty thousand more. During the past summer and autumn, I should estimate the average quantity of gold dug daily at eight dollars to a man; for although it is by no means uncommon for an individual to "strike a lucky place," and some days take out from a hundred to a thousand dollars, others spend whole days in search and labour, without finding more than two or three dollars a day. From my own experience in the mines I am, however, satisfied, that, during six months in the year, a stout man, with health, energy, and perseverance, can average sixteen dollars a day in almost any portion of the placers; and that, for twenty years, from three to ten dollars a day can be made by individual labour. Still, I would advise all who are in good positions at home to remain there. The labour and hardships consequent upon the life of a gold-digger are of the most severe and arduous nature. Prying and breaking up huge rocks, shovelling dirt, washing it with wet feet all day, and sleeping on the damp ground at night, with nothing above but a thin covering of canvass, or a leaky log roof, are not by any means agreeable to one who has been accustomed to the civilized life of cities. Richelieu says that "the pen is mightier than the sword." Many a fine, spruce young clerk coming to California with golden dreams of wealth before him has proved, to his sorrow, that the crowbar is heavier than the pen. I hesitate not to say, that the labour of gold-digging is unequalled by any other in the world in severity. It combines within itself the various arts of canal-digging, ditching, laying stone walls, ploughing, and hoeing potatoes,—and adding to this a life in the wilds of the mountains, living upon poor provisions, continually exposed either to the burning rays of the sun, or the heavy dews of night, and the occupation becomes anything but a pleasant one. But to a man endowed with a constitution to endure hardship, with hands that have been accustomed to labour, and with a heart which suffers not itself to be sorrowed with disappointment, there was never a better opportunity in the world to make a fortune, than there is at present in California. To mechanics, especially, there are great inducements; for if they do not choose to labour in the mines, with the wages which I have previously stated as being paid to them in San Francisco and the other towns of Northern California, they may, in one year, save more money than in five in any other portion of the United States. . . .

A great mistake has been made by people who have emigrated to California, or who have desired to emigrate, in considering it merely as a temporary home, a sort of huge goose, out of which a few feathers were to be plucked, and then forsaken. It is for this reason that the life of the miner is at present tenfold more arduous than it otherwise would be, and never was there a more egregious error in regard to the character of the country. Gold is not the only product of the soil in California. Her fertile valleys and rich prairies are capable, when cultivated, of producing an untold store of agricultural wealth. Her lofty pines and spreading oak trees afford an abundant supply of material for the erection of comfortable dwellings. Her thousand streams, pouring down every hillside and winding through her plains, furnish an inexhaustible supply of water-power, and her forests, mountains, and lakes abound with game of every description. In the immense valleys of the Sacramento and San Joaquin, are millions of acres of land entirely unreclaimed, upon which any man may settle and make a fortune in a few years by the cultivation of the soil. . . .

California is a habitable country, and should be looked upon no longer as a mere temporary residence. A state government has been organized, the sheltering hand of law stretched over its borders, and life there can be made as comfortable as life in any other portion of the world. Let then the gold-digger come, and from the never-failing hills gather a rich supply of treasure. Let the farmer come, and from the abundant soil produce the necessaries of life, and enrich himself from them. Let the mechanic and labourer come, and build up the towns of this new country, and let the ladies of our land come, and with their smiles bring peace and happiness into the wilderness.

CHRONOLOGY

1783

A peace treaty is signed by the United States and Great Britain; Loyalists move to New Brunswick and Prince Edward Island in Canada; America's first daily newspaper, the *Pennsylvania Evening Post*, begins publication; Noah Webster publishes *The American Spelling Book*.

1784

The U.S. government negotiates the Treaty of Fort Stanwix with the Iroquois, taking more land for white settlement; Spain closes New Orleans to American shipping; Father Junipero Serra dies after founding nine Spanish missions in California.

1786

Virginia enacts the Statute for Religious Freedom drafted by Thomas Jefferson; Shays's Rebellion erupts in western Massachusetts; Charles W. Peale opens the first American art gallery.

1787

The Philadelphia Convention meets and drafts a new constitution; Congress passes the Northwest Ordinance, establishing governing procedures (and banning slavery) for lands north of the Ohio River.

1788

The Constitution goes into effect after New Hampshire becomes the ninth state to ratify.

1789

In America's first presidential election under the new system, George Washington is elected without opposition; the first Congress under the Constitution convenes in New York, where it approves the Bill of Rights; the French Revolution begins.

1790

The first U.S. census is held, revealing a U.S. population of 4 million; Samuel Slater, a British immigrant, designs and constructs a water-powered cotton mill in Rhode Island; the U.S. capital moves from New York to Philadelphia.

1791

The Bill of Rights is ratified by the states; Congress charters the Bank of the United States; Vermont enters the Union as the fourteenth state; Toussaint-Louverture leads a slave revolt against the French in Santo Domingo (Haiti); U.S. forces are defeated by the Western Confederacy of Native American tribes in present-day Ohio; Congress passes the first internal revenue law, an excise tax on whiskey.

1792

Kentucky becomes the nation's fifteenth state; election of 1792: President George Washington is persuaded to run again and is elected without opposition.

1793

Eli Whitney invents the cotton gin; Washington proclaims the United States to be neutral in the war between Great Britain and France; Congress passes the Fugitive Slave Act, making it a crime to aid runaway slaves.

1794

American forces defeat the Western Confederacy of Native Americans during the Battle of Fallen Timbers, destroying Native American control of the Ohio region; a rebellion breaks out as farmers refuse to pay federal taxes on whiskey; the first major turnpike, or toll road, begins operations from Philadelphia to Lancaster, Pennsylvania.

1795

The Senate ratifies Jay's Treaty with Great Britain, establishing the U.S.-Canadian boundaries, and Pinckney's Treaty with Spain, securing navigation rights in the Mississippi River; the Treaty of Greenville cedes Indian lands in the Ohio region to white settlement.

1796

Tennessee becomes the nation's sixteenth state; Washington's Farewell Address is published; election of 1796: In the first contested presidential race between political parties, John Adams (Federalist) is elected president over Thomas Jefferson (Republican), who, as runner-up, becomes vice president.

1798

Amidst growing U.S.-French tensions, Congress passes the Alien and Sedition Acts, which restrict speech and press freedoms.

1799

George Washington dies; Handsome Lake begins a religious movement among the Iroquois.

1800

The U.S. capital moves from Philadelphia to Washington, D.C.; election of 1800: Incumbent president John Adams (Federalist) finishes behind Thomas Jefferson (Republican); Jefferson and vice presidential candidate Aaron Burr are tied in electoral votes, the House of Representatives picks Jefferson as president.

1801

Tripoli declares war on the United States; John Marshall becomes chief justice of the Supreme Court.

1803

Jefferson buys the Louisiana Territory from French leader Napoléon; Ohio becomes the seventeenth state; the Supreme Court establishes its right to declare acts of Congress unconstitutional.

1804

Aaron Burr kills Alexander Hamilton in a duel; Meriwether Lewis and William Clark begin their expedition; the Twelfth Amendment changes how America elects presidents by placing presidential and vice presidential candidates on separate ballots; election of 1804: Thomas Jefferson (Republican) wins reelection over Charles C. Pinckney (Federalist).

1806

Zebulon Pike discovers Pikes Peak in what is now Colorado.

1807

Robert Fulton's steamboat sails up the Hudson River; Congress passes the Embargo Act, banning trade with England and France.

1808

Congress bans the importation of African slaves; election of 1808: James Madison (Republican) is elected president over Charles C. Pinckney (Federalist).

1810

The third U.S. census shows the population to be 7.2 million, including 60,000 immigrants and 1.2 million slaves.

1811

Venezuela is the first South American Spanish colony to declare its independence; William Henry Harrison attacks and destroys the Indian settlement of Prophetstown in the Battle of Tippecanoe.

1812

The War of 1812 between Great Britain and the United States begins; Louisiana becomes the nation's eighteenth state; Napoléon invades Russia with disastrous results, altering Europe's balance of power; election of 1812: President James Madison (Republican) is reelected over DeWitt Clinton (Federalist).

1813

Native American leader Tecumseh, fighting for the British, is killed.

1814

Frances Scott Key writes the lyrics for "The Star-Spangled Banner"; British troops occupy and destroy much of Washington, D.C.; the Boston Manufacturing Company constructs America's first fully mechanized textile mill; Andrew Jackson leads Tennessee militia troops in defeating the Creek Indians in the Battle of Horseshoe Bend; the Treaty of Ghent between the United States and Great Britain is signed.

1815

Andrew Jackson leads a resounding victory over the British in the Battle of New Orleans, fought before word of the Treaty of Ghent reaches America; Congress authorizes a peacetime army.

1816

Congress establishes the Second Bank of the United States; Indiana becomes the nation's nineteenth state; the American Colonization Society, which supports sending emancipated slaves to Africa, is founded; election of 1816: James Monroe (Republican) is elected president over Rufus King (Federalist).

1817

Mississippi becomes the nation's twentieth state.

1818

Spain sells its Florida territory (which includes present-day Florida and parts of Alabama and Georgia) to the United States; Connecticut is the first state to ban property qualifications for voting; Illinois becomes the nation's twenty-first state; regular transatlantic shipping lines are established between New York City and Liverpool, England.

1819

Alabama becomes the nation's twenty-second state.

1820

Congress passes the Missouri Compromise, which results in the admission of Maine (a free state) as the nation's twenty-third state and Missouri (slave) as the twenty-fourth state; election of 1820; James Monroe (Republican) is reelected without Federalist opposition.

1821

James Fenimore Cooper publishes the first of his American novels, *The Spy*; the first public high school in the United States is founded in Boston; the Republic of Mexico wins independence from Spain; the first college for women is founded by Emma Willard.

1822

A planned slave rebellion in Charleston, South Carolina, is discovered and prevented; its leader, Denmark Vesey, is tried and executed; the first cotton mill powered by water begins production in Massachusetts; President James Monroe and Congress agree to formally recognize as independent nations former Spanish colonies in Latin America; Liberia, West Africa, is founded as a colony for liberated American slaves.

1823

Monroe issues the Monroe Doctrine.

1824

The Supreme Court, in *Gibbons v. Ogden*, extends Congress's power to regulate interstate commerce; election of 1824: Four regional candidates, all officially Republicans, fail to win electoral majority; John Quincy Adams is elected by the House of Representatives despite receiving fewer popular and electoral votes than Andrew Jackson.

1825

Erie Canal is completed, sparking economic growth and a canal construction boom; Monroe calls for voluntary removal of Indians to lands west of the Mississippi River; the "Second Great Awakening" begins as evangelist Charles Grandison Finney leads religious revivals in the state of New York; Mexico opens Texas to settlement by U.S. citizens; Thomas Cole establishes the Hudson River School of landscape painting.

1826

The American Society for the Promotion of Temperance is founded; the first railroads are constructed.

1827

Massachusetts requires that a high school be established in every town; *Freedom's Journal*, the nation's first African American newspaper, begins publication.

1828

Cherokee Phoenix, the nation's first Native American newspaper, begins publication; California residents revolt against their Mexican governor; South Carolina asserts its right to nullify federal laws; election of 1828: Andrew Jackson (Democrat) is elected president over incumbent John Quincy Adams (National Republican).

1830

The *Tom Thumb*, the first steam locomotive built in America, begins service; Congress passes the Indian Removal Act; Joseph Smith founds the Mormon church; Mexico bans further immigration of U.S. citizens into Texas.

1831

Nat Turner leads a slave insurrection in Virginia; abolitionist William Lloyd Garrison begins publication of the *Liberator* newspaper; Cyrus McCormick invents the mechanical reaper.

1832

Jackson vetoes a bill to recharter the Bank of the United States; the South Carolina legislature votes to nullify the federal tariff; election of 1832: President Andrew Jackson (Democrat) wins reelection over Henry Clay (National Republican).

1833

Congress passes the Force Bill, authorizing Jackson to enforce federal law in South Carolina; Slavery is abolished in the British Empire; the American Anti-Slavery Society is founded.

1835

President Jackson calls for suppression of abolitionist mailings; John Marshall steps down as chief justice of the Supreme Court; the Seminole War begins in Florida.

1836

Texas proclaims independence from Mexico; Abolitionists send antislavery petitions to Congress, which are automatically tabled under the Gag Rule; Arkansas becomes the nation's twenty-fifth state; Ralph Waldo Emerson publishes *Nature*; election of 1836: Vice President Martin Van Buren (Democrat) is elected president over William H. Harrison (Whig).

1837

A financial panic causes an economic depression and sets back the burgeoning labor movement; Michigan becomes the nation's twenty-sixth state; Nathaniel Hawthorne publishes *Twice-Told Tales*.

1838

Northern states enact personal liberty laws, which obstruct enforcement of the federal Fugitive Slave Act; four thousand Cherokees perish on the Trail of Tears while being forced to move from their homelands to Oklahoma; blacks lose the right to vote in Pennsylvania.

1839

Mormons establish the city of Nauvoo, Illinois; Charles Good-year discovers vulcanized rubber.

1840

The first regularly scheduled transatlantic steamship line is established; election of 1840: William H. Harrison (Whig) defeats incumbent Martin Van Buren (Democrat).

1841

Harrison becomes the first U.S. president to die in office; John Tyler is the first vice president to succeed to the presidency; Brooks Farm, a transcendentalist utopian community, is founded; the first pioneer wagon train from Missouri reaches California.

1842

The Webster-Ashburton Treaty between the United States and Britain establishes the boundary between the United States and Canada from Maine to the Lake of the Woods; the U.S. Supreme Court in *Prigg v. Pennsylvania* rules that no state has responsibility of enforcing federal fugitive slave laws; Phineas T. Barnum opens his American Museum in New York; the Seminole war ends with surviving Seminoles removed to Oklahoma.

1843

The first overland caravans trek from Missouri to Oregon; General Santa Anna of Mexico warns that the U.S. annexation of Texas will be viewed as an act of war.

1844

Inventor Samuel F. Morse successfully demonstrates the telegraph; the Senate rejects the annexation treaty with Texas; Congress repeals the Gag Rule regarding antislavery petitions; election of 1844: James K. Polk (Democrat) is elected president over Henry Clay (Whig); James G. Birney of the antislavery Liberty Party polls sixteen thousand votes in New York, helping tip that state from Clay to Polk.

1845

Florida is admitted as the nation's twenty-seventh state; the Republic of Texas is annexed by a joint resolution of Congress, becoming the nation's twenty-eighth state; Mexico breaks off diplomatic relations with the United States; the *Narrative of the Life of Frederick Douglass, a Slave,* is published; a potato famine in Ireland stimulates mass immigration to the United States; *Scientific American* begins publication.

1846

The war with Mexico begins; a U.S.-British dispute over Oregon is settled by treaty; California breaks from Mexico and is claimed by the United States; the Wilmot Proviso, calling for the banning of slavery in territories gained during the Mexican War, is debated in Congress; Elias Howe patents the sewing machine; Michigan abolishes capital punishment.

1847

U.S. forces under General Winfield Scott capture Mexico City; Mormons arrive in the Great Salt Lake Valley; John C. Calhoun proposes Senate resolutions asserting the right of slave owners to take their property into any U.S. territory; annual Irish immigration increases three-fold to 105,000.

1848

Gold is discovered in California; the Treaty of Guadalupe Hidalgo ends the war with Mexico and gives America the provinces of California and New Mexico; European revolutions of 1848 occur; men and women meet in Seneca Falls, New York, to discuss women's rights; Karl Marx publishes the *Communist Manifesto*; Chinese laborers are imported to California to work on railroads; Wisconsin becomes the nation's thirtieth state; election of 1848: Zachary Taylor (Whig) is elected president over Lewis Cass (Democrat); Martin Van Buren (Free-Soil Party) receives 10 percent of the popular vote.

1849

The gold rush transforms California; Elizabeth Blackwell is the first woman in the world to receive a medical degree.

1850

The U.S. population reaches 23 million; President Taylor dies and is succeeded by Millard Fillmore; Levi Strauss begins selling canvas pants for miners; California is admitted as the nation's thirty-first state; Congress bans the slave trade in the District of Columbia.

FOR FURTHER RESEARCH

THE CONSTITUTION

Bernard Bailyn, ed., *The Debate on the Constitution*. New York: Library of America, 1993.

Richard B. Bernstein and Kym S. Rice, *Are We to Be a Nation? The Making of the Constitution*. Cambridge, MA: Harvard University Press, 1987.

Lydia D. Bjornlund, *The Constitution and the Founding of America*. San Diego: Lucent Books, 2000.

Clinton Rossiter, *1787: The Grand Convention*. New York: Macmillan, 1966.

Frances N. Stites, *John Marshall: Defender of the Constitution*. Boston: Little, Brown, 1981.

Garry Wills, *Explaining America: The Federalist*. New York: Doubleday, 1981.

CULTURAL AND SOCIAL DEVELOPMENTS

Daniel Boorstin, *The Americans: The National Experience*. New York: Random House, 1965.

David Brion Davis, ed., *Antebellum American Culture: An Interpretive Anthology*. Lexington, MA: D.C. Heath, 1979.

Reginald Horsman, *Race and Manifest Destiny: The Origins of American Racial Anglo-Saxonism*. Cambridge, MA: Harvard University Press, 1981.

Walter Huggins, ed., *The Reform Impulse, 1825–1850*. New York: Harper & Row, 1972.

Jack Larkin, *The Reshaping of Everyday Life, 1790–1840*. New York: Harper & Row, 1988.

Ira M. Leonard and Robert D. Parmet, *American Nativism, 1830–1860*. New York: Van Nostrand Reinhold, 1971.

Russel B. Nye, *Society and Culture in America, 1830–1860,* New York: Harper & Row, 1974.

William J. Rorabaugh, *The Alcoholic Republic.* New York: Oxford University Press, 1979.

Anne C. Rose, *Transcendentalism as a Social Movement.* New Haven, CT: Yale University Press, 1981.

Ronald G. Walters, *American Reformers, 1815–1860.* New York: Hill and Wang, 1978.

FOREIGN RELATIONS

John M. Belohlavek, *Let the Eagle Soar! The Foreign Policy of Andrew Jackson.* Lincoln: University of Nebraska Press, 1985.

Donald B. Chidsey, *The Lousiana Purchase.* New York: Crown, 1972.

Howard Jones and Donald R. Rakestraw, *Prologue to Manifest Destiny: Anglo-American Relations in the 1840s.* Wilmington, DE: Scholarly Resources, 1997.

Lawrence S. Kaplan, *Entangling Alliances with None: American Foreign Policy in the Age of Jefferson.* Kent, OH: Kent State University Press, 1987.

Daniel G. Lang, *Foreign Policy in the Early Republic: The Law of Nations and the Balance of Power.* Baton Rouge: University of Louisiana Press, 1985.

Ernest R. May, *The Making of the Monroe Doctrine.* Cambridge, MA: Belknap Press of Harvard University Press, 1975.

David M. Pletcher, *The Diplomacy of Annexation: Texas, Oregon, and the Mexican War.* Columbia: University of Missouri Press, 1973.

INDUSTRIALIZATION AND THE MARKET REVOLUTION

Joyce Appleby, *Capitalism and a New Social Order.* New York: New York University Press, 1984.

Stuart Bruchey, *Enterprise: The Dynamic Economy of a Free People.* Cambridge, MA: Harvard University Press, 1990.

Thomas Cochran, *Frontiers of Change: Early Industrialism in America*. New York: Oxford University Press, 1981.

Brook Hindle and Steven Lubar, *Engines of Change: The American Industrial Revolution, 1790–1860*. Washington, DC: Smithsonian Institution, 1986.

Charles Sellers, *The Market Revolution: Jacksonian America, 1815–1846*. New York: Oxford University Press, 1991.

Sean Wilentz, *Chants Democratic: New York City and the Rise of the American Working Class, 1788–1850*. New York: Oxford University Press, 1984.

MANIFEST DESTINY

Norman Graebner, ed., *Manifest Destiny*. Indianapolis: Bobbs-Merrill, 1968.

Sam W. Haynes and Christopher Morris, eds., *Manifest Destiny and Empire: American Antebellum Expansionism*. College Station: Texas A&M University Press, 1998.

Thomas Hietala, *Manifest Design: Anxious Aggrandizement in Late Jacksonian America*. Ithaca, NY: Cornell University Press, 1985.

Allan O. Kownslar, *Manifest Destiny and Expansionism in the 1840s*. Lexington, MA: D.C. Heath, 1964.

Frederick Merk, *Manifest Destiny and Mission in American History: A Reinterpretation*. New York: Knopf, 1963.

Anders Stephanson, *Manifest Destiny: American Expansionism and the Empire of Right*. New York: Hill and Wang, 1996.

NATIVE AMERICANS

Gregory Evans Dowd, *A Spirited Resistance: The North American Indian Struggle for Unity, 1745–1815*. Baltimore: Johns Hopkins University Press, 1992.

John M. Dunn, *The Relocation of the North American Indian*. San Diego: Lucent Books, 1995.

R. David Edmunds, *Tecumseh and the Quest for Indian Leadership*. Boston: Little, Brown, 1984.

John Ehle, *Trail of Tears: The Rise and Fall of the Cherokee Nation*. New York: Doubleday, 1988.

Grant Foreman, *Indian Removal: The Emigration of the Five Civilized Tribes of Indians*. Norman: University of Oklahoma Press, 1953.

Steven Mintz, ed., *Native American Voices: A History and Anthology*. St. James, NY: Brandywine, 1995.

Bernard W. Sheehan, *Seeds of Extinction: Jeffersonian Philosophy and the American Indian*. Chapel Hill: University of North Carolina Press, 1973.

Anthony F.C. Wallace, *The Death and Rebirth of the Seneca*. New York: Knopf, 1970.

Richard White, *The Middle Ground: Indians, Empires, and Republics in the Great Lakes Region, 1650–1815*. New York: Cambridge University Press, 1991.

POLITICS AND GOVERNMENT

Donald B. Cole, *The Presidency of Andrew Jackson*. Lawrence: University Press of Kansas, 1991.

James T. Flexner, *George Washington and the New Nation, 1783–1793*. Boston: Little, Brown, 1970.

Paul Goodman, *The Federalists vs. the Jeffersonian Republicans*. New York: Holt, Rinehart, and Winston, 1967.

Richard Hofstadter, *The Idea of a Party System: The Rise of Legitimate Opposition in the United States, 1780–1840*. Berkeley and Los Angeles: University of California Press, 1969.

Daniel Walker Howe, *The Political Culture of the American Whigs*. Chicago: University of Chicago Press, 1979.

Lawrence Kohl, *The Politics of Individualism: Parties and the American Character in the Jacksonian Era*. New York: Oxford University Press, 1989.

John Niven, *Martin Van Buren and the Romantic Age of American Politics*. New York: Oxford University Press, 1983.

Merrill D. Peterson, *The Great Triumverate: Webster, Clay, and Calhoun*. New York: Oxford University Press, 1987.

Merrill D. Peterson, ed., *Democracy, Liberty, and Property: The State Constitutional Conventions of the 1820s*. Indianapolis: Bobbs-Merrill, 1966.

Robert V. Remini, *Andrew Jackson and the Course of American Democracy, 1832–1845*. New York: Harper & Row, 1984.

John William Ward, *Andrew Jackson: Symbol for an Age*. New York: Oxford University Press, 1983.

SLAVERY AND ABOLITIONISM

John Ashworth, *Slavery, Capitalism, and Politics in the Antebellum Republic, 1820–1850*. New York: Cambridge University Press, 1995.

Ira Berlin, *Slaves Without Masters: The Free Negro in the Antebellum South*. New York: Pantheon, 1974.

Drew Gilpin Faust, ed., *The Ideology of Slavery: Proslavery Thought in the Antebellum South, 1830–1860*. Baton Rouge: Louisiana State University Press, 1981.

Elizabeth Fox-Genovese, *Within the Plantation Household: Black and White Women in the Old South*. Chapel Hill: University of North Carolina Press, 1988.

John Hope Franklin and Alfred A. Moss, *From Slavery to Freedom: A History of African Americans*. Boston: McGraw Hill, 2000.

Henry Mayer, *All on Fire: William Lloyd Garrison and the Abolition of Slavery*. New York: St. Martin's, 1998.

Eric McKitrick, *Slavery Defended: The Views of the Old South*. Englewood Cliffs, NJ: Prentice-Hall, 1963.

Gary B. Nash, *Race and Revolution*. Madison, WI: Madison House, 1990.

James Oakes, *Slavery and Freedom: An Interpretation of the Old South*. New York: Norton, 1998.

Benjamin Quarles, *Black Abolitionists*. New York: Oxford University Press, 1969.

Kenneth M. Stampp, *The Peculiar Institution: Slavery in the Ante-Bellum South*. New York: Vintage, 1964.

James Brewer Stewart, *Holy Warriors: The Abolitionists and American Slavery*. New York: Hill and Wang, 1976.

Donald R. Wright, *African Americans in the Early Republic, 1789–1831*. Arlington Heights, IL: Harlan Davidson, 1993.

Arthur Zilversmit, *The First Emancipation: The Abolition of Slavery in the North*. Chicago: University of Chicago Press, 1967.

THE WAR OF 1812

Roger H. Brown, *The Republic in Peril, 1812*. New York: Columbia University Press, 1964.

Donald R. Hickey, *The War of 1812: A Forgotten Conflict*. Urbana: University of Illinois Press, 1989.

J.C.A. Stagg, *Mr. Madison's War: Politics, Diplomacy, and Warfare in the Early American Republic*. Princeton, NJ: Princeton University Press, 1983.

Reginald C. Stuart, *United States Expansionism and British North America*. Chapel Hill: University of North Carolina Press, 1988.

Wesley B. Turner, *The War of 1812: The War That Both Sides Won*. Toronto: Dundurn Group, 2000.

Stephen Watts, *The Republic Reborn: War and the Making of Liberal America, 1790–1820*. Baltimore: Johns Hopkins University Press, 1987.

THE WAR WITH MEXICO, 1846–1848

Paul H. Bergeron, *The Presidency of James K. Polk*. Lawrence: University Press of Kansas, 1987.

Seymour V. Connor and Odie B. Faulk, *North America Divided: The Mexican War, 1846–1848*. New York: Oxford University Press, 1971.

John S.D. Eisenhower, *So Far from God: The U.S. War with Mexico*. New York: Random House, 1989.

Donald S. Frazier, ed., *The United States and Mexico at War: Nineteenth-Century Expansionism and Conflict*. New York: Macmillan Library Reference, 1998.

Robert W. Johannsen, "America's Forgotten War," *Wilson Quarterly*, vol. 20, no. 2, 1996.

Don Nardo, *The Mexican-American War*. San Diego: Lucent Books, 1999.

John H. Schroeder, *Mr. Polk's War: American Opposition and Dissent, 1846–1848*. Madison: University of Wisconsin Press, 1976.

Richard Winders, *Mr. Polk's Army: The American Military Experience in the Mexican War*. College Station: Texas A&M University Press, 1997.

WESTERN EXPLORATION AND SETTLEMENT

Stephen E. Ambrose, *Undaunted Courage: Meriwether Lewis, Thomas Jefferson, and the Opening of the American West*. New York: Simon and Schuster, 1996.

Ray A. Billington and Martin Ridge, *Westward Expansion: A History of the American Frontier*. New York: Macmillan, 1982.

John Mack Faragher, *Sugar Creek: Life on the Illinois Prairie*. New Haven, CT: Yale University Press, 1986.

Reginald Horsman, *The Frontier in the Formative Years, 1783–1815*. New York: Holt, Rinehart, and Winston, 1970.

Patricia Nelson Limerick, *The Legacy of Conquest: The Unbroken Past of the American West*. New York: W.W. Norton, 1987.

Michael V. Uschan, *Westward Expansion*. San Diego: Lucent Books, 2001.

Richard White, *"It's Your Misfortune and None of My Own": A New History of the American West*. Norman: University of Oklahoma Press, 1991.

WOMEN IN ANTEBELLUM AMERICA

Barbara J. Berg, *The Remembered Gate: Origins of American Feminism: The Women and the City, 1800–1860*. New York: Oxford University Press, 1978.

Virginia Bernhard and Elizabeth Fox-Genovese, eds., *The Birth of American Feminism: The Seneca Falls Women's Convention of 1848*. St. James, NY: Brandywine, 1995.

Jeanne Boydston, *Home and Work: Housework, Wages, and the Ideology of Labor in the Early Republic*. New York: Oxford University Press, 1994.

Bruce Dorsey, *Reforming Men and Women: Gender in the Antebellum City*. Ithaca, NY: Cornell University Press, 2002.

Lori D. Ginzberg, *Women in Antebellum Reform*. Arlington Heights, IL: Harlan Davidson, 2000.

Miriam Gurko, *The Ladies of Seneca Falls: Birth of the Women's Rights Movement*. New York: Macmillan, 1974.

Sylvia D. Hoffert, *When Hens Crow: The Women's Rights Movements in Antebellum America*. Bloomington: Indiana University Press, 1995.

Nancy Isenberg, *Sex and Citizenship in Antebellum America*. Chapel Hill: University of North Carolina Press, 1998.

Lora Romero, *Home Fronts: Domesticity and Its Critics in the Antebellum United States*. Durham, NC: Duke University Press, 1997.

GENERAL

William L. Banning, *The Passage of the Republic: An Interdisciplinary History of Nineteenth-Century America*. Lexington, MA: D.C. Heath, 1987.

Don E. Fehrenbacher, *The Era of Expansion: 1800–1848*. New York: John Wiley & Sons, 1969.

Robert Leckie, *From Sea to Shining Sea : From the War of 1812 to the Mexican War, the Saga of America's Expansion*. New York: HarperCollins, 1993.

Robert V. Remini, *The Jacksonian Era*. Arlington Heights, IL: Harlan Davidson, 1989.

Arthur M. Schleslinger Jr., *The Age of Jackson*. Boston: Little, Brown, 1988.

Robert H. Wiebe, *The Opening of American Society: From the Adoption of the Constitution to the Eve of Disunion*. New York: Knopf, 1984.

Sean Wilentz, ed., *Major Problems in the Early Republic, 1787–1848*. Lexingon, MA: D.C. Heath, 1992.

INDEX